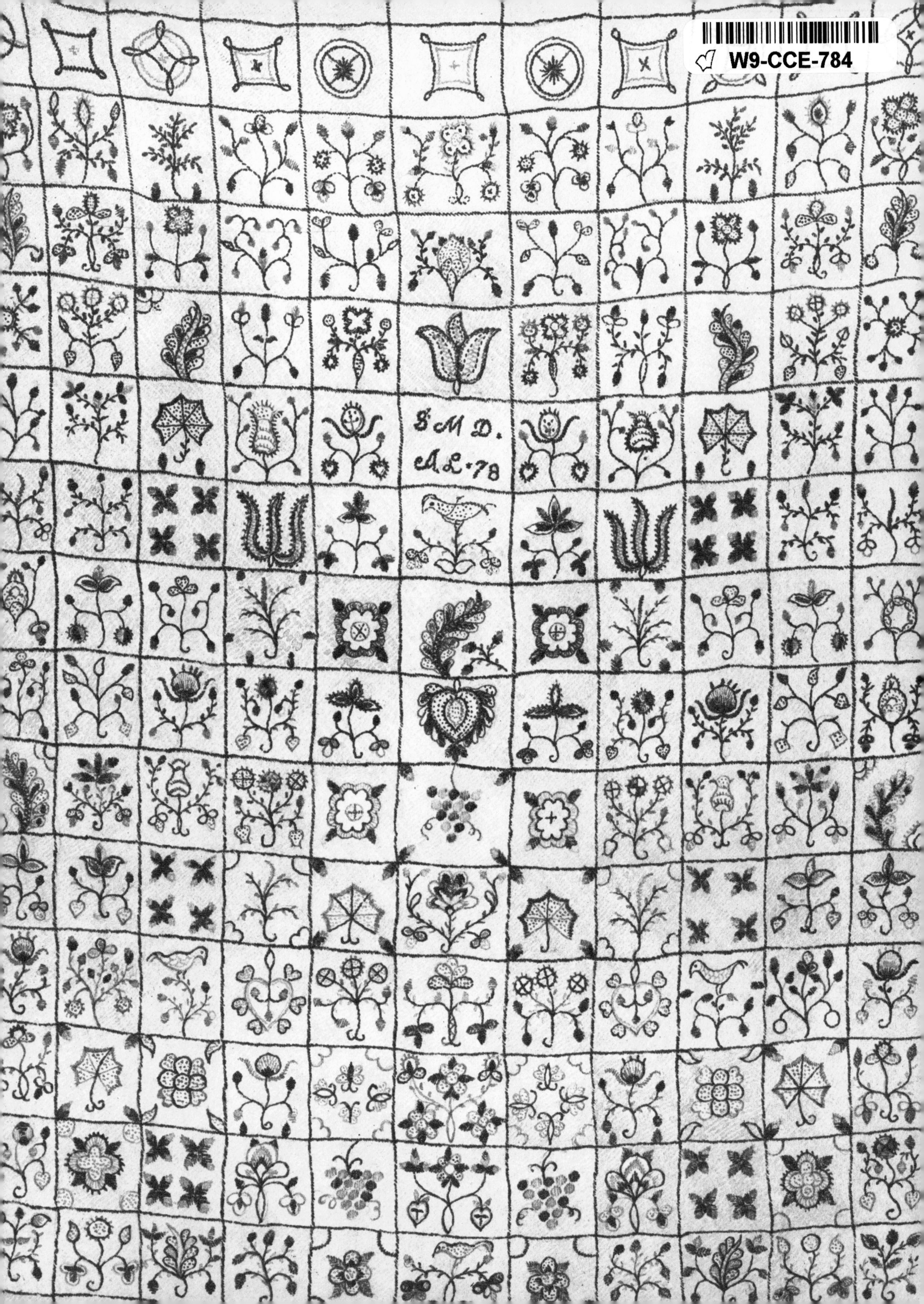
S M D.
A L • 78

THE INDEX OF
AMERICAN DESIGN

THE INDEX OF AMERICAN DESIGN

ERWIN O. CHRISTENSEN

INTRODUCTION BY HOLGER CAHILL

THE MACMILLAN COMPANY: NEW YORK
COLLIER-MACMILLAN LTD., LONDON

NATIONAL GALLERY OF ART
SMITHSONIAN INSTITUTION, WASHINGTON, D. C.

The Macmillan Company, New York

Collier-Macmillan Canada Ltd., Toronto, Ontario

PRINTED IN THE UNITED STATES OF AMERICA

PREFACE

In this book we examine the crafts and popular and folk arts of the United States as they have been recorded by the Index of American Design. The objects range from well-known museum specimens to new discoveries made by the artists who did the watercolors. Almost four hundred plates were selected from the many thousands contained in the whole Index collection. Not only furniture, silver, glass, ceramics and textiles are included but also tavern signs, figureheads, cigar-store Indians, carrousel horses, toys, pots and pans, and many other items. A sewing machine and an early phonograph are characteristic novelties of the era when the crafts gave way to the machine.

Painting, practiced as a home art, is included as well as the work of sign painters and decorators who painted walls or produced easel pictures in their leisure hours. There is little stone sculpture, but much of the wood carving is virtually sculpture.

Objects known to have been imported have mostly been omitted. You will find no Lowestoft china, no Staffordshire ware, no "Gaudy Dutch," and no textiles of Revolutionary subjects, printed in Paris or London. Obvious foreign-looking toys, presumably from Nuremberg or Berchtesgaden, were also avoided. But occasionally an imported article has been included and a few may have slipped in unrecognized. On the other hand, if a native of old Mexico painted a chest of a superior quality in New Mexico, or if a settler from south Germany made a clock that still looked Germanic, chest and clock have been admitted as long as they were produced within the borders of the United States.

With riches to choose from, the decision as to which figurehead or which quilt to include was made largely on the basis of the artistic merit of the original work. The craftsman who made the chest, the housewife who stitched the quilt had thought of its usefulness as well as its beauty. Now that they have become collectors' items, we are concerned with artistic considerations. As for the renderings, only those of superior quality were included, in any case. Where several renderings of the same type and of equal merit were available, the one was selected that fitted best with other drawings on the same page or in the same chapter.

After a few limits had been decided upon, the chosen plates had to be grouped according to some plan. A few minority groups like the Pennsylvania Germans, the Shakers, and the Spanish in the Southwest were singled out and presented in connection with the background out of which they grew. What they produced stands out in contrast to the dominating Anglo-Saxon culture. In the first section of the book ("Our Wide Land") we have the arts of transplanted groups and other more acclimated works in a geographic arrangement. To balance this geographic section there is an historic arrangement of subject matter at the end of the book ("The Years Pass"). In the middle section ("About the House") are the objects associated with life at home. What fits into the sterner living of the first part of the nineteenth century, frontier life, shipping, and business of the towns ("Pioneers and Traders"), precedes the section on the house. Aspects of the more comfortable living of the later nineteenth century ("For Profit and Pleasure") come after the house section.

The question is often asked, "What is the American element in our folk and popular arts?" In some crafts there developed a type of functional design which is truly American. On the other hand, some time may elapse before we can define what is peculiarly American in many of the objects here reproduced. At times, simplification stands out as a common denominator, in such diverse objects as Shaker furniture and carved *bultos* from New Mexico. Simplification is basic to the country; it grew out of the native environment.

Another question, "Is it good art?," can be settled more readily, and often the answer is definitely in the affirmative. In the last analysis it is their artistic quality that makes these objects worth-while.

A number of persons have given valuable assistance in connection with the preparation of the manuscript.

I gratefully acknowledge the help given me by Ann W. Woods, who has assisted in the various editorial tasks relating to the text, including checking and proofing, and has also made constructive criticisms in connection with the selection of the plates and the preparation of the dummy. I also thank my assistants Jean Watkins, Virginia Holland, Elizabeth Benson, Martha Parker, and Nancy Leech for their able checking and proof-reading, and Nancy Leech for her work on the index to the text.

I am indebted to Holger Cahill for his detailed and expert criticism; to Faulkner Lewis and Cecil Scott, of The Macmillan Company, for many helpful suggestions on the selection of the illustrations and on the text; to Penrose Berman, of the Beck Engraving Company, who was responsible for the color plates; to Dr. Preston A. Barba for his critical reading of the sections on Pennsylvania German art; to Dorothy Vaughan for introducing me to historic Portsmouth (N. H.); to Estella T. Weeks for information on the Shakers. Joseph Downs, Adolph C. Glassgold, Macgill James, June H. Gardner, Romana Javitz, Frances Lichten, Jean Lipman, George S. and Helen McKearin, Pauline A. Pinckney, Charles Messer Stow, Alice Winchester, and

Joseph B. Eggen have contributed various suggestions. For constructive criticism on the whole manuscript I am particularly grateful to my wife, Edna Florance Christensen.

I am also indebted to each person who answered questions on particular details, to the authors in the bibliography, and finally to the many research workers, not otherwise mentioned, who in the days of the projects sought out basic information on many of the objects here reproduced.

The real creators of this book are the men and women who made the extraordinary renderings from which the illustrations were reproduced. It is they who made this book possible, and their names will be found in the List of Illustrations on page 197.

Erwin O. Christensen

ACKNOWLEDGMENTS

The author wishes to express his gratitude to the many friends who by their knowledge and advice have helped him in the preparation of this book, and in particular to those listed below:

John H. Bailey, Davenport (Iowa) Public Museum; Florence P. Berger, Wadsworth Atheneum, Hartford, Conn.; Carl Beust, Dayton, Ohio; Harry MacNeill Bland, New York City; Mrs. Davis Bohon, Lexington, Ky.; Henry S. Borneman, Pennsylvania German Society; E. Boyd, Los Angeles; M. B. Brainard, Hartford, Conn.; Alfred Mansfield Brooks, Cape Ann Scientific, Literary and Historical Association, Gloucester, Mass.; James L. Bruce, Old State House, Boston; Jerry Bywaters, Museum of Fine Arts, Dallas; Charles F. Carey, Herbert W. Krieger, F. M. Setzler, Frank A. Taylor and Malcolm Watkins, Smithsonian Institution; Lucien Cazebonne, New Orleans; Charles M. Christenson, County Historical Room, Racine, Wis.; Laurence V. Coleman, American Association of Museums, Washington, D.C.; Cyrol Colnik, Milwaukee; Mrs. Elizabeth T. Davis, Worcester Historical Society; Alberta Thorne Daywalt, Western Reserve Historical Society, Cleveland; E. J. Drake, New York City; Kenneth H. Dunshee, New York City; A. N. Dyer, Grangeville, Idaho; J. Selden Fisher, Rochester, N.Y.; Joseph W. P. Frost, Kittery, Maine; Charles P. Fox, Oconomowoc, Wis.; Rev. M. Geiger, O.F.M., Old Mission, Santa Barbara, Calif.; Elmer A. Goessl, Milwaukee Public Museum; George Graf, Peru, Ind.; Samuel M. Green, Middletown, Conn.; Rawson W. Haddon, Mattatuck Historical Society, Waterbury, Conn.; R. F. Haffenreffer, King Philip Museum, Mount Hope, R.I.; Talbot F. Hamlin, Columbia University; Frederick F. Hill, Mariners' Museum, Newport News, Va.; Edwin J. Hipkiss and Gertrude Townsend, Boston Museum of Fine Arts; Henry Russell Hitchcock, Middletown, Conn.; O. M. Hovde, Norwegian-American Museum, Decorah, Ia.; Alfred F. Hopkins, Chicago Historical Society; Mrs. DeWitt V. Hutchings, Riverside, Calif.; L. W. Jenkins, Peabody Museum, Salem, Mass.; R. P. A. Johnson, U.S. Forest Products Laboratory, Madison, Wis.; Marion E. Kent, Concord Antiquarian Society, Mass.; Reidar Kjellberg, Director, Norwegian Folk Museum, Bygdø, Oslo, Norway; L. V. Landry, New Orleans; Mrs. Clair F. Luther, Amherst, Mass.; W. F. Mangels, American Museum of Public Recreation, Brooklyn, N.Y.; Horace Mann, Bucks County Historical Society, Doylestown, Pa.; Grace M. Mayer and Janet Pinney, Museum of the City of New York; John D. Meyer, Tyrone, Pa.; J. E. Miller, Philadelphia; Clifford T. Monahon, R.I. Historical Society; M. Nason, New York City; Roger Hale Newton, New York City; Mendel L. Peterson, U.S. National Museum, Washington, D.C.; N. H. Randers-Pehrson, Library of Congress; Charles van Ravenswaay, Missouri Historical Society; Elizabeth Wells Robertson, Chicago; Nile C. Schaffer, Florida State Museum, Gainesville; J. D. Scott, Zoar (Ohio) Village State Memorial; John Spargo, Bennington (Vt.) Historical Museum and Art Gallery; William B. Thomson, Philadelphia; William H. Tripp, Whaling Museum, New Bedford, Mass.; Elsbeth Trotter, Kennebunkport, Maine; Mrs. Lawrence J. Ullman, Tarrytown, N.Y.; H. Walker, Elmira, N.Y.; Mrs. Donnell B. Young, Bethesda, Md.

CONTENTS

INTRODUCTION

The Index of American Design is a record made by artists of a chapter in American history which is largely anonymous. It is the story, told in pictures, of articles of daily use and adornment in this country from early colonial times to the close of the nineteenth century. In the main it is devoted to the craft traditions which dominated American production for more than two hundred years and left their heritage to our developing mass-production technology which has impressed its forms upon our contemporary culture. Phases of this technology are represented in the Index, especially from the second half of the nineteenth century when mass-production methods were in the making and the machine was taking over even the more complicated handicrafts.

The Index is the result of a conjunction of circumstances during the depression of the 1930's. It was organized in response to several needs: the need of artists for employment, the need of the Government work program to devise projects which would maintain the skills of the unemployed, and public need for pictorial information on American design and craftsmanship. Demand for information on this phase of our history had been growing for some years before the Index came into being. It made itself felt insistently during and after the First World War, partly because of the rapid expansion of visual education, partly because American industry realized during the war its too close dependence on European design.

Behind these developments and sustaining them was a wide interest in American decorative and domestic art which had been steadily building up since the seventies and eighties when the work of early American craftsmen began its journey from farm sheds, town attics, and secondhand dealers' storerooms toward the art museum. The Centennial Exposition at Philadelphia in 1876 had something to do with it, but its contribution was in the spirit of the log cabin tradition fixed in popular consciousness since the campaign of the first President Harrison. The Centennial, like most American fairs, was devoted to contemporary enterprise and "modern improvements." In a period when the design of articles of everyday use was at a low ebb it is not surprising that the American artifacts most admired at the Exposition were trotting wagons, agricultural implements and clocks, all of which were more clearly related to handicraft traditions than to our rapidly developing machine technology. There were some exhibits of early American furniture and utensils. A house, built in "imitation of a New England log house" of 1776, contained, among other things, Peregrine White's cradle, John Alden's desk, Governor Endicott's folding chair, chests of drawers, bedsteads, quilts and kitchenware. Twenty ladies in costumes of the Revolutionary period conducted visitors through the house "explaining with courtesy the wonderful articles of furniture and cooking utensils whose very simplicity made them incomprehensible to the victims of modern improvements."

Interest in early American craftsmanship was not altogether new in the 1870's. Museums had concerned themselves with it to a degree, though the primary interest of most was history, natural history, or ethnology. Among these institutions one may mention the Charleston (South Carolina) Museum founded in 1773, the oldest institution of its kind in the country, the Massachusetts Historical Society (1790), the Albany Institute of History and Art (1791), the New-York Historical Society (1804), the American Antiquarian Society in Worcester (1812), the Peabody Museum and the Essex Institute in Salem, the Pennsylvania Historical Society, in Philadelphia, and various state and city museums and historic houses.

Pioneers in the late nineteenth century development were such men as Dr. Henry Chapman Mercer of Doylestown, Pennsylvania, who gave up archaeology and began collecting early American material in the 1880's; Dr. Edwin Atlee Barber, early writer on ceramics and glass, effective discoverer of Pennsylvania German pottery and Bennington Ware and founder of the collections that bear his name at the Philadelphia Museum of Art; John Cotton Dana, founder of the Newark (New Jersey) Museum and of the first library picture collections in this country; Mr. and Mrs. Robert W. De Forest, founders of the American Wing of the Metropolitan Museum of Art; Henry W. Kent, of the Metropolitan staff, who was behind most of the Museum's activities in the early American field; R. T. Haines Halsey, Henry W. Erving, Eugene Bolles, and other collectors and writers who were calling attention to the American tradition in design before the turn of the century.

In the early 1900's great impetus was given by such events as the Boston Museum's important exhibition of colonial silver in 1906; the Hudson-Fulton celebration in New York in 1909 when the Metropolitan Museum exhibited a collection of early American decorative art; the foundation in 1910 of the Society for the Preservation of New England Antiquities, whose editor, George Francis Dow, did pioneering studies of arts and crafts; the *Werkbund* exhibitions at the Newark Museum (1912 and 1922) that brought to this country the message of an organization which was one of the most important links in the progression from William Morris to modern design; and the activities of collectors like Mr. and Mrs. De Forest, Francis H. Bigelow, Howard Reifsnyder, Judge Alphonso T. Clearwater, and Henry F. du Pont. The "manufacturer and designer" exhibitions begun in 1917 at the Metropolitan Museum under the direction of Richard F. Bach, and the survey of American resources in industrial art by Charles Russell Richards at the beginning of the twenties, while they took note of all resources no matter what their origin, served to call attention to the quality of the indigenous contributions. In 1924 when the American Wing of the Metropolitan was founded the most conservative museums were beginning to see that early American furniture, ceramics, glass, silver, metalware, textiles, tools, and utensils were worthy of serious attention. The tricentennials beginning with that of Jamestown in 1907, and the New England tricentennials of the twenties and thirties, projects like Henry Ford's Wayside Inn, opened in 1928, and the important Williamsburg restoration begun by John D. Rockefeller, Jr., in 1927 were high points in the development. In the late 1920's it was not unusual to see early American furniture which had been disregarded two generations before sold for many thousands of dollars. At a New York sale in April, 1929, three eighteenth century Philadelphia pieces were bid up to $103,000 by collectors. Another New York event of 1929 more appealing to the general public was the exhibition of early American art held for the benefit of the Girl Scouts.

Appreciation of American folk and popular art, which forms one of the major categories of the Index of American Design, grew more slowly. It has two main sources: the ethnological collection which has made us aware of design horizons beyond our own Western tradition, and the rise of modern art. Each is involved to some extent in the other. Modern artists helped educate ethnologists and the museum public to the esthetic quality of primitive, folk and popular art. The ethnological collection exerted an influence on the early development of modern art. Study of the art of primitive peoples led to an interest in the art of peasants, artisans and amateurs. These ideas made themselves felt in the United States in the second decade of this century in the work and writings of artists returning from European study, in small collections, and in the pages of such magazines as R. J. Coady's *The Soil,* and *The Arts* founded by the painter Hamilton Easter Field, one of the early collectors of American folk art. Between the mid-twenties and the mid-thirties folk and popular art was brought into the focus of national consciousness through such notable collections as those of Mr. and Mrs. Elie Nadelman, Mrs. Isabel Carleton Wilde, and Mrs. John D. Rockefeller, Jr., and through a series of exhibitions at the Newark Museum, the Whitney Studio Club, the Museum of Modern Art, the Whitney Museum of American Art, and Colonial Williamsburg.

These various developments provided a matrix for an index of American design. They also pointed up the need for it. Despite the enthusiasm of collectors, and possibly because of it, American material in the arts has always been widely scattered. No really comprehensive collections exist here such as one found in Germany before World War II and may still find in Sweden. The scattering of American material is due in part to the factor of distance, the extent of the country as compared with European nations, the wide separation of the Colonies, and transportation difficulties in early days. More fundamental reasons were the comparatively broad base of patronage in colonial times and the diversity of traditions that existed here at one and the same time.

The rapid growth of interest in visualization around the turn of the century led public libraries to gather pictorial information to meet the needs of education and industry. The first of these public library collections of documentary pictures was organized by John Cotton Dana at Denver in 1891, and later at Springfield, Massachusetts, in 1898, and at Newark, New Jersey, in 1903. In 1916 the New York Public Library set up its Picture Collection following Mr. Dana's ideas. Though not devoted exclusively to American subjects these picture collections were called upon to answer questions similar to those asked in the preface of this book: "What is American? Is there anything recognizably American aside from Indian material? Where can I see it? Have you a picture of it?" European visitors had been asking such questions for a long time. It seems probable that some of our self-consciousness about what is American, aside from the stream of fashions which we have imported and appropriated as our own, has been stimulated by questions asked by European visitors from the middle of the nineteenth century and repeated with growing insistence after the First World War. During the 1920's more and more Americans were asking them, not only collectors, artists, designers and educators, but also manufacturers made keenly aware of the drying up of European design sources during the war. The New York Public Library Picture Collection in its reports during the early 1930's makes note of the increasing demand for American material and the difficulty in meeting it.

The idea for an Index of American Design crystallized into a plan in the spring of 1935. It was not a new idea. European nations had made large collections of their native design material and published richly illustrated books on the subject. With us well-illustrated publications have been few until recent years. Pioneers in this type of publication in the United States were historical museums, private collectors, and amateurs. Some of the earliest documentary drawings of American artifacts—of Benjamin Franklin's stove, for instance—were published in *The Transactions of the American Philosophical Society* in the last quarter of the eighteenth century. A hundred years later one finds William C. Prime writing on pottery and porcelain (1878); John H. Buck on old silver in 1888; Dr. Edwin Atlee Barber, writing on American ceramics, glass, and the tulip ware of the Pennsylvania German potters as early as 1893; Irving W. Lyon on colonial furniture in New England, 1891; R. T. Haines Halsey on pottery, 1899, and on silver, 1906; Luke Vincent Lockwood on furniture, 1901; Frances Clary Morse; and Alice Morse Earle who began writing in the nineties and probably did more to popularize early New England than any other writer. N. Hudson Moore and Clarence C. Cook also were writing on American domestic art, and many of those named were collecting it before the turn of the century. One of the important collectors and writers of the early 1900's was Alexander Wilson Drake, who wrote on American copper and brass in 1907 and showed a collection of samplers at the Cincinnati Museum of Art in 1909. Frederick William Hunter's book on Stiegel glass, which had wide influence, was published in 1914.

Among the historical societies, that of Bucks County in Doylestown, Pennsylvania, brought out pioneering illustrated books on the decorative stove plates of the eighteenth century, the art of illuminated writing among the Pennsylvania Germans, and ancient carpenter's tools. These books, written by Dr. Henry Chapman Mercer, were published in the twenties. Also published in the twenties were Albert H. Sonn's work on early American wrought iron, J. B. Kerfoot's book on American pewter, and the early writings of Mrs. Rhea Mansfield Knittle on handicrafts west of the Alleghenies. These and other admirable publications brought into view neglected chapters in the history of the useful and popular arts in the United States and called attention to what still needed to be done in research, in education, and in the organization of collections. Important contributions in these various fields were made by such men as Fiske Kimball, Royal Bailey Farnum, Leon L. Winslow, Valentine Kirby, Henry Turner Bailey, Theodore S. Woolsey, Howard D. Eberlein, William Laurel Harris, George Leland Hunter, and others.

When the Civil Works Administration was set up in 1933 unemployment in many professions was severe and nowhere more severe than in the arts. The first large Government project for artists, organized in December, 1933, and directed by Edward Bruce under the Treasury Department through a grant of funds from the Civil Works Administration, employed mainly painters, sculptors, and printmakers. Although it also employed designers and craftsmen the basic problem of unemployment among commercial artists remained. The Civil Works Administration and various State Emergency Relief Administrations tried to meet it through setting up handicraft and recording projects. The most valuable recording projects were the Historic American Buildings Survey carried out under the direction of the Department of the Interior through a grant of funds from CWA and later from WPA; and a record of American Indian design begun by Frederick Douglas at the Denver Art Museum in 1932 which employed Government project artists from 1933 until its work was completed in 1938. Another recording project, planned before the Index but organized later, was the Historic American Merchant-Marine Survey, which was under the joint direction of the Smithsonian Institution and WPA. Other similar projects were proposed in 1935. One such project, for recording decorative iron and bronze in New York, was put before Mayor La Guardia's Municipal Art Committee by Peter Larsen, who later carried it on under the Index of American Design.

These projects were the immediate forerunners of the Index, but it did not grow out of them. The Index idea as it was later developed by the WPA Federal Art Project resulted from discussions between Romana Javitz, head of the New York Public Library's Picture Collection, and artists who came to the Library for research. This was in the early spring of 1935. Miss Javitz and the Picture Collection staff had recognized for some time the need for a comprehensive source record of American design. Prominent among the artists who participated in the discussion at the Library was Ruth Reeves, a textile designer and painter. She brought the Index idea to Mrs. Frances Pollak, head of Educational Projects for the New York City Emergency Relief Administration, and suggested that artists employed on Government projects carry it out. Later Miss Reeves, who was the missionary of the Index idea, brought it to the attention of WPA officials in Washington and to Edward Bruce, head of the Section of Painting and Sculpture. Mrs. Pollak immediately saw the Index as a solution for the problem of commercial artist unemployment and asked Miss Javitz to formulate a plan. This plan was completed in July, 1935, but because of difficulties in finding public sponsorship, the Index remained largely in the planning stage until after the organization of the Federal Art Project in October of that year.

The Index of American Design was organized as a nationwide activity in two meetings of the Federal Art Project national staff, December 7 and 8, 1935. Certain activities of the nascent Index in New York City were ruled out. It was felt that Indian Arts should be left to the ethnologists who had been making pictorial records in that field. The Index was limited to the practical, popular and folk arts of the peoples of European origin who created the material culture of this country as we know it today. Architecture had to be ruled out because two other Government projects were concerned with it, the Historic American Buildings Survey and the Historic American Merchant-Marine Survey. The Index was placed under the direction of the Washington staff of the Federal Art Project. Constance Rourke was appointed national editor and Ruth Reeves national co-ordinator. A small central research staff was set up in Washington. A larger research staff had already been set up under the New York City project. In the spring of 1936 C. Adolph Glassgold succeeded Ruth Reeves as national co-ordinator of the Index and he was succeeded by Benjamin Knotts in 1940.

State Index projects of any size set up their own research staffs made up of persons familiar with the history of American crafts or expert in some particular field. Where employment was small the research was done by the project supervisor or by the artists themselves. It was the function of research staffs to make surveys of local material, to select from it the objects to be recorded, checking on their history and authenticity. Before an object was assigned to an artist for recording it was examined by the research supervisor and all information concerning it entered on the data sheet which would be pasted on the back of the completed drawing. The Index office in Washington checked on the quality of local project work and assisted in co-ordinating research. It might be found, for instance, that objects of the same kind were duplicated over wide areas and it became necessary for the state projects to determine whether material which they planned to record had been recorded elsewhere, whether the objects were the best available examples, and if any good purpose would be served by the duplication. Considering the extent of the Index, it is surprising how little duplication took place. In choosing objects for recording priority was given to material of historical significance not previously studied, which, for one reason or another, stood in danger of being lost. Regional and local crafts were emphasized; for instance, crewel work, Shaker design and the early colonial crafts in New England; the folk crafts in Pennsylvania and in the Southwest; pioneer furniture, tools, and utensils in the Middle West and in Texas; early Mormon textiles in Utah, and various community crafts in Ohio, Illinois, Iowa, and other states. In carrying on their work, research staffs received generous help from museums, private collectors, and dealers who owned the material recorded by the Index.

In January, 1936, a preliminary Index manual was issued by the Washington office of the Federal Art Project outlining the scope of the new activity, its purpose, plan of organization, methods of recording, research, classification and filing, together with specimen copies of data sheets to accompany each drawing. The research methods and data sheets were drawn up by Phyllis Crawford, research director of the New York City project, in collaboration with Miss Javitz. Two months later a supplementary bulletin on techniques was issued. This was based on the teaching of Suzanne Chapman who was loaned to the Massachusetts Index project by the Boston Museum of Fine Arts. Miss Chapman had studied methods worked out by Joseph Lindon Smith, who made pictorial records of the Museum's Egyptian expedition. Mr. Smith had devised a meticulous technique of documentary painting in water color. Miss Chapman taught Index artists this "Egyptologist's technique."

The Index plan as finally worked out in its objective and techniques of recording and research proved well suited to the program of the Federal Art Project. The Project was charged by the Government with finding useful employment for thousands of artists referred to the WPA by local agencies throughout the country. What work the Project could carry on depended on the skills of these artists, or skills which they might acquire through in-service training. The basic directive of the whole WPA program was maintenance of skills. There were other directives. Congress did not approve projects which were in competition with private enterprise. Some project supervisors found this opposition irksome, but it was, in fact, wise. Unemployment would scarcely have been relieved if Government employees had engaged in competition with others employed at higher wage levels in commerce, industry or the professions. It was in these circumstances that the Index came into existence. Here was a job that needed doing. The doing of it would maintain and improve skills. It would not compete with private enterprise but would, and in fact did, benefit private enterprise through providing it with a reservoir of pictorial and research material on American design and craftsmanship.

The Index of American Design as it exists today was produced by a great collaborative enterprise to which hundreds of persons contributed talent, ideas, techniques, research methods, and persevering, devoted effort. Some of these persons are mentioned in Mr. Christensen's list of illustrations. Others will become known to a wider public as more Index drawings are published. The names of some, especially of those artists, research workers and supervisors who perfected the techniques of the Index and guided it through its beginning years, are recorded only in Government archives. In its early stages the Index met with many difficulties. Since its drawings were to remain Federal property they could not be allocated in the states where they were made. This virtually eliminated local sponsorship. No Federal project could be set up in the states without the consent of the WPA administrations involved and so it became necessary to win the support of the state administrations for a project which would show no contribution to their sponsor's funds. WPA was required by law to show local contributions in cash or kind ranging from 10 per cent in 1935 to 25 per cent in 1939. Projects which had a high percentage of sponsors' contributions had to support projects which had little or none. This difficulty was considerably aggravated when the Federal program came to an end and the states took over administrative control of the Arts Projects. It must be said, however, to the great credit of WPA State Administrators, that with few exceptions they agreed to carry the Index both in its early stages in 1935-1936 and after the close of the Federal period in 1939.

Another difficulty was with museums, dealers, and private collectors who owned material which the Index sought to record. At first many of them were sceptical of Government projects and saw little value in the Index. Even when they admitted its worth they thought it might better be carried out by what they considered the cheaper and more expeditious method of photography. Museums were won over when they became convinced of the sound purpose of the Index, the quality of its drawings and its careful research methods. Dealers and collectors followed. Important in winning this support for the Index were Constance Rourke, Ruth Reeves, Mildred Holzhauer, Nina Collier, C. Adolph Glassgold, Thomas C. Parker, Pauline Pinckney, and Kathleen Clinch Calkins from the Washington office of the Federal Art Project; Richard C. Morrison and Gordon W. Smith in Massachusetts; Phyllis Crawford, Helen McKearin, Janet Rosenwald, Aline Bernstein, Carolyn Scoon, Millia Davenport, Elizabeth T. Riefstahl, Scott Graham Williamson, and Charles O. Cornelius in New York. Many of these were expert in various fields of American design. A strong supporter who helped convince collectors of the value of the Index was the late Homer Eaton Keyes, editor of the magazine *Antiques,* which he founded in 1922.

A third difficulty was with the artists. In the beginning many artists felt that the Index was dead copying. Index artists had to discipline themselves to meticulous rendering techniques and to the objects they recorded. They could not express themselves through the free use of form and color and so felt cheated of the creative assignments they had expected from the Federal Art Project. But they discovered that documentary art may become a free creative activity even within severe discipline and limitations. This change in the artists' attitude was brought about by the steady improvement of project standards and the missionary work of supervisors on the Washington staff of the Federal Art Project and in the states: Richard C. Morrison, Gordon W. Smith, Suzanne Chapman, Elizabeth Moutal, Ingrid Selmer-Larsen, Lawrence Peterson, and Alfred Smith in Massachusetts; Dorothy Hay Jensen in Maine; Donald Donovan in Rhode Island; William Warren in Connecticut; Lou Block, Lincoln Rothschild and Tillie G. Shahn in New York; Frances Lichten in Pennsylvania; Hildegarde Crosby Melzer in Illinois; Sylvester Jerry and Paul McPharlin in Michigan; Elzy J. Bird in Utah; Donald Bear in Colorado; R. Vernon Hunter and E. Boyd in New Mexico; and Warren Lemmon in California.

The Index prospered in New England and the Middle Atlantic states where a great deal of early American material was available for recording and artists of the highest competence could be employed. It lagged in the South and some parts of the West because of lack of material to record, but mainly because personnel trained in the techniques which the Index required could not be employed under Government regulations. The situation was improved somewhat by lending artists from Massachusetts, New York, and other northeastern states to teach Index techniques in the South and West. This was a complicated procedure involving the agreement of two state administrations, problems of quota, per diem and travel allowances, and rates of pay which differed considerably in various parts of the country. Another reason why the Index developed slowly in the South was that states like North and South Carolina, Virginia, Tennessee, Mississippi, and Florida were leaders in the Community Art Center movement. Most of their artists were employed in teaching and in bringing art to the general public. Because of these circumstances some states in the South had no Index projects. However, excellent Index drawings were made in Virginia, Kentucky, Louisiana, and Texas. In the West and the Middle West where problems of quota and pay rate were not so difficult many states benefitted by the eastern experience. Others did not, either because trained personnel could not be hired or because their Index material was duplicated in other states. The Index project was finally set up in thirty-five states and employed an average of three hundred artists from the time it was organized in December, 1935, until it was closed down shortly after the United States entered the war in 1941.

While expert supervisors from the metropolitan centers assisted many Index projects throughout the country, the best results achieved often depended on purely local developments. An example of this is Utah, a state with a small art project and a good source of material in the Relic Halls founded by the Daughters of the Utah Pioneers. The story is told by Elzy J. Bird, under whose direction the Index did some of its best drawings:

"When I became director of the project I had been working on an Index plate and I remember the amount of sweat that went into the finished product. Most of the artists seemed to feel as I did, that it was merely copy work and didn't give free rein to anything creative.

"At first I think the only artist who took the Index seriously was William Parkinson. I remember one artist doing a remarkable textile piece—just one. He said he'd sooner starve than do another. Finally I raided our silk screen department and found some of the boys who were very skillful with their hands. Frank Mace, Frank Maurer and Paul Vaughn were the ones who really enjoyed doing Index drawings. Mace was a journeyman printer, Vaughn a metal craftsman, Maurer a carpenter and ex-Marine. I put them to work with Parkinson and together they developed the wonderful painting of textiles, working from dark to light with transparent and opaque water color. Another of the group was Florence Truelson who devised her own method of producing textile textures. From time to time others came and went. There were, for instance, several cowboys who could sit down for days over a drawing of leatherwork or an old spur or gun. They were the saddle and spur type; wouldn't be caught dead doing a textile but you could certainly keep them out of trouble with something of the old West."

The Federal Art Project tried to channel Index techniques in the direction of quality, but no one technique was insisted upon. What was insisted upon was strict objectivity, accurate drawing, clarity of construction, exact proportions, and faithful rendering of material, color and texture so that each Index drawing might stand as surrogate for the object. This ideal was not always carried out in practice. The best drawings, while maintaining complete fidelity to the object, have the individuality which characterizes works of art. To find their peers in American art we must go back to the still-life of William Harnett and the *trompe-l'œil* painters of the nineteenth century. The lesser drawings represent steps in the training of artists who later produced better work. This training was carried on by expert supervisors, in Boston, New York, Philadelphia, Chicago and the larger Index projects generally. Miss Chapman and her pupils in Boston taught their technique throughout New England and were called upon to teach it in other parts of the country. Techniques were also taught through touring exhibitions of the best drawings, and of drawings in various stages of completion illustrating the method step by step.

The technique recommended in the Index manual (WPA Technical Series, Art Circular No. 3) for most categories of objects was a transparent water-color method. The object was first carefully studied and a light outline drawing made. The lighter passages of color were then washed in, gradually working up to the darkest passages. One wash might be applied directly over another, allowing the first wash to dry thoroughly, or a glaze might be applied and new washes of color laid in over the glaze. High lights and shadows were simplified and accidental reflections and cast shadows eliminated. Another method described in the Index manual was the opaque water-color method in which the darkest undertone passages were laid in first, then the lighter tones, with the darkest and lightest accents picked out last. This was the technique of the Utah artists. New York used a variant of this method, underpainting in Chinese ink and laying in the color over this monochrome wash. Oil technique was preferred for certain types of objects. Michigan used it in recording tobacconists' signs and Pennsylvania in recording Pennsylvania German folk art. Another method favored in New York and New Jersey for certain kinds of textiles was scratchboard done by scratching with a steel pen through a water-color wash into the soft chalk and wax surface of a prepared drawing paper. Pen and ink, and pencil were used where color was not important. Photography was also used. Some critics argued that photography should have been employed exclusively. However, aside from the fact that the Index was part of an employment program for artists, there were many reasons why photography did not become its leading technique. The camera, except in the hands of its greatest masters, cannot reveal the essential character and quality of objects as the artist can. Problems of distortion and of lighting are difficult. The camera cannot search out the forms of objects deeply undercut or modeled in high relief, match color as closely as the artist, or render the subtle interplay of form, color and texture which creates the characteristic beauty of so many products of early American craftsmen. Color photography approximating the quality of Index drawings is an expensive process with many problems which have not been fully solved. The color photograph is perishable, while water color is one of the most durable of art media.

Erwin Christensen's text describes the Index accomplishment in such interesting detail that there is no need to discuss it further here. However, one may ask certain questions about its values and shortcomings. Its most obvious value is historical. The Index, in bringing together thousands of particulars from various sections of the country, tells the story of American hand skills and traces intelligible patterns within that story. In documenting the forms created by the tastes, skills, and needs of our ancestors it brings a new vitality and warmth into their everyday history, whether they were the founders of colonies and states, or political, religious, or economic refugees who came here to find a new free way of life, "a chapter of harmony and perfection" in the relations of men.

In one sense the Index is a kind of archaeology. It helps to correct a bias which has tended to relegate the work of the craftsman and the folk artist to the subconscious of our history where it can be recovered only by digging. In the past we have lost whole sequences out of their story, and have all but forgotten the unique contribution of hand skills in our culture. As early as the eighteenth century little remained above ground of seventeenth century Jamestown. When the Williamsburg restoration began in 1927 a good deal of the research into that eighteenth century town had to be done by digging in old sites. These excavations recovered more than forty tons of material other than brick, including fragments of ceramic ware, glass, bone, iron, brass and pewter. Colonial Williamsburg is authority for the statement that an accurate reconstruction "would not have been possible without this very intensive archaeological exploration, just as it could not have been done without the most intense sort of research work with surviving documents and records." "Artifacts are of inestimable value in giving us a broad over-all impression of the culture and taste of colonial people." In the damp earth of the peninsula between the York and the James rivers, wood, textiles, leather, clothing, and floor coverings disintegrate quickly. Consequently some of the history of Jamestown and Williamsburg is lost and can be reconstructed only from conjecture and analogy supported by surviving written documents. The same may be said of other early towns. Some of the houses in Plymouth, before they could be restored, had to be freed from constructions laid over them through the generations. This sort of digging into the American past has been necessary not only for the early period but even for developments in our machine technology in the nineteenth century. Siegfried Giedion and John Kouwenhoven in their researches into the history of mechanization and mass-production methods have shown how much we have forgotten about the development of techniques which have given contemporary American civilization its character.

As we study the drawings of the Index of American Design we realize that the hands that made the first two hundred years of this country's material culture expressed something more than untutored creative instinct and the rude vigor of a frontier civilization. This need surprise us only if we forget the ageless tradition that may lie behind the making and decoration of the simplest article of everyday use. The artifacts recovered at Jamestown are far from crude. The earliest houses at Plymouth have a direct and simple manner of construction which shows that they were built by men who knew exactly what they were about. While the tradition of the early American craftsman is basically English, it shows in its beginnings an interweaving of influences made more complex by immigration and intercolonial migration. This helps to explain the variety of handicraft and popular art styles in certain sections, in Pennsylvania, New Jersey, New York, Virginia, the Carolinas and the settlements to the west. Pennsylvania Germans settled some towns in New England. The Moravians and other Palatine Germans followed the Shenandoah Valley through Virginia and into North Carolina and the Ohio River Valley to the west, carrying with them their typical handicraft skills.

The English tradition itself is far from single, even in the work of the artisans and craftsmen who came from Britain before the middle of the seventeenth century. These men were trained in ways of doing things that go back through late medieval times in Britain, France, and The Netherlands into Gothic and even Romanesque times. This medieval tradition lived a long time in Britain. Some phases of it were in existence in the hill towns of Gloucestershire as late as the twenties of this century; in the United States it lasted well into the nineteenth century. The men who carried this tradition in early colonial times and through the recurring primitivisms of the expanding frontier were sometimes specialists and sometimes jacks-of-all-trades not only because of the exigencies of life in a new land but also because their training made for flexibility. Joiners and shipwrights could turn their hands to architecture, the making of furniture, and the carving of tools and utensils. Some of the carvings which they made as shop signs and ship's decoration we now recognize as our earliest sculpture. Carriage makers and house and sign painters knew how to design and paint coats of arms, shop signs, portraits, and landscapes, some of which may still be found on the overmantels of eighteenth century houses. There is small question that the portraits of the 1670's which began the development that culminated in the eighteenth century came out of this anonymous and sturdy craftsmanship. Like early American articles of everyday use these portraits reflect a tradition of shop practice which looks back through Tudor painting to medieval manuscripts and Books of Hours. But they look forward also to our eighteenth century masters, Feke and Copley and Earl.

There is this double aspect in the work of the craftsman who is the bearer of folk memory in the arts. This folk memory, which is amazingly tenacious, is a storehouse of the technical and symbolic innovations of the past, and on more than one occasion has prepared the way for new developments. For this reason the Index of American Design which records American craftsmanship is more than a backward look. There is in it also the Davy Crockett "go ahead principle." It tells the story of creativeness and inventive change when traditional design failed to meet new problems. Dr. Henry Chapman Mercer, in his valuable study of early carpenters' tools, says that American tools do not appear as inventions but as European heirlooms "modified rather than transformed by a new environment." And yet the book in which he makes this statement gives evidence of real transformations. One is that of the American ax whose quality, both as tool and as design, was admired by European visitors to the Philadelphia Centennial in 1876. As early as 1828 Fenimore Cooper had noted the superior form, neatness and "precision of weight" of the American ax. In all previous European axes, with their heavy bits, the weight was poorly distributed so that the ax wobbled in delivering oblique blows and was both tiring and dangerous for the woodsman. Some time between 1744 and 1776 there developed the American ax in which the weight has been distributed so that the poll is heavier than the bit. This new "precision of weight" made the ax steady and much more effective. The thinning of the blade made it easier to withdraw after the blow. Later, in the first half of the nineteenth century came the lean and delicately curved handle. How did these changes come about? Undoubtedly they were stimulated by the needs of an agricultural civilization in a forest frontier where every acre of farmland had to be cleared of trees. Possibly useful hints came from the eastern Pennsylvania wedge-ax which had no cutting edge. Perhaps the two developments came independently. In any event we have here a tool transformed into something more useful and beautiful than anything in its ancestry.

The inventiveness that reshapes forms in response to the needs of a changing environment and the stimulat-

ing influence of one tradition upon another is reflected many times in the Index. The Shakers, most austere of our eighteenth and nineteenth century craftsmen, were English immigrants. Their design may be traced to English sources but in its severe integrity in handling materials, its discarding of ornament in favor of unadorned surface and its sense of fitness and function it is as much a forerunner of modern ideas as it is a reflection of the past. Pennsylvania German and Spanish Colonial which are related to peasant art seem further away from us. Yet, in their feeling for surface and their stimulating influence upon our all but lost sense of vivid and clear color in articles of everyday use they have much of value for the contemporary designer and the craftsman.

Today we are surrounded by so many and such powerful evidences of mass-production technology that we are apt to forget that this technology was born in a handicraft tradition. The forgetfulness may be an expression of our passion for obsolescence. It is one of the accidents of our history that modern design in the United States has developed in almost complete isolation from traditional craftsman's skills. Here the Index serves in the role of interpreter, calling our attention to the unique and irreplaceable contribution which these skills have made, and may still make, in our culture. We can see many ways in which contemporary design has been influenced by the hand skills of the past. Perhaps we may even be permitted to wonder if in the design of such modern things as the steamboat and the automobile, lustiest offspring of our mass-production economy, we have improved upon the work of the shipwrights and the wagonmakers whom Horatio Greenough admired a hundred years ago. Nikolaus Pevsner has pointed out our tendency to overestimate the contribution of the engineer and underestimate the craftsman and the artist as factors in modern design. We need not follow William Morris and Walter Crane and insist that handicraft is the one true root and base of the arts. But it is no mere Luddism to maintain that the hand skill is one of the main roots. This is true today not only in broad areas of industry which have a craft base, textiles, furniture, ceramics, glass, utensils, printing, and the building trades, but also in design for mass production and in the making of the machine itself.

The wide interest in American craftsmanship that developed in the last quarter of the nineteenth century, and which is part of the ancestry of the Index, was not antiquarian. Men like John Cotton Dana and Henry W. Kent made no separation between the machine and the hand tool but insisted that the machine could become an instrument of man's creative skill in making articles of everyday use—one as sensitive as the hand tool and much more powerful, after it had been fully mastered. But they felt that we must not forget what the craftsman had learned in the dialectic of shop practice, his sympathy with materials and his knowledge of their possibilities and limitations. The Index of American Design is a repository of the skills of craftsmen who thought out their design in the material itself; it may well become a steadying influence and a source of refreshment to the designer who brings his ideas to life on the drawing board and the craftsman who models and tools the pattern.

The Index, as it stands, is the largest and most nearly comprehensive collection of its kind in the world. But it is not complete. The Second World War brought the activities of the project to an end before its work was done in any state and before much had been accomplished in the South. The first need of the Index is completion. The second is a wider distribution of its pictorial information. The National Gallery of Art has tried to meet this through making Index material available to students through exhibitions. The present magnificent volume, which is the fullest presentation of the Index thus far, is the best kind of answer to the problem of making its information easily available. The question of availability is important, for the Index has value not only for the designer, the craftsman and the manufacturer, but even more for the historian, the educator, the student and the general public. As the late Constance Rourke, one of the soundest students of American culture, has phrased it: "Not the least of the revelations of the Index may be those offered to the student of American social history. Fresh light may be thrown upon ways of living which developed within the highly diversified communities of our many frontiers, and this may in turn give us new knowledge of the American mind and temperament. Finally, if the materials of the Index can be widely seen they should offer an education of the eye, particularly for young people, which may result in the development of taste and a genuine consciousness of our rich national inheritance."

Holger Cahill

1. Earthenware Dish, sgraffito decoration, Pennsylvania German; made by
Georg Hübener, probably in Montgomery County; dated 1786.

This is a splendid example of Pennsylvania German ceramics, showing the best efforts of the potter.

The dish was dedicated to Katharine Raeder, no doubt as a love gift, a sort of ceramic valentine. Her name appears in the inscription, and two doves unite in one heart-shaped figure. This might be a lover's coat of arms, with the doves replacing the imperial double eagle of heraldry. It seems clear the potter has identified himself with the tender message, because the initials GH, for Georg Hübener, are closely woven into the design. The inscription reads: "Cadarina Raeder her dish. From clay and many skills the potter fashions what he wills."

OUR WIDE LAND

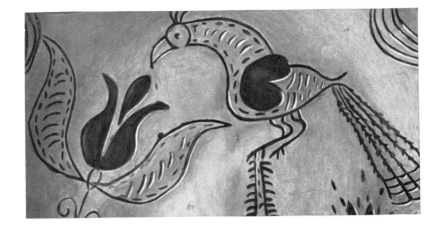

2. Earthenware Plate (detail), sgraffito decoration, Pennsylvania German; dated 1812.

1. Bird and Tulip

The colonies on the eastern seaboard had been settled largely from England and eventually the Anglo-Saxon tradition became the predominating influence everywhere. But here and there, East and West, there were other racial groups. Smaller in number, they were held together by a common faith, and developed styles that differed from the prevailing pattern. The fact that these groups lived in regions or communities isolated from the rest of the population favored artistic originality.

One of the most exuberant of these local styles is the Pennsylvania German. The Spanish art of the Southwest is ornate, but it can also be severe. No other region produced a folk art so fresh and homogeneous in character. Here we have a style that is pleasantly decorative; it enriches surfaces, it is colorful and at times childlike in its untutored simplicity.

As if eager to decorate, the design spreads across the surface, freely and boldly. One feels the luxurious richness of gay colors, yellow, intense green, purple and flaming red, that seem to speak of a delight in the good things of life. Applied to objects of everyday use, the art of the Pennsylvania Germans is wholly utilitarian. It is a true folk art, largely unconcerned with the niceties of technique. The artists depended on talent rather than academic training.

Folk art is not linked to the current historic styles as exemplified in architecture, sculpture and painting. Being chiefly rural and isolated, it is unrelated to the changing period tastes that ruled the towns. Philadelphia might have its Chippendale, its classic revival, its Victorian Gothic; Bucks County and Berks, Montgomery, Lancaster, York, Dauphin, Lebanon, Schuylkill, Lehigh, and Northampton continued the traditions of their forefathers. These independent, freedom-loving farmers adhered to their cultural heritage as tenaciously as they conserved the fertility of the soil. The rich farms, with their large barns, today reflect the conservative trend of their owners' thrift and husbandry, the wish to keep what they have and to provide for the future. In the same way a desire to cling to what is theirs reveals itself in the continued and unchanged use of the same motifs.

This adherence to tradition is shown in the use of the tulip as a floral motif. It occurs on chests and boxes, it is found on wood, tin, cast iron and paper.

In the chest painted to order by the itinerant decorator, in the baptismal or marriage certificate illuminated by a schoolteacher or village pastor, and even in earthenware crocks and stove plates purchased from pottery or foundry, we recognize a common artistic expression. It is this expression, rather than origin or purpose, that produces the character of folk art.

Just as the language of the Pennsylvania Germans is a German dialect, interspersed with English words, so is their art an offspring of a European tradition. From 1683 up to the time of the Revolution these newcomers took up land in the eastern and southern counties of Pennsylvania. Leaving villages in which the native crafts were flourishing, they transplanted a European peasant style to the new world, where it lived on undisturbed for a century and a half. Traditions isolated from outside influences were kept intact and strengthened through fresh immigration, as the first arrivals were joined by friends and relations.

The motifs used were not inventions of the artist. They belonged to a common stock handed down from one generation to another, and were used by all who practiced the arts. Simple shapes and dots, lines, circles, stars, chevrons, rosettes, and even flowers and birds, appear in the designs of many peoples at various times. These motifs came to Pennsylvania with the immigrants, who brought them from the Palatinate, the upper Rhine, Swabia and Switzerland. Though the same motifs are used, the decorations differ from one county to another, pointing to differences in the styles of individual decorators.

Pottery, chests, painted tin called toleware, illuminated manuscripts or Fraktur writings, and cast-iron stove plates are here illustrated. There are two kinds of pottery, the so-called slip-decorated and the sgraffito ware. Both were for display rather than for use and represented but a portion of the common homemade pottery. In slip-decorated pottery, the slip, a white clay mixed with water, was applied to the surface to form various designs in relief. In sgraffito decoration the concave surface was entirely covered with slip, and the design was scratched into this covering coat. A lead glaze, transparent and yellow, softened the slip and brought out the red of the clay. The potteries were small and largely concentrated in Montgomery and Bucks counties near deposits of suitable clay. Here and there in the state are the remains of early kilns, and the ruins of furnaces that once produced the stove plates may still be seen at Durham, in Bucks County.

In furniture, the dowry chest and bride's box have a special significance. The young bride took her chest filled with household linens to her new home. At the time of the wedding, the groom gave her a smaller, often oval-shaped box, made of thin strips of pliable pine, for personal belongings. Chest and box were gaily decorated in color on the exterior, and so were salt boxes, chairs and cupboards.

Fraktur, so called after the name of the Gothic type, is the art of illuminated writing, elaborated with pen-drawn decorations in color. The elements were taught in the schools, and this art was widely used for various documents, including certificates of baptism and marriage, pious inscriptions used as house blessings for wall decorations, bookmarks, valentines, and decorations of songbooks.

What these sturdy people created, to bring the joy and satisfaction of artistic expression into their lives, is now treasured by public museums and private collectors.

3. Salt Cup, pine, Pennsylvania German; lathe-turned, and painted by Joseph Lehn, Lancaster County; 1860–1880.

4. Oval Dish with Scalloped Edge, earthenware, sgraffito decoration, Pennsylvania German; made by Samuel Troxel, in Montgomery County; dated July 17, 1823.

5. Water Whistle, earthenware, Pennsylvania German; nineteenth century.

In this oval dish the compactness of the design contrasted against the openness of the rim is particularly pleasing. The light strokes of the letters of the inscription form a delicate border, subordinated to the main decoration. As on Hübener's dish, it reads: "From clay and many skills the potter fashions what he wills."

The whistle, shaped like a hen, is about ten inches high. When used it is filled with water and is blown through the head, the length of the neck governing the pitch. The zigzag line of the saw-tooth edge is an ancient decorative motif, and color applied to the glaze in spots and streaks is characteristic of the Pennsylvania German style.

6. Pie Plate, earthenware, sgraffito decoration, Pennsylvania German; made near Tyler's Port, in Montgomery County, by Johannas Neesz; dated 1805.

Correct anatomical representation of animals and human figures lies beyond the interest of folk art. Nevertheless, the drawing is fresh and spontaneous, the line unhesitating in the contours of horse and rider and in the freely-drawn floral sprays. The Continental soldier is believed to be George Washington. This motif may be based on a European folk-art tradition, for the jumping horse is well known throughout popular ceramics. The inscription reads: "I have ridden over hill and dale, (and) have found disloyalty everywhere." Green and orange have been used in the red glaze to fill in the floral sprays and rider.

7. Dough Trough with Lid, poplar, Pennsylvania German; painted decoration attributed to Christian Selzer of Jonestown; eighteenth century.

8. Candlebox with Sliding Top, pine, Pennsylvania German; painted in 1777.

In troughs of this type the dough was put to rise before being kneaded into loaves. Articles of use when produced through the handicrafts were often elaborated with painted decoration. Stylized tulips growing out of vases were thought to be as suitable for a dough trough as for a bride's box. Christian Selzer takes high rank among the chest painters. Though he frequently used the same motifs, he constantly varied his adaptations. The trough is twenty-eight inches long, and gives some idea of the amount of baking which was done. The food and good cooking of the Pennsylvania Germans have become almost legendary, and bread was the staff of life.

What is so attractive about the design on the box is its sumptuous vigor. A few shapes are used, and large masses with sharply rendered contours stand out in boldly rendered sprays. This box is carefully constructed; the sides are dovetailed and the upper rim is rounded to form a groove for the lid. Tulips, set into panels and circles, form a well considered decorative scheme and stand out in striking contrast against a light ground. Before chests of drawers and dressing tables were in common use, low chests and small boxes were used. Those the bride received on her wedding day were elaborately painted and became valued possessions.

[5]

9. Dish, earthenware, slip decoration, Pennsylvania German; made in Bucks County by David Spinner (1758–1811). Signed.

10. Bowl, earthenware, Pennsylvania German; made in Bucks County, nineteenth century; probably designed by David Waring.

Appreciation of a fine relationship of shapes is shown in the way the inscription, borders and birds of the dish harmonize with one another. The facile stroke that spells out the potter's name is echoed in the adjacent wavy-line border. Birds and tulips are laid in lightly with white slip, like sugar icing on a cake. In applying the slip, a cup was used from which the creamy fluid trickled out through a quill onto the reddish clay. Splashes of green appear in the lead glaze; the outer border is orange. The inscription reads: "Every morning I like to eat fried sausage with sour gravy. D. Spinner."

In the bowl the surface is perforated with a kind of openwork suggestive of lace. The potter thereby displayed his skill so that the contents of the dish, perhaps red apples or purple grapes, would show their color against the clay. An acorn forms the knob on the lid, and the handles suggest wickerwork. An imitation of natural and other forms in art is typical of eighteenth century ceramics.

Dowry chests with designs of birds come from Lancaster County. Doves and peacocks are here set among tulips and blossoms. The artist was more interested in

11. Dowry Chest, Pennsylvania German; from Lancaster County, inscribed with the name of the first owner, Jacob Rickert; dated 1782.

12. Dowry Chest, Pennsylvania German; from Berks County; dated 1784.

spots of bright color than in making the flowers and birds lifelike. A decoration in two panels was no doubt suggested by the intrusion of the wrought-iron key plate and the space reserved for the name. The low base and the narrow lid, in their contrasting colors, call attention to the chest's spaciousness. The effect of the design depends on the plain, unbroken surface, in which one feels the restraining hand of a person sensitive to the beauty that lies in simplicity.

The most ornate of Pennsylvania marriage chests come from Berks County. The one illustrated here is exceptionally elaborate. The surface is covered with a splendid array of intricate designs. There is boldness in the large floral shapes and delicacy in the leaves and branches that fill the panels in a closely spaced carpet-like design. Unicorns, symbols of the Virgin Mary in medieval art, are characteristic of Berks County folk design. On the lid we find a star, a design also used on the barns where it was meant to keep out evil spirits. Designs of such artistry are the works of itinerant craftsmen, who traveled from one farm to another, often accepting food and lodging in payment.

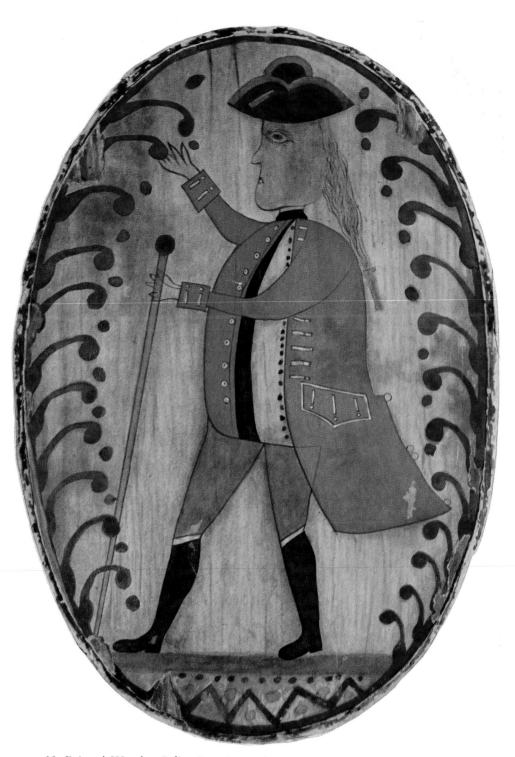

13. Painted Wooden Splint Box, Pennsylvania German; eighteenth century.

This box, about sixteen inches long and less than a foot wide, was intended for keeping wearing apparel. The cheerful decoration, the red frocked man with cane and tricorn hat, suggest the festive character of the occasion, for such boxes were known as gift boxes, dressing boxes, or brides' boxes. They continue a tradition of European peasant art; similar boxes painted by experienced craftsmen are found in Bavaria, Austria, and Switzerland. Berchtesgaden was a center of manufacture that also furnished the toy industry with splint boxes as containers.

Judging from the awkward character of the drawing, this box belongs to rural Pennsylvania. Painted splint boxes, that are sometimes mistaken for Pennsylvania German, were also imported. As they were attractive and practical for storage purposes, and no doubt valued for sentimental reasons, many must have come over with the baggage of the immigrants. They can be recognized by the more professional character of the decoration.

Though this box was painted by an amateur artist, the layman is usually not responsible for Fraktur writings. The text in Fraktur writing was executed with the quill pen, elaborated with pen-drawn ornaments, and embellished with painted designs in color.

14. Birth and Baptismal Certificate, Fraktur Writing, Pennsylvania German, Whitehall Township, Lehigh (formerly Northampton) County; dated 1808.

15. Water Color, on paper, by Heinrich Otto, Pennsylvania German, Lancaster County; eighteenth century, last quarter.

Manuscript illumination died out in Europe after the adoption of printing with movable type, but it lingered on in Pennsylvania and in other states till about the middle of the nineteenth century. It received particular emphasis at the Ephrata Cloisters, where we may speak of a revival.

This example shows a fine appreciation for style in its decoration, and its skill suggests the professional writer. Such certificates were made by itinerant writers, usually some time after the event. Calligraphy was also an accomplishment of the schoolmaster, who was expected to write a good hand. Baptismal certificates were favored by the Lutheran and Reformed Churches, but not by sectarians like the Amish or the Mennonites, and others who did not believe in infant baptism. This certificate attests to the birth of Elizabetha Schlosser, January 10, 1808, and her baptism by the Reverend Johannes Gebrecht. Religious precepts are written into the two smaller hearts.

The peacock-and-parrot design may be a pattern for a chest decoration. The drawing is accomplished, and the elegance and precision of line are due to the practiced hand of the experienced artist. This design, like many others, demonstrates the love of folk art for symmetry.

16. Show Towel, Pennsylvania German, made by Magdalena Gross in Pennsylvania; 1829.

This towel shows traditional embroidery patterns, typical folk-art motifs, including stars, trees of life, and birds of paradise. Such motifs are close to basic symbols that have been widely used throughout primitive art as charms to bring good luck or ward off evil. They are part of a common heritage and not consciously derived from nature. Even where folk art is no longer ostensibly symbolic, certain designs go back to a time when belief in magic affected the daily lives of the people.

Folk art is impersonal; there is no desire to achieve a personal expression. The same motifs are perpetuated and modified, as new materials bring about variations. Here the design takes on a rectilinear character because embroidery in cross-stitch encourages straight lines. The top is in red and green, whereas the border at the bottom was achieved by pulling threads in the homespun linen. This left a net on which the design was stitched with linen thread. This show towel is for decoration only, to cover the ordinary towels, and uphold the reputation of the farmer's wife for good housekeeping.

17. Chandelier, tinned sheet iron, Pennsylvania German.

18. Patch-box from a Kentucky Rifle, brass, Pennsylvania German; about 1790–1810.

19. Hinge, wrought iron, Pennsylvania German.

In the days of feeble candlelight, several candles were grouped for better illumination in a chandelier suspended from the ceiling. As tin was inexpensive, it was used in wide bands which make the fixture a trifle bulky; but the narrow strips, bent ribbonlike into curves, give it a fantastic character. The shapes as well as the motifs punched into the tin are appropriate to the material, as tin bends easily and takes impressions readily.

Before the days of standardized, interchangeable parts each handmade flintlock rifle was different. The ornate brass lid of the patch-box with its scrolled design, cut and chased, was also individual. A patch is a piece of greased leather or cloth wrapped around the ball to keep it out of contact with the barrel. Thereby less cleaning was necessary, making faster shooting possible. The Kentucky rifle that helped to conquer the wilderness was made in Pennsylvania; it got its name through association with Daniel Boone after his return from the country beyond the Cumberland Mountains, then called Kentucky.

In the wrought-iron hinge, the medieval Gothic tradition persists. In the scrolls, we sense the delight of the craftsman who could hammer the malleable metal into fantastic shapes.

20 and 21. Toleware Bread Tray and Coffee Pot, from Lebanon, Pennsylvania.

22. Utility Box, wood; Pennsylvania German, from Ephrata, Pennsylvania; about 1800.

The term japanned tinware or toleware is applied to such household utensils as trays, coffee pots, tea caddies and the like made of thin sheets of tinned iron painted. These decorations are executed in varnish color on opaque, almost black ground. Chinese vermilion, yellow, green-blue, white and bronze powder are used. Originally this technique was introduced from China; it spread to Europe and the United States, where it achieved its greatest popularity in the nineteenth century, lasting until after the Civil War.

In the eighteenth century, toleware was also imported from England. The designs show the firm line and sure touch of the experienced artisan who worked for a larger market. At a later period the quality of the decorations deteriorated at the hands of inferior artists who used stencils.

The bright color and bold decoration, using flowers, bands, and dots, are in the folk-art tradition. In these broad, expansive motifs that cover the surface in all directions, you still feel the flavor of a European peasant design. Toleware was also made in such centers as Berlin, Connecticut, and Stevens Plains, Maine.

Characteristic of folk art are the simple designs on the coffee pot: flowers, wave bands and stars. It was made by hammering flat sheets of tin in separate sections over molds, hence the angular profile. Though handmade, it

23. Coffee Pot, decorated with a design punched into the metal, Pennsylvania German; nineteenth century.

24. Toleware Tea Caddy, from Reading, Pennsylvania.

25. Basin of a Three-Piece Washstand Set, sheet iron with cast-iron handles; made between 1867 and 1884 in New York City.

foreshadows a later machine age, since here the craftsman is concerned with rapidity of manufacture.

Toleware, commonly called Pennsylvania German, often shows this type of expert brushwork in the decoration. Such painted tinware was used by the Pennsylvania Germans; the brilliant color and the light weight made it popular. Like "Gaudy Dutch" Staffordshire pottery, it was imported from England and sold to the Pennsylvania farmers.

The humble basin is so striking, in its blaze of color, that one hardly questions its appropriateness. This de-

sign reflects European peasant art, in spite of classical scrolls and rosettes. These designs were added to painted surfaces and stenciled borders through a mechanical transfer from prepared paper, called decalcomania, a process much in vogue in the early sixties. In 1867 a certain Louis Fitzmaier patented an improved method of transferring a design from lithographic paper to a metal surface. Though industrial methods of circumventing the artist's handiwork did much to debase taste, in this instance, at least, the combination of techniques still retains its effectiveness.

26. Religious Inspirational Drawing, Shaker; made by Polly Reed, New Lebanon, New York; April 11, 1847.

These fascinating though little known "spirit drawings" belong to a period (1837–1847) when the Shakers were gripped by an intense emotionalism that expressed itself in elaborate rituals, in visions and various psychic experiences. What the Shakers' millennial laws ordinarily would have banished could express itself in pious symbolism. Those who made these drawings were looked upon as inspired recipients of "divine gifts," expressing spiritual messages in graphic form. Here a talent bursts its bonds, revealing a yearning heart seeking an outlet in art, veiled in mysticism.

Throughout there is a sense of purity, but also a frank delight in the ornamental. In pristine whiteness the dial of a clock stands out above a heart surrounded by a floral decoration. Blossoming roses are set within a rigid en-

closure, and the tender branches droop down as they meet the sidewalls of a prisonlike box, so that the free and natural mingle with the rigid and systematic. The line, threadlike and brittle, suggesting writing rather than drawing, breathes a sensitive, delicate beauty.

The whole drawing is steeped in religious symbolism. The names of Father James and Father William, who worked with Mother Ann Lee, are placed beside the trees. Altars and tables of shewbread relate to the Scriptures; the heart is a universal symbol of love, lamps and candles mean heavenly light; and doves, little birds and the falling feather reflect the daily speech of the Shakers, for by such symbols they would refer to the inspirations coming from Heaven.

27. Spinning Wheel, oak and ash, iron spindle, Shaker; Pleasant Hill, Mercer County, Kentucky; nineteenth century.

2. Work and Faith

A rich heritage of the arts and crafts has come to us from the religious communities established in America largely after the Revolution and in the decades before the Civil War. As we have seen, the Pennsylvania Germans at Ephrata established one of the early religious settlements. Toward the end of the eighteenth century a few English Shakers founded the first of their communities in America. Among the settlements that followed were a Swedish one at Bishop Hill, Illinois, which had a short but dramatic existence, and a German one at Zoar, Ohio.

Only in a country that offered freedom from persecution and poverty was it possible to form these independent, self-contained communities, where those of the same faith might live, work and worship together. Communal settlements of various religious groups were scattered from Maine to Pennsylvania, west as far as Oregon, and south through Kentucky into Tennessee. A fertile soil provided sustenance, and an atmosphere of tolerance encouraged experiments in reforms. As all property was held in common, the welfare of every member was assured, and he could consecrate himself wholeheartedly to labor in the spirit of religion. Each

settlement secluded itself from the outside world, leaving to the church trustees all matters of commerce and finance, the sale of produce and the purchase of supplies. However communities might differ in name, they all advocated a return to the ideals of primitive Christianity and to a new conception of the dignity of labor.

The founder of the Shaker church in this country, Ann Lee, came from England in 1774, with eight followers. After an early settlement at Niskeyuna, later named Watervliet, near Albany, the first Shaker colony was founded at New Lebanon, New York, in 1786, and it became the seat of central authority of all Shaker societies. Between 1825 and 1850, at the time of greatest development, there were six thousand members in about twenty settlements in seven states. The name "Shaker" came from the group dancing, a part of the religious service, the purpose of which was to shake sin out of the body through the finger tips. The official name of the Shaker group was the United Society of Believers in Christ's Second Appearing.

Of the various Shaker societies only a few members remain, but the contributions the Shakers made to American culture have endured. Their furniture, particularly, represents a native American style of distinction and originality.

It was a Shaker belief that "True Gospel simplicity . . . naturally leads to plainness in all things." This affected their designs for architecture, furniture and textiles; to make these things simple was a kind of worship. Beauty was not consciously sought, but was synonymous with utility. The Shakers cared nothing for art; ornamentation was considered superfluous. Their walls had no pictures, but their floors were immaculate and their rooms were kept in the best of order. Work and faith were linked in Mother Ann's saying, "Put your hands to work and your hearts to God."

To promote the comfort and happiness of their fellows was also the aim of the craftsmen. Once a form had been found that best served the purpose no further experimentation was needed. Hence Shaker design had a basic permanence; individual preferences were subordinated to the religious principles sanctioned by the group. This meant a degree of uniformity in the search for standards of excellence.

Essentially this is also the modern point of view. Before a machine age had given a new meaning to the idea that form should follow function, the Shakers were applying this principle, and our methods of production have brought back the ideal of simplicity that makes us sympathetic to the kind of beauty found in Shaker design.

Whatever the Shakers did, they did well. They believed in using to the fullest extent the gifts that God had given each individual. Personal ingenuity and talents were consecrated to practical use. Whether in the improvement of agriculture, the building of a house, or the construction of furniture, they avoided waste of labor and materials. Ever seeking the most economical solution of a problem, they invented many labor-saving devices. As these improvements were not patented, they were of immediate benefit to all, but their Shaker origin has frequently been forgotten. Among the many inventions credited to the Shakers are the circular saw, the screw propeller, a new type of wood stove, a washing machine, a windmill, and numerous other machines and devices used in home and shop.

The Shakers were known for their integrity and for the quality of their goods. The demand for their products was such that thriving industries were developed for garden seeds and medicinal herbs, for canned fruits and vegetables, as well as for chairs, benches, footstools, brooms and other things.

Another religious community was that of the Janssonists, of Bishop Hill in Henry County, Illinois. Starting with four hundred settlers who came from Sweden in 1846, under the leadership of Eric Jansson, the colony increased to eleven hundred in two years. Their economy, too, was based on agriculture, and their crafts furnished not only field implements and household furnishings but also the tools with which to make them. Buildings in the village were constructed of bricks burnt in community kilns and lumber cut from black walnut trees common in the neighborhood. Home-grown wool and flax were spun into thread and woven into cloth. Men and women worked together in fields and shops, supplying their own necessities and selling the surplus.

We do not know the names of the individuals who made the beds, chairs, and wooden pitchforks, but from their work we can see they were skilled in their several trades. Some of the objects reproduced are still in the original buildings; others are in museums or private collections. The German Separatists of Zoar, Ohio, under their leader Joseph Michael Bäumler, later called Bimeler, are here represented by a peasant bench and an elaborate calendar. Dating from the time the Mormons were settled at Nauvoo, Illinois, a relic from the Mansion House is here reproduced.

28. Man's Beaver Hat, made by the Shakers; nineteenth century.

29. Dressmakers' Counter, maple and pine, Shaker; Watervliet, New York; nineteenth century.

Works of the Swedish settlers at Bishop Hill find a counterpart in another work of Scandinavian origin, a large carved altarpiece from Decorah, Iowa. This Norwegian-American example is of a later date, and not connected with a religious communal settlement. Of these works, it is the only one that represents the established church and a religious subject.

But more important than subject matter were the convictions that inspired the religious communities and permeated the whole mode of life. In the case of the Shakers, these moral precepts gave direction to the craftsmen who produced the style we admire today.

The drop-leaf top, the tapered legs, and the red color of the dressmakers' counter are typical Shaker features.

Construction is light but sturdy, and as inlays and veneers were thought to be deceitful, they were never used. Instead, Shaker furniture depended on proportions and the natural grains of the wood, as in the contrast of ungrained maple posts against pine panels and curly maple drawers.

Like all early settlers, the Shakers made their own wearing apparel. As their advancing economy, with their labor-saving inventions, yielded more than they could consume, the surplus was sold in the open market. They produced the raw materials, flax, wool, and hides, from which they manufactured anything from carpeting, horse blankets, worsted cloth, and checked linen, to felt hats.

30. Interior with Stove, Shaker; New Lebanon, New York; nineteenth century.

31. Shaker Basket; nineteenth century.

32. Stool, pine, Shaker; made in Hancock, Massachusetts; nineteenth century.

Shaker rooms are sober but cheerful. Pegboards line the walls. They are for wearing apparel and for hanging chairs off the floor at cleaning time. Plain baseboards lack the usual moldings. Stoves exhibit the Shaker genius for simplicity at its best in a design that is low and horizontal, so that heavy logs can be handled with the least effort.

The excellence of their handicrafts is in the Shaker craftsmanship, but they also selected the finest materials and used the best tools. Basket-making was one of the many smaller industries in which they excelled. Where there was so much produce, baskets of various types were always in need, and some were made into sieves.

To give access to high drawers, the Shakers used stools with two or three steps of light but sturdy construction. The steps are dovetailed, and the edges are reinforced and cross-braced for rigidity. An orange shellac brings out the natural color of the wood.

33. Dipper, wood with natural finish, Shaker; made in New Lebanon, New York; about 1800.

34. Child's Chair, maple, Shaker; New Lebanon, New York; first half nineteenth century.

35. Armed Rocking Chair, maple and cherry, Shaker; New Lebanon, New York; nineteenth century.

One would like to keep this dipper just as a source of delight to the eye. In addition to the fresh sparkle of the grain of the wood, there is a sense of satisfaction from the tension felt in the thin wood bent into a circle.

Shaker chairs combine elegance and simplicity with comfort; they are as strong as slatback colonial chairs but lighter in weight. The back posts have finials, since Shakers were not against ornamentation that grew structurally out of the wood itself. Their craftsmen were inventive and attached a ball-and-socket device to the ends of the back posts, to prevent slipping when the chair was tilted back. Shakers were among the first to make rocking chairs and they made chairs for children. Though Shakers had renounced family life, they took care of children left in their charge and they were interested in education.

36 and 37. Man's Suit and Woman's Dress, Shaker; nineteenth century.

Fashions in dress vary but the Shakers adhered to their own conservative styles. In the cut of this nineteenth century man's suit there is a lingering suggestion of the eighteenth century. The subdued color reflects a humble, self-effacing spirit, but in spite of all sobriety, the vest is blue, the trousers brown and the coat purple.

The woman's costume is modesty itself; a triangular kerchief is combined with a bell-shaped skirt. The sleeves are tight and narrow. These almost geometric shapes are unrelated to the lines of the figure, for the designer has successfully obscured almost all semblance to nature, and even the collar looks as if it were part of a uniform. Yet this severity is relieved through the use of orange and white. A purplish red, made from butternut bark, was a favored color, something in the nature of a "universal" dye, being used on wood and fabrics alike. On one occasion, when a Shaker sister was dipping chairs into a large kettle of dye, the similarity of the colors of her chair and dress was pointed out and she replied, "Shaker dyes dye everything."

38. Rug, Shaker; made in Pleasant Hill, Kentucky; nineteenth century.

This rug is made of bits of woolen homespun rags, strung on threads like beads and sewn to a heavy canvas until the surface is covered; the outer border is braided. The design is unsophisticated; it grew under the hands of the worker. Rug corners could be round or square, depending on convenience or the impulse of the moment. The Shaker artist paid little attention to realistic drawing, and hardly differentiated between horse and cow. More elaborate naturalistic renderings would have been inappropriate. Simple borders, placed side by side in contrasting colors, were combined into an attractive pattern. Created in the midst of a group that fervently believed in simplicity, the design is in good taste.

Such abstract design is essentially the language of the spirit. This was true when Shakers made their rugs, as it is today and as it was in the neolithic period. Things of the spirit are invisible and do not depend on representation; symbols suffice. Pure line and form seem unworldly, hence even a religious community, that thought it had rejected art, could indulge in artistic creation in an abstract, chastened form.

39. Weave-Chest or Sill Cupboard, pine with natural finish, Shaker; made in New Lebanon, New York; nineteenth century.

40. Tall Clock, Shaker; made by Benjamin Youngs in Watervliet, New York, in 1806.

The splendid effect of this cupboard is due to an immaculate quality in the velvety surface, a pronounced pattern in the grain of the wood and a sense of amplitude in the proportions. These drawers were made to hold quantities of weaving material. Though severely plain, monotony is avoided.

In the clock, the usual division into base, shaft and capital, after the manner of classic architecture, is retained. The columns flanking the dial are reduced to slender spindles; the few moldings accentuate the plainness and all carvings have been suppressed. The straight bracket foot continuing into the base without break is in the Shaker spirit. Benjamin Youngs was a descendant of a well known Connecticut family of clockmakers. He made this work and signed it. Even though his signing a work of his hand suggests worldly pride, whatever scruples the Shakers might have had did not prevail against this firmly established practice.

41. Blanket Chest, pine, stained red, Shaker; Canaan, New York; 1836.

42. Sewing Table, Shaker; nineteenth century.

43. Bed, pine and maple, Shaker; made in New Lebanon, New York; nineteenth century.

This chest in general character is like the New England type, but simplified. The open, dovetailed corners, the base cut at the corners in angular fashion, and the bone key plate are in the Shaker manner. This plate was intended solely to protect the wood from being marred by the key, for the Shakers studiously refrained from making the key plate an ornamental feature in the usual manner. Being meant for utility only, it was small and inconspicuous.

The design of the sewing table is a simplified version of an earlier colonial tripod table that had an elaborately carved center support. By fitting the table with two drawers, the practical Shakers made it convenient for two sisters to work on a single piece.

In this bed, design has been stripped of all superfluities; only those parts that are justified by use have been retained. Light in weight, this bed was made movable by the addition of large casters.

44. Center Panel from Altarpiece, carved of maple and black walnut applied to oak planks,
by Lars Christensen of Benson, Minnesota, formerly of Iowa; 1880-1890.

What is attractive in this altarpiece is the ornamental effect gained from the mingling of carving, wood grain and color; each panel seems precious. The emphasis is on detail and in the altarpiece itself there is no connection between the panels. One is placed abruptly beside another and the spaces between are filled in with finials, scrolls, flowers and Norwegian inscriptions. This is the work of an artisan who makes the most of decoration. He has a sense for the ornamental, he emphasizes contours and works with masses, and presents his ideas with delicacy as well as boldness and good taste. Figures are like emblems, unrealistic and, except for the central panel, subordinated to the enframing ornament. The design in horizontal panels and the pointed gable (not included in our illustration) suggest an influence from the country churches of Norway; and some of the ornamental carving resembles woodcarving in eastern Norway.

45. Painting, "Harvesting with Grain Cradles," by Olof Krans of Bishop Hill, Illinois; 1875–1895.

Something of the vastness of the prairies carries over into this picture, with its yellow harvest fields against a luminous sky. The primitive artist is impressed with the desirability of expression and he exaggerates. Men stare as if in grim determination and women move awkwardly. Krans was not interested in variety in the action of his figures. Instead he makes us feel that farm labor is here organized to function with the regularity of a machine. In his youth Olof Krans had been a member of the Bishop Hill community where belief in the dignity of labor was part of the religious creed. Late in life, as a house and sign painter of Galva, Illinois, he painted a number of reminiscences from Bishop Hill.

Folk painters like Krans go to no art school. When a daily routine of work gives them no satisfaction, they may turn to painting for pleasure. They work at their own level, and one cannot judge them by academic standards. In this case the artist returned to the scene of Bishop Hill as a pleasant pastime during a period when he was convalescing from a leg injury due to a fall.

The Swedes at Bishop Hill were excellent craftsmen. The shears, made by the local blacksmith, are large and heavy, and may have been used in the tailoring shop.

Even if their religious fervor did not produce a new style, their furniture has a flavor of its own. The bed is rugged and heavy, with round rails and old-fashioned

46. Shears, steel; made in Bishop Hill, Illinois; nineteenth century.

47. Bed, maple; made in Bishop Hill, Illinois; nineteenth century.

48. Bench; made in Zoar, Ohio; nineteenth century.

49. Hotel Lantern, sheet iron and glass; made about 1854 for the Bjorklund Hotel, Bishop Hill.

cords, after the manner of the more modest furniture of the period. The turned sections are the same on all four posts.

This lantern has a pleasing thinness and leanness characteristic of sheet iron. As sheet iron comes to the craftsman in a finished state, part of his work is done for him; he only bends the material into final shape. In the word "Hotel" on the glass pane, round dots sprout like buds, replacing more functional serifs. Adapted to neither brush nor pen, such playful adornments have not survived.

In this bench from Zoar we have a folk manner trans-ferred from southern Germany to northern Ohio. These religious settlers were simple peasants with modest aspirations; their rustic furniture was designed for utility rather than comfort. Where the leg is mortised into the seat additional thickness is needed, which tends to make the bench top-heavy, so the legs spread out for stability. Labor and material are used economically, demonstrating another variety of simplification. Old traditions are continued so that here the Middle Ages reach almost into our own period. The style is attractive and as functional as any that grew out of the divergent backgrounds of these American religious communities.

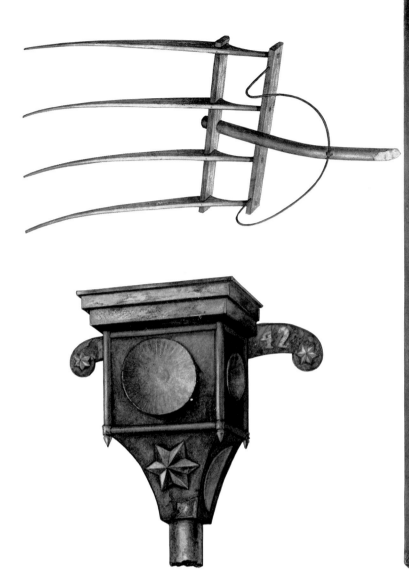

50. Barley and Straw Fork, hickory; Bishop Hill; nineteenth century.

51. Downspout Head, painted tin, originally gilded; made for Joseph Smith's Mansion House in Nauvoo, Illinois; dated 1842.

52. Calendar, wood; made in Zoar, Ohio in 1836.

The hickory fork from Bishop Hill is tough and suggests the thinness of metal. These prongs, so perfectly adapted for digging into a bundle of hay, are also pleasing to look at; their purity of form is most satisfying.

A downspout head is a box connecting a gutter to a downspout to carry a sudden rush of rain water. This one follows the style of the Greek revival, and sun, moon and star are emblems of the Mormon Church.

Perpetual calendars were useful before mass production gave us a yearly supply of printed calendars. This one has a case like a clock with dials on the back. It tells the month, the time of sunrise and sunset, the length of the day, fixed holidays, and the days of the week and month; the names are in German. The decoration of flowers and castles perched on hills is in the manner of painted peasant furniture common to the villages from which these newcomers had emigrated. The astronomical symbols beside the weekdays remind us that the days were named after the planets. Sunday has the sun, Monday the moon, Tuesday shield and spear, for Mars the god of war. The caduceus is for Wednesday or Mercury's day, the Z for Thursday, the day of Zeus or Jupiter. Friday has a mirror for Venus, goddess of love, and Saturday a scythe or sickle for Saturn, god of time.

53. Saint Francis, *bulto*, carved and painted wood; made in New Mexico; late eighteenth or early nineteenth century.

54. Sidesaddle, leather and white felt; made on Nipomo Ranch, San Luis Obispo County, California; mid-nineteenth century.

3. Saints and Saddles

In our southwestern states there grew up a folk art, Spanish in character with some Indian elements intermingled. Here the Indians were not so quickly displaced by landseeking settlers as in the East; they remained and were converted to Christianity. The Catholic Church brought them from Spain not only a new religion but a new way of life. Taught by Spanish priest or craftsman, the natives became familiar with new techniques; to work in metal, to carve and build in stone and to use paint in the European manner. In the resulting style a simplified Spanish element is conspicuous, but an Indian contribution is also present.

In contrast to the artisans of Massachusetts or Virginia, who were of European origin, the natives of California, like all American Indians, had but recently emerged from a Stone Age. In the East the craftsmen were trained and experienced; they merely continued in a new country what they had previously practiced. The Indian of California formerly had gathered acorns for a living, and many skills had to be newly acquired. The tribes in New Mexico and Arizona, indeed, had enjoyed a highly developed material culture, but here the Indians lived in pueblos separate from the Spanish communities. The country was isolated; manufactured goods had to be brought on muleback across mountain trails. What little the Indian and the Spanish craftsmen saw of European art and what guidance they received hardly compared with the rich cultural resources of a New England craftsman. Their works of art could not, therefore, be duplicates of Spanish art. Even when they based their work directly on European models they did not produce exact copies. Either they lacked the necessary tools or they preferred something that corresponded more nearly to their own experience.

New Mexico was poor and afforded but a meager livelihood. The California Indians lived on berries and roots and had only a few utensils, yet they were among the finest basket-makers in North America. Moreover, the folk arts that later came out of the Southwest are artistically equal to folk arts elsewhere.

This geographical area may conveniently be divided into two parts: New Mexico and Arizona, with their century and a half of Spanish-Mexican rule, and California. Here white settlement came later, for the first mission, San Diego de Alcala, was not founded until 1769. Our religious carvings and panels are largely from New Mexico, while doors, fountains, water basins, candleholders and wall paintings reflect life under the Franciscan missions of California. Saddles and spurs here illustrated are from the end of the Mexican or the early American period.

Historically, three divisions may be distinguished: Spanish rule, from the reconquest of New Mexico to Mexican independence (1692–1820), the Mexican Republic (1820–1850), and the American period, after these regions came into the Union (1850). It was the Spanish mission that first gave the southwestern style its essential character. In the ranch or pastoral period of the great landed estates of California (1820–1850) the influence of the missions decreased. Separated from Church control, they fell into decay. The Indians were dispossessed and became peons or cowboys; craftsmen who survived practiced their crafts outside the church or mission, and with the coming of industry, folk art gradually disappeared.

The Spanish period was responsible for the missions, particularly in California where a once splendid array stretched from San Diego to San Francisco along the *Camino Real,* or King's Highway. Community functions revolved around the mission or parish church, and those priests who were artistically inclined took charge of building the church and making its furniture. They were the first to make *bultos* and *retablos* in New Mexico, and to teach the craft to the natives. A *bulto* (literally bulk) is a figure of a saint or holy person in the round; a *retablo* is a religious image, painted, carved or printed on a flat surface.

In the early period the Spanish influence was pronounced, as the priests had in mind the sculpture of Spanish churches. The early *santos,* representations of saints, were probably made by priests and showed lively gestures and expressive features. As the native craftsman, Spaniard or Indian, became independent of his teachers he developed a style of his own. His figures took on something of the character of puppets, yet they are serious and dignified. They were no longer statues for churches but statuettes for house altars, for every adobe had its patron saint. As is often the case in archaic art, an emphasis on simplicity of form produces a monumental character. This is true of the *bultos* in spite of their small size; they are usually under two feet high. To the mind of the native, the image itself was the source of supernatural power; its magic could heal sickness and benefit crops. However, a saint who ignored the prayers of his worshipers might be punished by having his face turned to the wall.

The *santero* carved figures for a livelihood, traveling from one New Mexico community to another, like the New England itinerant portrait painter. The amateur *santos*-maker, on the other hand, made his *santo* as an exercise in religious devotion.

In California, painted mission walls from which the whitewash had been removed indicate that, in addition to painted altars of purely Spanish inspiration, the native artists of the Southwest produced mural decoration. European ideas, pilasters and arches are fused with some of the simple motifs that appear in the petrographs or rock paintings of this region. There are also large easel paintings, like the Stations of the Cross, which are exceptional in folk art.

Distances in the Southwest were great, and stylistic differences considerable. The painted chest from the Rio Grande Valley is quite unlike the mission basket from the Pacific coast; they were made by artists of different races and in places about as far apart as New York and Florida.

55. Gold Pin, dove, made by Celestino Trujillo in Monterey, California; nineteenth century.

56. Basket, made in 1822 by Anna Maria Marta, Mission of San Buenaventura, California.

This is one of the finest California Indian baskets in existence. Its design is unified, even though it combines Indian designs like blocks, diamonds, V shapes and the like, with the Spanish royal coat of arms, the castles and lions of Castile and León. The lions are hardly recognizable, partly because the technique of weaving gives to any representation a geometric character. An inscription woven into the border becomes a part of the design itself. It reads: "Made by Anna Maria Marta, Neophyte of the Mission of the Serafic Doctor, Saint Bonaventure." The basket is made in the usual Indian manner of coils covered with rush and sewn together. A tall, thin grass is used for the body of the coil, but only the covering rush appears on the surface. At the missions, basket-making was done by the women. For weaving they sat on the ground; the only tool they used was a bone awl, a spine of cactus or a nail.

The wooden stirrup goes back to the days of the California rancher, when the country was given over to vast cattle-raising estates. Horseback riding was both sport and necessity, and much attention was given to finely tooled leather for saddles. The ornamental stirrup, though made of wood, suggests an influence from leather in the carved pattern. The inside was hollowed out like a box; this gave the foot a firm rest and must have added to riding comfort.

The native furniture of the old Spanish Southwest looks heavy as if something of the thickness of the adobe

57. Carved Wooden Stirrup, mounted with silver, made in California; nineteenth century.

58. Chair, cypress, from the Spanish Governor's Palace at San Antonio, Texas.

59. Small Chest, pine, covered with deerskin, from New York State; nineteenth century.

walls had been carried over into the wood. Chairs were primitive, consisting of hardly more than posts and boards mortised and pegged together without the use of nails. Tools were scarce and so was paint, so that the surface of the wood was left unfinished.

This small chest suggests in its materials the meeting of the frontier with the resources of the eastern factories. Deerskin is stretched over wide pine boards and finished with brass upholsterer's tacks, strips of patent braid, and cast-iron handles. It is already in the manner of the trunk as our grandparents knew it.

The charm of the *retablo,* on the following page, lies in its precise shapes and elegant curves. The artist has used lines that combine into a pattern, like the arms which echo the garlands above. Because the Christ Child is important, he is large; the hands are tiny, for primitive

60. Holy Family, *retablo,* made in New Mexico.

art often neglects hands and feet. Here we have extreme simplification; *retablos* tend to be unrealistic; the flat surface of a panel is, by itself, removed from the reality of a statue in the round. The dark colors, chiefly red, black, and brown, make the panel appear gloomier than when it was originally painted, at which time the background was light and fresh.

According to legend, Saint Acacius or San Acacio, one of the early martyrs, suffered death with 10,000 Christian soldiers at Mount Ararat. To symbolize this army, a half dozen soldiers are lined up at the foot of the cross, and each one wears a serious expression. The

61. Saint Acacius, *bulto,* wood; made in New Mexico, eighteenth century.

saint, with arms outstretched, merely stands against the cross. Bright, cheerful colors in a tragic subject may seem contradictory, but probably no such scruples troubled the artist. Had he given any thought to pain and death, he probably comforted himself in the belief that a saint triumphs over death. Here no suffering is shown, though the red streaks on the yellow coat suggest blood. In spite of such details, this is still a devotional image. Children can delight in what is apt to appear gruesome to adults. Lacking experience, they take it as make-believe and find it amusing. Though folk art is not child art, in this instance it is close to the childhood level. Realism and abstraction appear quite commonly side by side in the folk art of New Mexico.

Bultos were carved of cottonwood, and covered with gesso and paint. Where the legs show, as here, they were made separately and mortised to the body by wooden pegs.

62. Saint Isidore, *bulto,* wood, painted; made in New Mexico.

We are told of Saint Isidore, patron saint of farmers, that while he prayed an angel worked for him in the fields. An angel with a team of oxen is here added, so that all may know this is Saint Isidore. The group is intended for a house altar; the saint faces his worshipers, ready to listen to those who pray before him.

This is New Mexican folk art after it had passed through an earlier, more emotional stage dominated by European influences. The carving of *bultos* was taken up by local craftsmen, who reverted to a simpler manner more in keeping with their own experiences.

The saint's trousers and jacket are brown, edged in yellow, and the green of the vest is repeated in the angel. Saint Isidore is given an elegant costume worthy of his importance as a sacred figure. Our modern custom of regarding such statues as art objects and placing them in museums would have seemed irreverent to the original owner.

63. Wall Painting, Mission House of San Fernando Rey de España, California; presumably after 1822.

This is part of a wall decoration executed by native artists. In matters of art where no question of religion was involved the Franciscan fathers allowed the Indians freedom to follow their own ideas. Where the native artist uses the cross he repeats it many times, contrary to the usual church custom, because he attaches to it a magical significance. Other motifs show a distinct resemblance to motifs that appear in certain neolithic rock paintings in California and adjacent states.

In this hunting scene painted over a door, the hunter, disguised in a pelt, is stalking a deer. One arrow has found its mark, as shown by the dots representing blood, and another is being aimed. The delicate zigzag line, another folk-art motif, forms an attractive border that fits in well with the pictorial part. Red is repeated in the wavy lines in the center of the door boards, giving unity to the whole design.

64. Virgin and Child, *bulto;* made in New Mexico.

65. Painted Chest, pine; made in New Mexico, first half nineteenth century.

The figure of the Virgin on the opposite page is expressive, her features are animated and the tilt of the head and the gestures of the arms give her an additional liveliness. The swinging curve of the Madonna's arm and shoulder carries over into the Christ Child. In New Mexico the Virgin, Nuestra Señora, was represented in at least a half dozen versions which differ in their attributes. One version, The Most Holy Virgin of Guadalupe, represents her standing on a crescent moon and a cherub. She is also surrounded by a nimbus of rays. According to a popular legend the Virgin appeared to the Indian Juan Diego in a vision from heaven. In another version, Our Lady of Sorrows, she is weeping and has her hands folded as she stands under the cross; a later, more restrained type is Our Lady of Solitude. These two are European interpretations that penetrated into the folk art of New Mexico. *Bultos* have often lost their

attributes and have been restored besides, so that we cannot be sure which version is here represented. The upper part of the figure is solid, the lower is a hollow framework built up of an armature of sticks. Bound together, they are fastened to waist and baseboard, and covered with cloth dipped in gesso. The bell-shaped skirt gave the artist his opportunity for splendid decoration. Figures such as this, each about two feet high, were carried in procession at church festivals.

The chest decoration shows the gay spirit of a fiesta with its bright colors, its exuberant figures and its lush foliage suggestive of the exotic vegetation of a southern climate. The design on the chest is closely packed, yet is vigorous and freely drawn. This chest is one of a series painted by an itinerant artist, who probably learned his craft in Mexico.

66. Ecclesiastical Candlestick, pine; made for the Mission Santa Ines, California; 1817 or thereafter.

67. Caballero Suit, owned by Don Antonio Franco de Coronel; mid-nineteenth century.

The pedestal of the candlestick is made in one piece, turned on a lathe. A new form has emerged; the native workman has simplified moldings, suppressed sharp edges, and made the profile soft and flowing. In the freshness of the cool blues and greens and in the warmth of the orange we seem to feel something of the pleasant California climate. Bright color is not restricted to any one region or period, but the supporting pedestal painted half green and half blue is unusual. Color is commonly used to bring out structure; here color cuts structure in two.

At a time when masculine clothing in the East al-

ready was turning toward its present drab monotones, the Dons of California were devoted to colorful apparel. For the owners of the ranches, life was a continuous holiday of fiestas and social activities, as gay and comfortable as Don Antonio's jacket and trousers. Rarely do we find in costume such a happy combination of extravagance and ease. In spite of the elaboration, there are no encumbrances to interfere with freedom of movement. The use of dark blue for accents and the arrangement of braid and buttons made this suit a model of good design.

68. Baptismal Font and Stand, copper and pine; made for the Mission San Luis Obispo; about 1812.

69. Altar Tabernacle, pine; made for the Mission San Luis Obispo; late eighteenth century.

70. Missal Stand, pine; made after 1797 for the Mission San José.

The artist who carved the baptismal stand may have had little to do with the design. In its shape, with a shell bowl and an octagonal base, it goes back to the late Gothic. Perhaps a native craftsman selected the colors and arranged them in broad, contrasting areas. The carving shows good workmanship; both stand and copper bowl are fine examples of work turned out by the Indians.

Tabernacles were placed on the altar to hold the sacred Eucharist. Instead of the more elaborate marble tabernacles of Europe, the Indians used wood covered with a painted decoration on a gesso ground. The cubical form is like an adobe house in miniature, but the pretentious arched doorway suggests the mission itself.

The missal stand has a native flavor; except for shelf and frame it seems to be free from a close imitation of European motifs. The curves of the front are vigorous and weighty, and are repeated on the back; a European design has taken on a native flavor. A soft pink and a yellow, which is perhaps an imitation of gilt, give it a pleasing color effect.

71. The Third Station of the Cross, one of a series, painted on sailcloth by Indians under the guidance of mission fathers, about 1779; two and a half feet by four feet.

72. Spur with Leather Toe Strap; made in Southern California; nineteenth century.

According to tradition, the fourteen incidents of the "Stations of the Cross" occurred on the road between the house of Pilate and the place of Crucifixion. They were represented by paintings in European churches, so that those who could not undertake a pilgrimage to Jerusalem might exercise their devotions at home. The artist here tells his story in a fresh, childlike manner. The design, based on freely intermingling colored shapes, is effective, particularly in the expressions of the soldiers beside the passive head of Christ.

In the spur a striking effect is achieved by the contrast of polished wrought iron and a textured surface of short, incised strokes. The craftsman selected light-colored leather, and increased this lightness by using white thread stitched in border fashion.

73. Woodcarving, "Lumberjacks Sawing a Log," nineteen inches long; made in Eau Claire, Wisconsin; nineteenth century.

4. Life on the Frontier

A growing native population moved the frontier steadily to the west, and after the War of Independence many individual settlers sought new homes beyond the Appalachian Mountains. In the second decade of the nineteenth century, the migration became so great that the roads were filled with those who made their way westward by wagon, on horseback, and afoot. As distances lengthened, improved transportation became a vital necessity. At first, trails were used by pack trains, but when horses with packsaddles could no longer carry the ever-increasing freight, the trails from east to west were widened into roads.

Conestoga farm wagons became the customary carriers of freight, particularly in the turnpike and tollgate era between 1790 and 1830 when road building was in the hands of private companies. Even before 1800 these wagons made regular trips between Baltimore, Philadelphia, Lancaster and across the mountains to Pittsburgh. These boat-shaped wagons were named after the Conestoga Valley in Lancaster County, Pennsylvania, where they were first made. We are more familiar with another type with straight, boxlike bodies, the "covered wagons," that transported eastern settlers and freight to the Ohio country, and later to California and Oregon. Of all draft vehicles, the Conestoga six-horse wagon acquired the greatest renown because it was large, well made and driven by men noted for their courage and self-reliance.

The first national road, built by the Federal Government in 1818, ran from Cumberland, Maryland, to Wheeling on the Ohio River. Here the home-seekers transferred their belongings to boats and rafts, and floated them down the river. Much traffic was by river steamboats, and in 1842, when Charles Dickens visited this country, the tonnage of Mississippi steamboats exceeded the total British steamboat tonnage. When the Erie Canal was opened, the Great Lakes were connected with the Atlantic through the Hudson River.

Wagons used in New England were smaller than the Conestoga, and the two-wheeled Red River cart of the Northwest was more primitive. This cart goes back to the eighteenth century. It came to what is now North Dakota through the Hudson Bay Company by way of Pembina. The Red River Valley was then still separated from the East by vast stretches of undeveloped territory.

Wherever the farmer appeared, forests were cut, log cabins were built, and a settled agricultural life began. In making his first clearing and building his first shelter, the pioneer used the tools he had brought with him. As settlements grew, he depended on the local cutler, wheelwright or blacksmith. What could not be made locally was purchased from peddlers or imported from eastern factories. By the middle of the nineteenth century about one half of all hardware used in this country was made here, mostly in New England.

Axes were probably the first tools to be made for general sale. Collinsville, Connecticut, had in 1828 what became the largest ax factory, and Philadelphia had one of the largest saw factories in the world. Equal in importance to the ax was the plow. In the eighteenth century only the share was made of iron. An improved plow, a solid piece of iron except for beam and handles, existed before 1800, but farmers did not take to it, claiming as one disadvantage that the iron poisoned the soil.

Most of what the frontiersman used for conquering the wilderness no longer exists. Wagons wore out on the farms, new and better tools replaced the old ones, and there was no incentive to preserve what had served its purpose. Even after the railroads came, canals were still used. The early steamboats, though, were short-lived; many were wrecked or burned before they had grown old. Fortunately, pioneer vehicles and implements have survived in our historical museums, and a few typical ones are here reproduced.

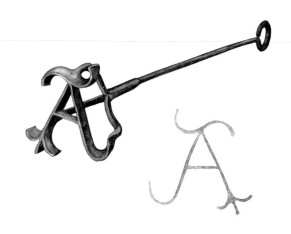

74. Branding Iron, about thirty-four inches long; made in Arizona, in 1891.

75. Conestoga Wagon; length, over 14 feet; wagon bed, 10½ feet; wheel diameters, 42 inches and 33½ inches; about 1800.

The Conestoga wagon was impressive with its vermilion-colored wheels, blue body and white homespun top. There are even those who believe it was the Conestoga wagon which suggested the colors for the American flag rather than George Washington's coat of arms.

Conestoga wagons were the long-distance overland freight carriers before the coming of the railroad. For a full load these sturdy vehicles carried from thirty to thirty-five barrels of flour. The driver did not sit in the wagon but rode on a saddle horse to the left of his team, or stood on a footboard on the side of the wagon.

Designed for lightness and strength, it was so well constructed that it withstood ruts, swamps and steep mountain roads. The bottom curved toward the center, sometimes in both directions, depending on the intended use, thereby preventing the load from shifting. This gave the body a shiplike design that may have facilitated the fording of streams in the early days.

The wheelwright designed and built the wagon; the blacksmith reinforced it with iron at all points subject to strain. He also added to the ornamentation by giving his iron a decorative turn. On the inside, iron strips lined the studding, and flat-head rivets fastened the iron to the frame. The toolbox especially was ornate, showing the artistry of the blacksmith. Conestoga wagons varied in size, but eight bows was common. The most important part of the wheelwright's work was the shaping of axles and the making of the wheels. Great care and skill was used to construct a strong wheel. To withstand side thrusts, and prevent the wheel from collapsing, spokes were made to point out from the hub and were held in place by the heavy iron tire. The distance the tire projects out beyond the hub is the dish. As the wheel was structurally the most important part it was made of the best materials. Each spoke was first roughly cut with a hand ax, and then shaped with a drawknife. The end that fitted into the hub was made from a template. All parts had to fit perfectly; a slight deviation might result in a broken wheel. Strong wood was used, which had been seasoned at least for three years—white oak and hickory for the frame, gum for the hubs, and poplar for the boards.

At one time the custom prevailed that a wagon which had to accept assistance from another teamster, had to give up its bells mounted on the horses. From this tradition we have the expression "with bells on" to signify that one is in fit condition. Our practice of driving on the right side of the road, with the driver on the left-hand side of the vehicle, began with the Conestoga wagoners.

76. Red River Ox-Cart, wood; 1845–1870.

77. Drawknife, wrought iron, maple handle; second half nineteenth century.

78. Broadax, wrought iron, oak handle; dated 1745.

This cart drawn by a single ox was used by the fur traders in the Dakota territory along the Red River of the North. Because the railroads did not reach these regions until the eighties, the pioneers here were dependent on their own resources later than in other parts of the country. The cart was therefore made entirely of wood; only the adze, saw and auger were used in its construction. As no grease was used on the axles the groaning of the carts could be heard for long distances. The high wheels allowed easy passage through the tall prairie grass. By stretching a hide over the cart, it was made into a shelter; by stretching one underneath, it was converted into a boat for crossing streams.

Drawknives were commonly used to smooth shingles after they had been split from the block. Basically, drawknives have changed but little since the time of the Romans. With its curved blade, this one demonstrates that an efficient, well balanced tool has a beauty of its own.

The old broadax was a finishing tool for smoothing planks and timbers, and was used in place of saw or plane in house and ship building. This one, an early, primitive type, has the date cut into the blade; it is without poll, and therefore a true hewing tool.

The adze is an ancient tool, developed long before it was brought to this country. It was used for planing timber and for hollowing out kitchen utensils.

The peavey is of American design, named after Joseph

79. Adze, wrought iron; second half nineteenth century.

80. Peavey, cast-iron socket, wrought-iron hook; made at New Superior, Wisconsin, second half nineteenth century.

81. Packsaddle, wood; nineteenth century.

82. Plow, hickory with iron share; made in Massachusetts, mid-eighteenth century.

83. Sharps Rifle, basic patent granted to Christian Sharps in 1848; later made in quantity in Hartford, Connecticut.

Peavey, the inventor. It is a hook with a spike and a curved lever for gripping logs, and is still a common tool in lumbering.

Before roads were built, the horse with packsaddle in trains of from two to twenty horses brought furs and hides to the towns, returning to the frontier with hardware and small articles. It was the packmen who opposed turning the trails into roads for wagon traffic, just as a generation later the boatmen on the canals opposed the railroads.

With this plow, made by carpenter and blacksmith, the plowing of an acre was a good day's work. Though lighter than plows brought over from England,

it is still primitive, with its wooden moldboard and attached iron share. A modern plow was gradually developed, based on such scientific studies as Thomas Jefferson's description of a moldboard of least resistance. A steel plow with a smooth, hard surface did not come into use until after the Civil War, when steel was produced by the Bessemer process.

Designed by Sharps in 1848, this single-shot breachloader was the most powerful black powder rifle ever made. It served in the Civil War and was popular in the West, where it was used to kill off the buffalo. This rifle was known as a "sharpshooter."

84. Printed Cotton; second quarter nineteenth century. One scene from a
larger piece depicting modes of travel.

This printed cotton is interesting for several reasons. It shows the Mississippi river travel of more than a decade after the first successful trip of the *Etna* upstream from New Orleans to Louisville. Here are the early stern- and side-wheel steamboats, and a cotton plantation with moss-covered trees. This is a sketch a landscape painter might have done for canvas; a designer would probably have emphasized the decorative rather than the pictorial aspects of the same motifs.

Printed cottons, so-called chintzes, appeared in Europe and North America after the East India trading companies had introduced them from the Orient. These India fabrics were highly prized in colonial times, but they were not in general use. After the Revolution, cottons printed in England became unpopular, few were made in North America and they have rarely survived.

The new country with its vast distances inspired this memorial to transportation. A second fragment of this travelogue, not reproduced here, shows figures on horseback, Conestoga wagons and a stagecoach; another fragment depicts a canal scene and it is known that a fourth section represents the railroad. Together these four pieces illustrate early nineteenth century travel. Anyone leaving Philadelphia for New Orleans would have used these conveyances, as he started inland toward Lancaster and Pittsburgh, making the largest portion of his journey by boat on the Ohio and Mississippi rivers.

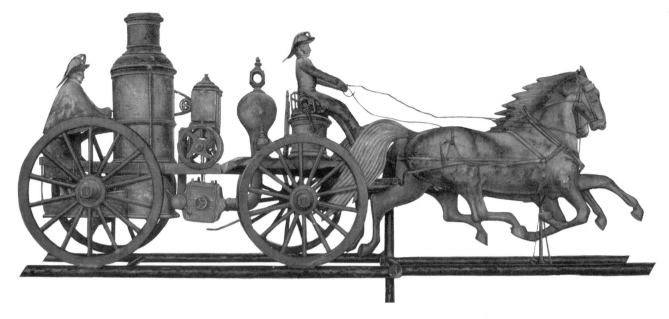

85. Fire Engine Weathervane, brass, copper, zinc and iron, from a fire engine house; made after an Amoskeag engine of the period 1860–1880.

5. FIRE

Fire companies form a spectacular chapter in American life. Many people today recall the old horse-drawn steam fire engines, racing down the streets with smoke and sparks belching from their boilers. But the volunteer fire companies hark back to an even earlier period. The colorful regalia of those days has been preserved for us: engines, hose carts, buckets, helmets, hats, badges, belts, trumpets and various fire marks. The firemen are remembered for their parades, picnics and fights, the ballads dedicated to them, and the songs and dances composed in their honor.

Fire fighting in this country began with leather buckets. Near the front door of each house was a bucket, bearing the owner's name. When church bells rang out the alarm, the call of "Throw out your buckets!" was quickly heeded. The bucket brigade formed in two lines between the fire and the nearest well or brook; the men passed the full buckets as the women and boys returned the empty ones.

When two-story houses became numerous, hand pumps came into use. They were tanks on wheels, and had to be filled by buckets and operated by handles called "brakes." The tanks were drawn by the firemen themselves, some twenty or more, as it required that many to man the brakes. Compressed air forced out the

water in a continuous stream through a stationary nozzle. Though this tub pump was more efficient than intermittent splashes from buckets, there was as yet no hose, and the firemen could not get close to the flames. Hand pumps were improved around 1819, when suction pumps which drafted their own water supply were introduced, together with substantial leather hoses.

The volunteer firemen occupied an important place in the community and frequently wielded considerable influence. Individual companies had their names and insignia. Firemen wore red shirts, colorful helmets, and fancy belts. The engines and hose reels were ornate and splendid, with brilliant colors and brass trimmings. The engines were even fitted with panels painted by leading artists and paid for by the firemen themselves.

Competition between different fire companies was keen. The water supply was often some distance from the fire, so that several engines might have to pump the water from one to the other. If one crew pumped faster than the next, they could overflow, or "wash" the other's cistern, and that was cause for deep humiliation.

One enterprising volunteer, arriving first at a fire, concealed the only fire plug with a barrel upon which he sat to reserve it for his own company. He enjoyed seeing his rivals search for the plug, but when his trick was discovered, such a beating followed that he had reason to regret his ingenuity.

The insurance company's fire mark on a building meant a reward to the company that put out the fire. It thus served as an incentive to greater effort and it often took a fight to settle the rival claims. Designs on fire marks were sometimes symbolic—clasped hands, guardian figures or eagles. A few remain that have a contemporary flavor, like the green tree or the bust of William Penn; others show engines, hydrants or merely the company's name.

As a young man, Benjamin Franklin organized the first Philadelphia fire brigade, and later, in 1752, he became a founder of the first American fire insurance company, the "Philadelphia Contributionship for the Insurance of Houses from Loss by Fire."

The horse-drawn steam engine was the last step in the development of fire engines, before the motorized equipment of our own day. Steam engines appeared around 1850, when machine production was getting under way, and after large cities had installed water supply systems with hydrants connected to underground mains. The term "fire plug" for hydrant derives from the early wooden main that had a stopper or plug at the street level.

After the Civil War, the volunteer fire companies declined. Firemen received regular salaries and fire marks were replaced by tin advertising signs. Though the trappings of the early fire fighters were gradually supplanted by sober uniforms, the tradition of bright colors and polished metal has continued to our own day.

As it was difficult to extinguish a fire in colonial days, it was equally laborious to kindle one. A strip of pine dipped in melted sulphur had to be ignited by a spark from flint and steel. A reluctant fire might be coaxed into a blaze with bellows, or if this failed, a flame was brought from another fire in a Cape Cod lighter, or smoldering coals were transferred in an ember carrier.

Houses were never uniformly warm. Although the glow of the open fire may have suggested comfort and cheer, even those who stood close to the fireplace would still feel cold. The fireback no doubt reflected some heat into the room, but its attractive design was perhaps as important as its heating value; and andirons that held the fireplace logs served a decorative as well as a useful purpose.

Except for the jamb stoves of Pennsylvania, there were no stoves until 1742 when Benjamin Franklin revolutionized heating by designing the Franklin stove. Heat had to be concentrated where it would do the most good. There were portable heaters or foot warmers for cold bedrooms, and warming pans to remove the chill from sheets and blankets.

Today we expect neither glamour nor art from our heating devices, but the era of the handicrafts combined the practical with the artistic. A warming pan may be inferior to a radiator, but its engraved lid afforded a craftsman an opportunity for self-expression, and it gave pleasure to all who saw it.

86. Fire Engine, hand pump, built by Patrick Lyon, 1806, for the Pennsylvania Fire Company No. 22, Philadelphia; side panels from the Weccaco Fire Company No. 19.

87. Fire Mark, cast iron, painted and gilded; first made in 1817 for the Fire Association of Philadelphia.

88. Fire Mark, "The Green Tree," cast in lead, on wood and covered with plaster; originally issued in 1784, in Philadelphia, by the Mutual Assurance Company.

89. Bandbox, covered with wallpaper; label H. Barnes and Co., 33 James Alley, Philadelphia; period 1831–1844.

The fire engine on the opposite page used a hose to draw water directly to the pump. The carved and painted side panels, belonging to an earlier tub engine, and the gilt scrolls around the brass intake, reflect the transition from craft to machine production. Artistic and mechanical features have not yet achieved a unity of style, hence these two in combination may appear somewhat incongruous to modern eyes.

The fire mark, with FA for Fire Association, was once gilt and showed the painted green grass beneath the hydrant. The early streets with hydrants set in a plot of grass rather than on a cement pavement must have appeared rural indeed. This mark appears on Independence Hall in Philadelphia.

Because trees attract lightning, houses near trees were considered poor risks, and Benjamin Franklin's Company refused to insure them. Such property was about all there was left when the Mutual Assurance Company was founded, so the Mutual made a virtue out of necessity and embraced the tree as its special mark.

Volunteer fire departments were so popular that one is shown on a bandbox used for traveling purposes, in

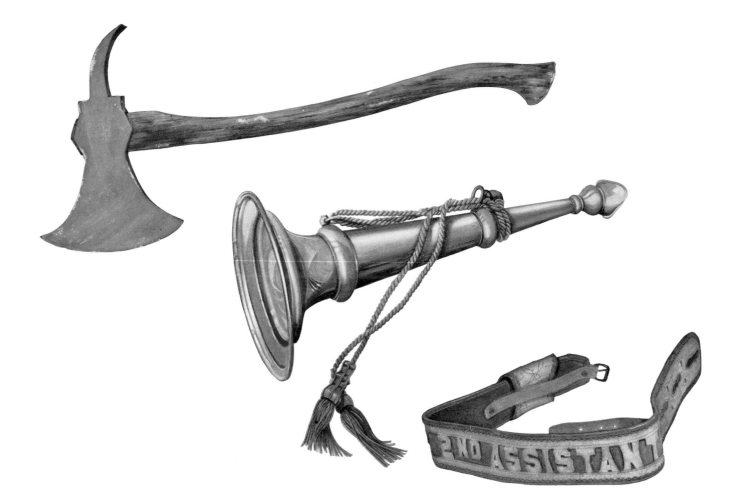

90. Fireman's Ax, from Niagara Hose Company No. 15, Philadelphia; before 1850.

91. Fire Marshal's Trumpet, nickel, silver- and gold-plated; made by John Elkins Jewelry Company, Racine, Wisconsin; dated 1877.

92. Fireman's Belt, cut leather, red and gray; from the Merchants' Hose Company No. 1, Fort Dodge, Iowa; nineteenth century.

a place where a well known landmark would often be illustrated. This is the goose-neck tub engine of the 1820's, in which the stream of water came from the goose-neck pipe on top of the air chamber, both visible in the illustration.

Early nineteenth century handicrafts continued to use traditional forms which clash with the more functional design of the mechanical age. Fire fighting equipment is here elaborated in the spirit of the handicrafts, yet an early fire engine is already a mechanical thing and before long will become an elaborate piece of steam-driven machinery. The results of these two methods of production when seen in the same work are in marked contrast. The painted panel on the fire engine looks out of place beside the brakes and so does the scroll decoration around the brass intake.

On the other hand, the ax presents a wholly unified solution of a tool that has developed its final form in the course of evolution. This well balanced tool with its curved handle is an American development of the straight-handled European ax. About the time of the Revolution the ax had achieved its present form. It was made in mass production on an irregular lathe. Here the poll is made into a hook for the use of firemen.

There is no superfluous decoration in the fireman's trumpet; the shape is developed out of the material itself. A trumpet is a megaphone used to amplify a man's voice in shouting orders or giving the call of "Fire!" A trumpet could also be a gift of honor and a token of esteem. When the speaking end was stopped with a cork, it became a drinking vessel and in a brawl an effective weapon.

What a fireman wore had to be suitable for his work, but that did not prevent hats and belts from being colorful. Even a second assistant had his rank blazoned in cut leather against a strawberry red background. The lettering set out in relief against the background anticipates the structural letters in vogue today.

93. Fire Helmet, sheet metal painted; made in Cincinnati, Ohio; about 1890.

94. Fire Hat, leather, with a portrait of Zachary Taylor; about 1850–1860.

95. Fire Bucket, leather, painted and with inscriptions; made in Massachusetts; mid-nineteenth century.

The helmet was for actual use. Its broad brim and channelled crown is for protection; its ornamental shield is comparable to the insignia on a soldier's uniform. The insignia on the helmet stood for the honor and reputation of his company. Though this badge was often only a number, it was highly regarded and given an artistic expression.

Fire hats follow the stovepipe fashion of the period. The one with a portrait of Zachary Taylor, hero of the

Mexican War and twelfth President of the United States, presumably belongs to the period around the middle of the century.

Buckets, made of the finest leather, afforded an excellent opportunity for decoration. The one above bears the owner's name, "John Tyler," and a painted ribbon inscribed, "Prompt in Danger," winds between bursts of flame, against a dark green background.

96. Ember Carrier, sheet iron with iron handle; eighteenth century.

97. Cape Cod Lighter, brass; early nineteenth century.

98. Warming Pan, brass, engraved and punched; wood handle.

The ember carrier was a humble container, designed to slant back so that the coals it held would safely settle to the rear. It had a lid, no doubt necessary when a fire might have to be carried from one house to another, at times through rain or snow.

A Cape Cod lighter consisted of a tankard holding oil, in which a rottenstone was dipped. This oil-soaked stone was ignited at a fire and carried about to light other fires. This tankard, made of brass and set on a brass plate, was designed as an attractive feature that added to the appearance of a room.

The warming pan, made by a brazier, continues a European tradition. With its polished lid it was an attractive utensil beside the fireplace. This one has an elegant chased and punched design in which the effect is achieved wholly through line, showing long, rhythmic curves of flowers and scrolls, and a cock with a flourishing tail.

99. Foot Warmer, zinc, with oak frame; first half nineteenth century.

100. Foot Warmer, tin, made in Wilmington, Delaware; early nineteenth century.

101. "Hessian Soldier" Andiron, one of a pair; cast iron, painted; late eighteenth century.

Foot warmers were metal containers set into wooden frames and decorated with perforated designs that allowed for draft. Inside was an iron pan for the smoldering coals, hot bricks or stones. This one has turned spindle supports at each corner. In colonial times it was common to see boys carrying prepared foot warmers to the women's side of the church before service.

This particular foot warmer was made for hot water and is "U" shaped to make it convenient for the foot to rest against. It could be used on wagons and sleighs, which probably explains its unornamental, utilitarian shape. It has a functional look although it was made

long before modern design was thought of.

The "Hessian Soldier" with his blue coat and straw-colored breeches was a colorful figure, though here his luster has worn with age. Ordinarily firedogs do not represent the human figure, but this one must have appealed to the imagination of his contemporaries. The part the Hessian Soldier played in the American Revolution may have been the reason for his being made to serve in this menial role. The eagle on his cap points to the German principality of Ansbach-Bayreuth, rather than Hesse-Cassel, after which these foreign mercenaries were named.

102. Eagle Head, pine, painted, from a sailing vessel; about 1850.

6. The Image at the Prow

At the front of the ship, under the bowsprit where the sides converge, was placed the figurehead, the symbol of the vessel. It served no practical purpose, yet hardly an American ship sailed without one. It was regarded by the seamen with an affection amounting almost to superstition. And this must have been so throughout history, for from earliest times vessels have been decorated with human or animal shapes.

Since shipping has always been one of our most important industries, it should not surprise us that the carving of figureheads ranks high among American crafts. The builder who launched a ship must have felt that he was sending forth an emissary to represent the young country in the harbors of the world. It became a matter of national pride that the ship should look her best.

American figureheads were unique in their variety. The most characteristic type was the full-length figure, often female, frequently larger than life-size. To be judged properly, a figurehead must be seen in its original position as part of the ship. What may seem awkward in a detached figure in a museum looked different when the figure was in its place intended by the designer. The contour, the silhouette, were more important than details. Figureheads were not superimposed

ornamentation; artistically and structurally they formed a unit with the bow. With outstretched arms, head lifted high and gaze fixed into the distance, the figure seems to fly forward, with the flowing draperies increasing the sense of speed.

Figureheads were carved in pine, painted and gilded. They were not always cut from a single block; usually several pieces were doweled together. Arms might even be detachable, so they could be removed during rough weather.

Figureheads were less subject than other kinds of sculpture to the influence of changing styles. The classic revival of the early nineteenth century affected the figureheads to some extent, but they never became as classical as sculpture in marble.

Ship carving was close to folk art, and flourished without benefit of academic training or European study. Nor was it confined to the imposing packet and clipper; whalers and smaller boats had their carved eagles and decorated trail boards.

Although much of folk art is anonymous, at least a few of the carvers of ships' figures are known. Shem Drowne, Isaac Fowle, Simeon and John Skillin of Boston were established craftsmen in the eighteenth century. Samuel McIntire, best known for his architectural carving on the fine houses of Salem, also did ships' carving, though only one existing figurehead is ascribed to him. William Rush of Philadelphia, who acquired a national reputation as a sculptor, did the carving for our newly created Navy, and others, like Sampson of Bath, were famous in their day. Late in the nineteenth century, when figureheads had gone out of style, less pretentious billetheads continued to be made by men like Bowers and Robb, who did work for steamboats and river craft around New York. Most of these men worked for private ship builders; others, like Bellamy, spent many years in the employ of the Navy. Bellamy, coming late in the period, added art school training to his shop experience.

Producing a life-size figure was no work for an amateur; it required years of training. Each master had his apprentices who carried on the craft, and the firms often passed from father to son.

Ship carvers lived near the water front. From their shops, often in old sail or mold lofts, they could look out on the harbor. They mingled with owners and captains, and among themselves they formed a closely knit group, a kind of fraternity, the members of which were scattered throughout the ports along the Atlantic seaboard. When work was scarce, carvers turned elsewhere for employment; some made cigar-store Indians or circus wagons.

As far as we know, no figureheads have come down to us from the seventeenth century. In the colonial period the craftsmen depended on English models, but after the Revolution a native development began, and early in the nineteenth century, achieved a freedom in the choice of subjects and a style that reflected the craftsman rather than the sculptor. The subjects of the figureheads were varied; symbolic figures, national heroes and statesmen, portraits of the owners, char-

acters from mythology and legend, even from literature and romance. Animals like sea serpents, dolphins, or alligators were used at different times. The name chosen for the vessel usually determined the subject of the figurehead.

The style in ships' figures changed with the styles in the ships themselves. The early ones were "bust heads" only; the full figure came later. At first they stood erect, for the rounded hull seemed to require a vertical figure. As vessels became narrower, figures accommodated themselves to the slant of the cutwaters, and leaned forward more and more. Finally, on the clippers, with their sleek hulls and sharply receding bows, figureheads were almost horizontal.

In the seventies and eighties, the down-Easters were among the last to carry full-length figureheads. Toward the end of the nineteenth century, the use of full figures declined. Simple billetheads, carved scrolls, or at best, eagles, took their place. As steam replaced sail, the carvings became flat, and in the Navy, state seals and scrolls seemed more in keeping with the times. Eagles survived on the pilot houses of river boats.

The eagle here reproduced is from a ship's prow, and probably belonged to a smaller vessel. The artist did not depend on color alone but used texture also by indicating feathers, without losing his bold and vigorous carving.

Finally, with the use of iron and steel in ship construction, carved wood was no longer suitable. In 1907 the United States Navy ordered that figureheads be removed from naval vessels and sent to the states for which the ships were named.

A much reduced decoration lingers on today in the carved trail boards, name plates and carved sterns of yachts.

103. Cat Head, cast iron, from the prow of a ship; nineteenth century.

104. Billethead, carved, painted, and gilded.

105. Figurehead, "Lady with a Rose"; before 1814.

Billetheads or fiddleheads, so called when the scroll turns up, were often used instead of figureheads for reasons of economy. Acanthus leaves, rosettes and C curves are combined effectively in a type of decoration that was common on land and sea.

In this early full-length figure, the jovial smile is in amusing contrast to the fashionable neoclassic dress. With all its striving for elegance, it is still folk art. Even though this figure may not have been cut out of a single piece, the carving looks bulky. The original block has been modified only enough to bring out the figure in rudimentary fashion. The method is not

unlike that of a carver on a medieval cathedral, who retains in his figure the feeling of the original stone. This lady is gawky and constrained; still we appreciate the vigor and unassuming simplicity of the carving.

What we actually know about an individual figurehead is usually very little. Where the costume is of a period, we may assume the carving to be of the time when such costumes were in fashion. In the case of this bust on the opposite page, hairdress, comb, puffed sleeves, and high belted waist suggest the twenties and thirties of the last century. One has the impression that

106. Figurehead, female bust, carved and painted; nine-teenth century.

107. Sea Serpent Head, carved and gilded, from the *Diadem* of Gloucester, built in Essex in 1855.

108. Figurehead, by Isaac Fowle of Boston; 1818-1853.

this probably represents the captain's wife, for what other figure in fashionable dress would have cross and anchor, symbols of faith and hope, carved on the scrolled base.

The sea serpent head was sawed from the tip of a ship's prow, and still shows some of the carved and gilt leaf-and-scroll pattern. In the early part of the nineteenth century there were persistent reports of the existence of a strange sea serpent. Though none are known to have been brought to the surface, the imagination of the ship carver had no difficulty in creating a striking specimen of the fabulous monster.

The freely posed woman with her billowy drapery is the work of a craftsman who was also a sculptor. It is

109. Figurehead, "Jenny Lind"; from the ship *Nightingale* of Portsmouth, New Hampshire; built in 1851.

110. Figurehead, male bust; early nineteenth century.

the only existing figurehead known to have been carved by Isaac Fowle of Boston, but it never went to sea, having been used only as his shop sign. This figure shows the influence of classical sculpture, and it is evident that the artist had a command of the figure. Fowle was one of the best of the early nineteenth century wood carvers. He and his sons were active in Boston over a period of sixty-two years.

This sweet, doll-like face, modish figure and elegant costume represents a celebrity of the mid-nineteenth century, Jenny Lind, "The Swedish Nightingale." Once her blond curls were gilt, and she carried a nightingale on her finger. Jenny Lind is perhaps the most romantic of famous persons carved in figureheads. From her first American appearance in 1850, her high soprano voice, charming personality and generosity won her a

tremendous success, and several ships bore her image. The vessel which carried this figurehead was designed to be exhibited as a model American clipper at the World's Fair in London. But instead she was sold, and proved to be one of the fastest of the California clippers. At one time she was relegated to the slave trade, and the figurehead of Jenny Lind was replaced by an eagle.

Figureheads are often cheerful or noticeably demure, as in this bust, for folk art is not given to subtleties. Here is freshness and charm and a sure touch in the carving of leaves and scrolls and the thick clusters of the sideburns. The craftsman ignored the neck but the haughty determination of the model caught his imagination. This must be a portrait of a person of importance in the contemporary life of the period, perhaps the ship owner himself.

111. Figurehead, female bust, from a schooner, built in Haverhill, Massachusetts; in 1815.

112. Figurehead, male bust, "Quaker"; nineteenth century.

113. Figurehead, carved and painted, about five feet tall; nineteenth century.

The size of the figurehead always bore some relation to the size of the vessel. It is known that this bust, which is little more than a head, comes from a schooner out of Salem, hence a smaller, two-masted sailing ship. This has been repainted at a fairly recent date.

In the "Quaker" figure there is stern reality, the force and determination of an actual person. The carving has a beautiful simplicity; it is broad, with very little detail.

The full-length figurehead shows a costume in which the neoclassic fashion merges with the early Victorian.

The hairdress is in a manner reminiscent of classic sculpture; the high waistline and the short sleeves of contemporary dress are combined with a wind-blown mantle that is treated as conventional drapery. The carving has the vigor and simplicity of folk art, typical of the manner of the figurehead carvers. The forward lean was probably still moderate, suggesting that this figurehead antedates the clipper period, when the figurehead became nearly horizontal to fit the raking bow.

114. Figurehead, perhaps "Commodore Perry," and possibly from an early packet of the same name, built in New York City; 1822.

Here we have a distinguished piece of wood sculpture that was certainly done by an able craftsman. The interest has been concentrated in the features, the broad surfaces of the half-length figure contrasting with the head. The artist has not been identified. The original paint is gone, but the costume fits the period of the 1820's. A comparison of this bust with portraits of Oliver Hazard Perry, the naval officer in command of the American ships in the Battle of Lake Erie (September 10, 1813), reveals a resemblance that makes this attribution plausible. It was in this engagement that Perry's flagship, the *Lawrence,* hoisted the battle flag inscribed with the words attributed to the dying Lawrence, "Don't give up the ship." A wood carving of this slogan is illustrated in the last chapter.

115. Figurehead, bust, "Solomon Piper," from the ship of the same name, Boston; made before 1854.

116. Sternpiece, carved and painted.

The contemporary life of the period furnished inspiration to the carver. Solomon Piper was a well known Boston merchant and shipowner. His bust is from a packet boat that plied between Salem and England. It belongs to the best period of the portrait bust and has a convincing lifelike quality.

This sternpiece illustrates a more modest type of decoration, a bust head within a circular frame. Perhaps it would not be fair to assume that this pudgy little face was meant to represent the owner's wife. This type of decoration, here somewhat hard and dry, must have been fairly common. The original piece is six feet long.

117. Navigator, wood; from shop of James Fales, nautical instrument maker of New Bedford, Massachusetts; nineteenth century.

The mariner with the huge sextant is just as compact as the nautical instruments that were packed away in snug-fitting cases. In his squat proportions, he follows an English tradition, for Dickens in *Dombey and Son* speaks of this type of shop sign as "a little . . . timber midshipman with an offensively disproportionate piece of machinery."

118. Cigar-Store Indian, wood, carved and painted; nineteenth century.

7. At the Sign of the Wooden Indian

In the old days, virtually every merchant and mechanic, every shop and tavern had a sign, either peculiar to the trade or personal to the tradesman. Even the town hall and post office had their emblems. The street then presented a lively picture of activities, with each barber pole or wooden Indian calling attention to services or goods offered for sale.

Though shop signs may well have helped those who could not read, that was not their sole purpose. They were not merely aids to the illiterate for when shop signs first appeared in this country they had already become traditional symbols. To sell goods and to advertise services were, of course, the basic reasons for signs, but other motives contributed to their enrichment. They reflected the taste, wealth or standing of trader or craftsman.

It is not accidental that many of these old signs are also fine works of craftsmanship. Inn signs frequently were well proportioned panels that used the same details as colonial architecture.

Among the most characteristic of the shop signs are those of the tobacconists. Tobacco was considered the gift of the red man, and the wooden Indian outnumbers all other cigar-store figures. The idea of the figures originated in England when the "Black Boys" stood on the counters of London smoke shops; the cigar-store Indian, however, belongs to this country. Although there were isolated figures in Baltimore before 1780, the real history of the wooden Indian begins in the forties of the nineteenth century. When cigar smoking increased, the tribe multiplied. By 1840 the making of these figures had developed into an industry; by 1860 every tobacconist had a life-sized Indian on the sidewalk in front of his shop.

Between two and three hundred were put on the market yearly. Firms in New York, Chicago and elsewhere kept a supply of figures in stock. In 1871 the largest known collection of wooden Indians was that of a New York dealer; we are told by an old man who remembers this storeroom that it was an awesome sight to see the hundreds of carved Indians in their fresh war paint. During the nineties the Indians became less common, as chain stores forced out the individual dealer and sidewalk regulations forbade obstructions.

The wood used was usually white pine. A foot a day was considered good carving. Since it took another day for each foot of finishing and painting, twelve days would be necessary for a six-foot Indian. An outline was drawn on the log and the wood was roughly hewn out with chisel and mallet, the grain being followed carefully. The trunk was made in one piece, the arms were attached separately. The carvers worked from old prints, colored lithographs, or from real Indian models. The figure was painted before it left the work shop and had to be repainted regularly by itinerant restorers. Details might be added to suit the individual customer. According to one story, a man from St. Louis ordered an Indian to resemble his mother-in-law, and sent a photograph to help the carver achieve a likeness.

The Indian chief is more common than the squaw; the generalized style at times makes it hard to distinguish one from the other. The typical wooden Indian is meant to represent the tribesman of the plains in tanned buckskin, knee-length shirt, belt, leggings and moccasins. He usually wears a feather headdress and a kilt of tobacco leaves or feathers, and holds in one hand a package or box of cigars. No particular tribe can be identified. The tobacconist's brave is strictly a white man's Indian, as the carver added fanciful details of his own invention, trimming shirts with beads, fringes, medals, feathers and tobacco leaves.

Though the Indian was by far the most popular of tobacconists' figures, there were others to add variety. Among them was the Highlander, who had been used in England where he helped to sell snuff, and the Turk, who came into vogue with Turkish tobacco. Others were baseball players, Buffalo Bills, clowns, drum majors, Humpty-Dumptys, policemen, soldiers and figures of Mr. Pickwick, Puck and Uncle Sam.

Early craftsmen who had been carvers of ships' figures turned to Indians when ship carving declined. The carvers varied from trained craftsmen to men who were little better than carpenters. In Michigan, Wisconsin, and Illinois there were German and Swiss settlers who had served apprenticeships in their own lands, whittling figures for Noah's Arks, and they took over the wood-carving craft in this country. Julius Melchers, father of the painter, Gari Melchers, had an academic background and was an outstanding carver. Through him Detroit became a center of the craft. William Demuth dealt in tobacconists' supplies and Indians as a sideline in a shop on Broadway, New York. He originated the cast zinc Indian, using wooden figures as molds.

Shop figures, like figureheads, represent a phase of native sculpture that functioned in everyday life. A cigar-store Indian was often ordered from a catalogue by a shopkeeper who felt he needed it for his business. The fact that in a very commercial age such fantastic figures successfully attracted customers shows how youthfully romantic these people of the nineteenth century really were.

119. Tavern Sign, "Temperance," figure (perhaps Aurora) in chariot, wood painted in oil; nineteenth century.

120. Felon, carved figure from Kent County Jail, East Greenwich, Rhode Island; second half eighteenth century.

121. Sign from Black Horse Inn, Saybrook, Connecticut, wood; eighteenth century.

122. Sign from Red Lion Inn, North Colebrook, Connecticut, wood; by William Rice; first half nineteenth century.

This handcuffed wretch, with pleading eyes and tight lips, is misery itself, and his plight arouses our sympathy. All the tension is in his face; his figure is limp. The carving is broad, revealing the tool marks, and it is not overly realistic except for the expression. As we become more familiar with our early folk carving, this figure may rank as one of the most significant works from the colonial period. It is only thirty inches high.

The delicately shaped pediments and spindlelike colonnettes are in keeping with the colonial architecture of the inn itself. The frame is as important as the design. A sharply delineated horse is finely related to the lettered word "Entertainment."

Two loyalties are combined on the lower inn sign, which has the American eagle on one side and the British lion on the other. The sign bears the signature of Rice, an itinerant sign painter of the period. Captain Arah Phelps, a soldier in the Revolution, was the owner of the inn at Colebrook, Connecticut.

123. Cigar-Store Figure, Highlander, wood, about four feet high; nineteenth century.

124. Bunch of Grapes, wood, painted and gilded, about one foot high, believed to be from the "Bunch of Grapes" Tavern, Boston; eighteenth or nineteenth century.

125. Cigar-Store Indian, squaw with papoose, wood, carved and painted; nineteenth century.

The Highlander was one of the most splendid of the types borrowed from abroad. In England he had already made a place for himself as an advertiser of snuff; and when used by the American manufacturers, he presented a package of cigars. This figure is one of the more accomplished pieces of carving. Its freedom and vigor suggest that the artist was an experienced, well trained craftsman. Some shop figures must have been done by immigrant craftsmen who had received their training in Europe, and such may be the case here. Look at the concentration of interest on the realistic head and at the bulky hands; it is clear that this is also folk art. A certain elaboration makes this figure look sophisticated, but the impression does not last as one becomes aware of the basic simplicity of the carving.

Bunches of grapes are typical signs for wine merchants and taverns, and this particular specimen is believed to have served for one of the early inns of Boston.

In contrast to many Indians with stolid faces and menacing gestures, this squaw with raised hand and papoose on her back is friendly. Her simplicity, and the restrained character of the ornamentation even lend her an air of elegance. This is a sensitive figure by an unknown carver.

The spirally striped barber pole originates in England at least as far back as the fifteenth century, when barbers were minor surgeons and were incorporated as barber-surgeons. Henry VIII separated the two professions,

126. Barber Pole, cedar; late nineteenth century.

127. Inn Sign, wood, presumably from the "Bell in Hand," Boston; Temperance Tavern of 1795.

128. Cigar-Store Indian, in posture of greeting, over six feet high; wood, carved and painted; late nineteenth century.

changing their name to the Company of Barbers and Surgeons, and restricted the barbers to the practice of dentistry. In the eighteenth century the two groups were divided into two distinct corporations. In the course of time the barbers were limited in their duties, but they never changed their shop signs, which still showed them as surgeons, for the spiral stripes denote bandages. The pole itself is usually said to represent the stick grasped by a patient to encourage the flow of blood during a blood-letting.

James Wilson is said to have established the "Bell in Hand" as a sort of temperance tavern because he deplored the drinking of rum and hoped to substitute for it malt liquors. He was town crier of Boston as well as a church deacon, so the town crier's bell serves as his personal emblem. Though this bell is a restoration it perpetuates the original design.

Rigid postures, as in this cigar-store Indian, may bring to one's mind archaic art as found in ancient Egypt or Greece. Arms raised stiffly or pressed close to the body are typical of early art, but the comparison goes no further. The cigar-store Indian is folk art, definitely of our period. The carver wants to make his figure seem alive. We get the suggestion of animation, through his hand raised to his forehead, but not of really free movement; the figure is still static and musclebound. Looked at superficially, it has realism; but actually the charm of the figure lies in the ornamental character of its design. There is an effective pattern in the rhythmic lines repeated in feathers and drapery.

129. Importer's Sign, carved and painted teakwood; nineteenth century.

130. Sign, wood; made by Isaac Fowle for shop of John Bradford, hardware dealer, Boston; early nineteenth century.

131. Locksmith's Sign, wrought and sheet iron; made in New Orleans by John A. Mangin in 1895.

Tea imported by clipper ship was sold in tea shops, for which the carved Chinaman was the characteristic figure. The gorgeous Chinese dress suggests the prosperous merchant. Like many shop signs, he stood on a small platform in front of the store.

Saws, hammers and other tools sold in hardware stores are arranged in orderly fashion. Hardware-store signs are comparatively rare, as few merchants exhibited them. This one, carved of a single piece of wood, is an individual design by the well known Isaac Fowle.

Ornamental ironwork, so profusely used in New Orleans, has contributed to the charm of the city. A simpler key might have sufficed for a shop sign; this craftsman shows his skill by creating an intricate design which grows out of the character of the material. The heated iron is hammered into elongated shapes, taking on an elegant linear quality.

There is a jaunty spirit in the little fellow on the opposite page holding the huge bunch of grapes, so much too big for his slender figure. It was done by a

132. Tavern Figure, man holding grapes, wood, carved and painted; fifteen inches high.

133. Butcher's Sign, painted wood, thirty-two inches long; first half nineteenth century.

134. Cigar-Store Figure, Turk, wood, carved and painted, fifty inches high; nineteenth century.

man who made no pretenses to anatomical accuracy and still produced a gay and carefree figure.

There can be no possibility of misunderstanding this sign, used as a weathervane on a slaughter house. The signmaker combines hog and cleaver with complete disregard for the pig's feelings.

With the introduction of Turkish tobacco, the man in turban and flowing robe took his place alongside the Indian. This is a fine example of the carver's art, done with a great deal of delicacy.

All shop figures, Indians and others, were articles of commerce that were sold in the market at established prices. A low price was $25, but these were trade-ins that had been repainted and reconditioned. Canal Street in New York City was a place where such bargains were available. Demuth sold Indians for $50, $75, and $100. Detroit Indians brought the highest prices; for them Melchers received $150 and even higher prices. A good metal Indian, called "iron" but made of cast zinc, cost from $125 to $300.

135. Mercury, wood, carved and gilded, three and one-half feet high; attributed to Simeon Skillin; second half eighteenth century.

136. Shop Figure, man in checkered coat and gray trousers, wood, carved and painted; nineteenth century.

The flying Mercury on the globe "was placed over the door of the [Boston] Post-Office in State Street" (Samuel Adams Drake, 1900). Mercury, the messenger of the gods, was appropriate for the postal service. The figure is slightly awkward, and in spite of the carver's attempts at classic sculpture he inclines toward the robust manner of the ships' figureheads. His traditional staff, the caduceus and a letter, which he once carried, have disappeared.

As shop figures approached the end of their career and Indians began to lose their appeal, tobacco stores went in for various types that stressed novelty. Among them was the fashionably dressed man of the day. The storekeeper who used the figure of the self-assured gentleman wanted to attract the best trade to his shop. His method of increasing his business is not unlike that of the duck hunter who sets out his wooden decoy.

137. Jockey Hitching Post, cast iron; about 1881.
138. Weathervane, wrought iron, banner and finial gilded; from First Church in Concord, Massachusetts; dated 1673.

8. Weathervane and Hitching Post

In the course of the nineteenth century, iron replaced wood in manufacture and construction, and industrialization invaded the arts. Where early craftsmen had depended on wood or stone for decorations, cast iron now made its appearance on the exterior of the house and in the garden. Previously the weathervane had been one of the few opportunities the owner had for personal expression; now ornamental hitching posts, iron fences and grilles, and all varieties of garden sculpture made their appearance.

The pioneer farmer had whittled his own weathervane, his son ordered one of copper or iron from the local smith, but his grandchildren in the city purchased theirs at a hardware store. The first metal weathervanes were wrought iron; later ones were cut out of flat sheet metal. Eventually copper vanes were made by hammer-

ing the sheet metal into a half-rounded, hollow form, and soldering the two sides together. Smaller parts like heads or tails were made separately and attached to the main piece. Frequently vanes were gilded, sometimes with 23-carat gold leaf.

The earliest weathervanes of the seventeenth century reflected the heraldic tradition of European aristocratic manors and medieval castles. Once the words "weathervane" and "weathercock" had been almost synonymous, but the eighteenth century gave us a variety of subjects, including fish and dragon, horse and cow. The ultimate was reached in the late nineteenth century when the new wonders of the age, the steam fire engine and locomotive, were reproduced in small scale to serve as weathervanes.

Wrought iron is essentially the province of a skilled

craftsman who beats the shape out of hot metal, producing his curves and scrolls, his spikes and tendrils, in a series of successive heatings of the iron. With hammer and tongs he flattens or thickens his metal and makes it round or square, or twists it into spirals. All this requires experience, ingenuity and taste. Our best ironworkers were Europeans who had already achieved mastery in their homelands. In New Orleans some of the finest work was done by Negro slave blacksmiths, who adapted Spanish and French patterns.

Europe, with its background of centuries of experience, produced masterpieces of wrought iron. Some fine wrought iron was also made in this country, though not abundantly. Wrought iron had to compete with the cheaper cast iron that came in with the 1820's and 1830's. Although ironwork was produced in this country in the eighteenth century and before, large scale production came only with the advent of cast iron.

Ornamental cast iron followed an indigenous American development. It is not the kind of folk art that adheres to simple geometric shapes. Instead, it reflects the style of the period, the Greek revival of the early nineteenth century, the Victorian Gothic, and after the Civil War, the Renaissance manner. Ornamental cast iron appears in the ponderous rails that still surround many of our public buildings. Its use was widespread in garden fences, and it enhanced many a porch rail and cemetery lot. In the South, it was used for galleries and balconies. Being brittle, cast iron required a massive treatment to create the bulk necessary for solidity. Even patterns in common use have an impressive surface; their exuberance catches the eye and assures them a decorative effect. Cast iron could not be simple; it had to extend itself; it was elaborate from the beginning.

Cast iron was peculiarly suited to the American temperament, as it achieved results quickly and lent itself to mass production. The demand was so great that there was no time for the slower methods of craftsmanship. Forms no longer grew under the hand of a sensitive artisan since a single model served to produce finished casts in quantities. It was sufficient if a hitching post had that prosperous look that would demonstrate worldly success. These were the decades that brought comfort and wealth to many who had but recently emerged from a pioneer life and had been without the leisure necessary to cultivate the arts.

In the horse-and-buggy days, hitching posts were necessities. At first simple posts served the purpose; the flourishing period of the hitching post began when cast iron came into its own. From the simple newel post a more elaborate type was developed with a molded base and a fluted shaft terminating in a horse's head. Tree trunks were imitated in cast iron, and finally pretentious figures, youthful jockeys, barefoot darkeys, or Chinese boys, held out the rings to which the reins were tied. In these late productions there is a sleekness, a delight in bright colors, good modeling, and easy postures.

Cast iron and cast zinc produced also an astonishing variety of animal life for the front lawn of the city mansion. These figures were made in halves, from one-quarter to one-half inch thick, screwed together and the holes filled with putty. Practical American ingenuity managed to supply the well-to-do with imitations of the zoo as well as works of sculpture. What deceptively lifelike creatures graced the Victorian garden! Turtles, dogs, life-sized deer, and statues of the human figure were neatly set out on the turf between beds of cannas, against the red brickwork of the house. The purchaser could select from a catalogue an angel, a nymph, an Amazon, Mercury, Flora, Pomona, or even a classic statue made after an original in one of the art galleries of Europe.

After this fashion had run its course, it eventually fell into disfavor. What had been considered desirable for the well dressed garden was later regarded as in the worst of taste. The generation that followed judged Victorian decoration harshly. That it was ostentatious and accompanied by a decline of craftsmanship was generally recognized. Its faults are undeniable, and yet we have softened in our attitude. The further removed we are from a period, the better we see its merits and the more we incline to overlook its faults. Time preserves the best, for what is well made lasts. Fortunately time also shrouds the worst; the shoddy soon disintegrates.

139. Numerals, wrought iron; made by original Dutch settlers for the Old Tile House, New Castle, Delaware; 1687.

140. Cross, wrought iron; made in Cahokia, Illinois; early nineteenth century.

141. Cross, wrought iron, from a fence in the Saint Louis cemetery of New Orleans; 1806.

142. Hitching Post, wrought iron; made by Calvin Nutting, Sr., Pioneer Iron Works, San Francisco; late nineteenth century.

The cross from the Church of the Holy Family in Cahokia, a French settlement in Illinois, is a thoroughly satisfying design. The ornamental ends, wrought in the lily motif from the French coat of arms, contrast with the simplicity of the arms of the cross.

The other cross has the character of wrought iron in its delicate flow of line. Large scrolls support the cross, and lily-shaped finials terminate the ends. Some of the best of our wrought-iron work is in the South, as in New Orleans. After 1830 cast iron gained in importance. Much of the ornamental iron work here as elsewhere throughout the country is cast iron, made in Philadelphia or after designs that originated in Philadelphia.

The straight bar is a reasonable solution of the problem of the hitching post. It fulfills its function by the simple means of a sturdy post and a ring to which the reins are tied. The form is made ornamental by the spiral twist in the middle section.

143. Eagle, copper, gilded, fifteen inches long; nineteenth century.

144. Weathervane, Indian shooting an arrow, painted sheet metal; late eighteenth to early nineteenth century.

145. Horse Head Hitching Post, cast iron, painted; made by J. W. Fiske Ornamental Iron Works, New York City; mid-nineteenth century.

Wherever eagles were used as this one, which is presumably from a flag pole or weathervane, the design was left to the individual artist who did not trouble himself with the rules of heraldry. These highly patriotic emblems, therefore, show great diversity of design. This particular posture, with wings raised as though for flight, was a common one.

The frontiersman who drew the contours of an Indian shooting an arrow, made a weathervane with the same confidence with which he built a house. He probably never thought of himself as an artist, but in his design he combined what seemed significant, the huge bow, the deadly arrow, the Indian shooting as he runs. He used enough sheet metal to offer a surface for the wind to blow against. This lumbering silhouette conveys something of the character of the maker, an element of the rude strength of the men who tamed the wilderness.

The baluster type of hitching post was inspired by contemporary architecture, which used a mingling of classic and Gothic motifs. It is a reflection of the late Victorian manner when designers borrowed and adapted from the historic styles of the past. It is the period that gave us the cast-iron façades that look like classic architecture carved out of gray stone. Almost any town and city is still well supplied with the remains of this taste, in which we are, today, developing a new interest.

146. Angel Gabriel Weathervane, copper, from Massachusetts; nineteenth century.

147. Fish Weathervane, metal; from Rhode Island.

In the winged Gabriel blowing his horn, the head, wings, and legs appear as if they had been pieced together from different sources, but this weathervane still makes an effective silhouette. An angel Gabriel, clothed in a flowing gown, was blowing his horn in 1814 on the steeple of the Baptist Church of Whiting, Vermont. No doubt, it came from the shop of a local blacksmith. The angel Gabriel here illustrated also bears the mark of a provincial craftsman, giving it a charm that is particularly appreciated today. This same motif, in a more conventional version, appears in commercial catalogues as early as 1840 and as late as 1883. By that time Gabriel had been transformed into a little cupid, on which the manufacturers took out a patent. When weathervanes were made by machines, they became more numerous. Old models were copied and many new designs appeared. The most familiar, perhaps, are the prize-winning cows and bulls, and the well known race horses adapted from Currier & Ives prints.

In the fish, much is made of the ornamental value of scales, fins, and tail. Once the fish was a Reformation symbol, and before that the fish was a significant element in early Christian symbolism. We do not know whether this Christian interpretation of the fish played any part in New England weathervanes. As this one comes from the coastal regions, it was probably on top of a wharf or fish market.

148. Cock Weathervane, copper; nineteenth century.

Probably the rooster is the earliest weathervane design in this country. His widespread European use on church steeples may explain this preference. The cock owed his place on church spires to Peter's denial of Christ and as a warning to the congregation not to do likewise. The copper roosters were made out of parts soldered together; some portions, like the legs, were cast solid. The fact that copper was so easily hammered gave the artist a good chance to get texture into the feathers. This was done more for the sake of variety than zoological accuracy. Metal weathervanes are made out of two sheets, hammered together over templates, and soldered into a single hollow form. We have to imagine the rooster with an arrow and the points of the compass below. The weathervane artists had an appreciation for fine contours; they made a lot of the sweep of the tail feathers and the erect posture of the rooster. On rare occasions the rooster is represented as crowing, and at times he is perched on a metal sphere.

149. Whale Weathervane, painted pine; made at Little Compton, Rhode Island; early nineteenth century.

150. Cock Weathervane, copper, gilded, over five feet high and one foot thick; made by Shem Drowne for New Brick Church, Boston; eighteenth century.

151. Deer, hollow cast zinc, three and a half feet high; made by J. W. Fiske Ornamental Iron Works, New York City; 1870.

The vane whittled in the form of a sperm whale perpetuates an earlier design. It was used by the captain of a New Bedford whaling vessel. The shape of the head shows that the carver knew his subject well. It is not surprising that New Bedford should favor the whale, as a large portion of the world's whaling was concentrated there in the decades before the Civil War.

In 1720 part of the congregation of a Boston church objected to the new pastor so violently that they left the church and formed what was nicknamed the First Revenge Church of Christ. On its steeple stood the splendid gilded cock by Shem Drowne, who is said to have hammered it from copper kettles. So large and so heavy was the "Revenge Cockerel" (it weighed 172 pounds) that when it was blown down in a storm it crashed through the roof and into the kitchen of a near-by house.

Shem Drowne was a famous weathervane maker of Boston. He made the brass and copper Indian shooting an arrow which stood on Old Province House, and the equally renowned grasshopper vanes for Faneuil Hall and Peter Faneuil's summer house. In the latter half of his life Drowne carved shop signs and figureheads, and became known as "Deacon Shem Drowne, the Carver." We are told of his work by Nathaniel Hawthorne under the title "Drowne's Wooden Image" in *Mosses from an Old Manse*.

152. Whirligig, painted pine, Pennsylvania-German; nineteenth century.

153. Gate, wood and iron; made by Hobart Victory Welton, Waterbury, Connecticut; mid-nineteenth century.

The body and head of the whirligig are made from a single piece of wood; the arms are separate to pivot and whirl on a rod which passes through the shoulders. There is little resemblance to a real person; a pole is merely shaped to suggest a rudimentary figure. The bold contours, the elongated forms and the painted costume bring out a linear rhythm, while lines and shapes emphasize subtle curves that flow up and down, and in and out. It measures thirty inches and was used out of doors, installed so that the arms would be made to rotate with the wind.

The same mechanism was also used for toys, of which there are three types. One is like a top; another is like a spindle turned by means of a string; and the third is like a miniature windmill with four arms which whirl when moved through the air. The whirligig is of Euro-pean origin, mentioned as early as the fifteenth century.

The gate design achieves an effect by using implements, plow, yoke, and sickle, that ordinarily do not lend themselves to purposes of decoration. Attempts to combine the practical with the decorative sometimes lead to such unfortunate expressions of taste as flower-beds set within cast-off automobile tires. The use of such realistic tools for purposes of design should by all precedent produce equally bad results, and yet this gate is surprisingly successful as a design. Perhaps the reason is that the artist created an orderly space division. Within each section the tool breaks the space in a carefully calculated manner so that the shapes and lines are inter-related. It is not so much the motifs used that are important for good design, but how they are combined to evolve artistically significant patterns.

154. Lion's Head, carved in stone by Hobart Victory Welton in Waterbury, Connecticut; mid-nineteenth century.

155. Carved Grasshopper Weathervane, wood, painted gray and yellow; about two feet long.

156. Weathervane, Cow, copper and zinc; possibly made by Harris & Company, Boston; nineteenth century.

This head shows a primitive sculptor's love of total bulk and smooth surfaces. Eyes, ears and mane are surface patterns superimposed on a generalized form. The sculptor's imaginative design is perhaps as satisfying as a more realistic rendition would have been. This head is one of a pair set on stone ramps, flanking the steps of the sculptor's house.

The primitive whittling of the grasshopper, the tendency to simplify and generalize, follows an early tradition rather than the accurate realism of a later period.

157. Weathervane, Horse, wrought and sheet iron; made in Pennsylvania; mid-nineteenth century.

158. Garden Urn, cast iron, painted; late nineteenth century.

159. Weathervane, Trotter Ethan Allen and Sulky, copper and cast iron; about 1871.

The weathervane represents an indigenous development, since the free choice of motifs is characteristically American. Though somewhat simplified, it is reasonably true to life. These weathervanes added to European subjects animals and various mechanical inventions.

The spirited horse, prancing and with bushy tail, is worked into a most effective weathervane. The vertical rod is set into a socket and is made to revolve. Its spearhead combines well with arrowhead and feather to round out the design. What adds to the silhouette is the fully rounded curves of the horse set against straight lines and serrated edges. The contour of the horse could be an adaptation from a Currier & Ives print.

The form of this urn is traditional, yet there is an individual element in the abrupt change of scale between the large ovals and the small flutes on the base. The artist has taken over the general shape of the vase and elaborated the details to his own liking.

This famous horse, named for the Revolutionary hero, may have also been made after a Currier & Ives print. It is noteworthy that a sporting event of the day should be made into a weathervane. A free country with few traditions creates new symbols that reflect the life of its own day.

160. Weathervane, Locomotive and Tender, copper, brass and iron, nine feet long; about 1870.

161. Weathervane, Horse, cast zinc and sheet copper; nine-teenth century. Over-all height, one and one-half feet.

The locomotive weathervane with many details is made in the round, virtually as a model of a real loco-motive. For a weathervane it is a mechanical wonder, the most elaborate development of its kind, and it is very large. Only a few of these designs were made, as the cost was prohibitive for popular use. Had appro-priateness and logic controlled weathervane design, locomotives would scarcely have been added to the list of subjects. The man who ordered this one must have been fond of railroads. The locomotive became his personal emblem which he hoisted proudly just as the knight flew his banner from the tower of his castle.

The magnificent horse weathervane is a striking con-trast to the locomotive. It is as conventional as the locomotive is unusual. One reflects the new industrial age, the other the passing day of the handicrafts. Be-cause of its clarity and simplicity of outline, the silhou-ette is effective even in the modest size of this example. The broad expanse of the muscular body, the small head, the ornate tail and the slender legs are all parts that individually and in combination are pleasing to look at.

162. Chalkware Deer; from Pennsylvania; nineteenth century.

9. From Parlor to Pantry

As the early settlers on the Atlantic seaboard replaced their primitive shelters with permanent dwellings, they patterned their houses and furnishings after those of England. Wood often took the place of stone and metal, but there was no basic change in the mode of living. Tankards and trammels, pots and pans, were like those at home, and cooking over the open fire continued in the old, familiar way. Utensils did not change greatly just because an ocean had been crossed, or a new government set up.

But one factor made for a decided change everywhere —the Industrial Revolution. As candles gave way to kerosene, as the hearth was replaced by the cookstove, and as home manufacture moved to the mill, life itself changed.

As long as household articles were made by crafts-men, they were beautiful, in America as elsewhere. As factory production increased, the handicrafts lapsed and taste declined. This was especially true in the decade after the Civil War. There was greater comfort and more wealth, but beauty gave way to ugliness. Still, even in this period of transition, when the factory was crowding out the crafts, an undercurrent of good design continued in unpretentious articles, whether made of wood, clay, metal or fabric.

It is not always easy to define what is peculiarly American. If any trend in design can be called American, it is a tendency to simplify the forms inherited from Europe. A new country, where much work must be done by few hands, does not encourage elaboration.

Among the utensils that retained a simple beauty were those of wood called "treen ware." Whittled at home or turned on the lathe and finished by hand, such treen ware served for common use well into the nineteenth century, especially for children and old people who might be likely to break the new precious porcelain.

Pottery-making was among the earliest of American crafts. For the kitchen, the potteries produced various types of glazed earthenware or redware; for storing food and liquids, jars and jugs of salt-glazed stoneware, hard and durable, were popular. Such stoneware was often decorated with an underglaze slip of cobalt blue. Because it was so widely used, this utility ware has been identified with this country. Certain pieces, astonishingly fine in shape and decoration, show that good things were being made, even while the handicrafts were receding.

Toward the middle of the nineteenth century, the so-called "Rockingham Ware," inspired by English tortoise-shell ware, reflected the Victorian love for elaboration in pitchers and creamers, in poodle-dogs, monks' bottles and the like. Some of these pieces were modeled by English craftsmen who worked in Bennington, Vermont, and elsewhere, to raise the standards of American ceramics. This type hardly achieved the distinction of some of the Greek or early Chinese ceramics, but the best of the brown, glazed, and mottled surfaces show an unusual brilliance and depth of color.

Before the period of large factory production, household wares were often produced in small shops. The village blacksmith, like the one immortalized by Longfellow, made all sorts of hardware, including iron locks, hasps and hinges, nails and bolts. The blacksmith who shod horses was called a farrier, and the whitesmith was one who worked with tin. Tinware, at first imported, by 1740 was produced in Berlin, Connecticut, and was peddled around the country from wagons by hawkers. Pewter, an alloy of tin with a small amount of copper, was still imported from England. The fact that the gunmetal molds were expensive made it difficult for this craft to get started in the colonies. After the middle of the eighteenth century pewter was made here, but it went out of fashion in the nineteenth century as porcelain became common. Copper in kettles and the like was in general use in the eighteenth century and brass was used somewhat less. In the late eighteenth century both were replaced by cast iron.

Some of the finest craftwork of the Colonial and early Federal periods was produced in silver, especially in Boston, New York, Philadelphia and Baltimore. People of wealth and culture had brought silver with them from England, and these pieces formed the models for the first Colonial designs. Here plain surfaces and severe contours reflect the Puritan reaction against elaboration. This love of simplicity affected even the florid rococo style that appears sober and restrained in comparison with the English variety.

Household silver, the aristocrat among the crafts, was essentially a luxury in which only the well-to-do could indulge. It appeared early in the history of the colonies because it was a convenient way of storing wealth when there were no banks, for the silversmith received the metal in the form of silver coin. Tankards and tea sets were both useful and ornamental, and when necessary they could be reconverted into coin. The owner had an added protection, that in case of theft utensils were easy to identify. The silversmiths were trusted, highly respected members of the community and many of them held public office. Paul Revere was a silversmith, and the silver he made is treasured for its historical as well as for its artistic value.

163. Pitcher, gray stoneware; made at Atwater, Ohio; dated 1862.

164. Painting on Velvet, basket of fruit; made in Wisconsin; mid-nineteenth century.

Designs painted on velvet were made with stencils called "theorems." They frankly emphasize line and pattern. The abstract character of these designs seems fascinating today, where formerly it appeared awkward. Books bearing such titles as *Hints to Young Practitioners in the Study of Landscape Painting,* and *Young Ladies' Assistant in Drawing and Painting, or Art Recreations, . . .* gave specific instructions on how to proceed in "theorem painting, Grecian painting, hair work, wax work, papier maché and aquarium-making." A young woman approached painting as she would follow a recipe, only she used pencils and brushes instead of pots and pans. At an earlier period this type of homemade decoration would have been embroidered. The daintiness of the water-color painting is a result of the teaching of the period. In the instruction books

the pupil was admonished to draw, which meant to copy, with utmost accuracy. Originality of design was not the object; copying was the accepted method of art study in the female seminaries. The fact that leisure-time activities had penetrated as far west as Wisconsin by the mid-nineteenth century shows that the harshness of frontier conditions was disappearing.

In ceramic decoration, as on the plate on the opposite page, the folk artist worked with surprising freedom; the freehand scrolls and tendrils are brushed in almost like writing. Their spontaneity combined with repetition, makes an effective design. This technique does not call for a great deal of skill, yet the results are attractive.

Eighteenth century bandboxes held the bands, ruffs or fancy neckwear of a professional man's attire. Women also had their bandboxes for articles of finery. Used

165. Plate, red earthenware; nineteenth century.

166. Bandbox, made by Putnam & Roff, Hartford, Connecticut; between 1823 and 1824.

167. Stoneware Ink Bottle; mid-nineteenth century.

168. Inkwell, gray salt-glazed stoneware; made for George Crawford by Clark & Fox, pottery at Athens, New York; 1828.

169. Pitcher, salt-glazed stoneware; nineteenth century.

for travel, bandboxes were light in weight, made of cardboard or thin wood covered with paper on which famous landmarks were often block-printed.

Even a century ago individual packaging in small quantities, which today we have come to regard as a standard technique, was still unknown. Ink and soda pop then came in the same type of bottle. Probably this one was made for a cork, and the incision below indicates that the cork was wired on. There is a spout on the upper rim to make the pouring easier. The surface is so pleasant in texture that it appeals to one's sense of touch.

Before the days of fountain pens, inkwells were more common than they are today. As this one was made before steel pens were used, we must imagine the goose quills, sharpened and slit at the ends for writing, left standing in the pen holes. This one was made for its first owner, who had his name stamped into the clay before the inkwell was finished.

This stoneware jug is satisfactory both from the utilitarian and the aesthetic point of view. Its massive body cannot be readily upset; it lifts easily and pours well from its ample spout. The broadly painted leaf and flower decoration is well suited to its sturdy character.

170. Tankard, silver; made by Edward Winslow, Boston; 1725–1750.

171. Tea Caddy, silver; made by Thauvet Besley, New York City; 1750.

172. Mug, silver; made by George Fielding, New York City; 1725–1750.

173. Mug, silver; made by Paul Revere, Boston; inscribed date 1768.

Silver, like furniture, follows historic styles, particularly those of England and Holland. The shape of the tankard comes from the beer-drinking countries of northern Europe, having evolved from a section of horn to which a metal base, lid and handle were applied. In this tankard the molded top and bottom contrast with the plain side. The polished surface of the silver, reflecting the surroundings, is attractive in itself. Handle, thumbpiece, spout and finial are cast.

This tea caddy was made in New York in a style that had been fashionable in London a decade or more before 1740, the date engraved on the base. Such a tea box was called a "caddy," after *kati*, the Malay word for pound, because it held about a pound of tea. The scrolled monogram with its flowing curves reflects the rococo manner, the initials CLR being those of Catharine Livingstone Reade.

Mugs were often shaped like small tankards without lids. This one shows a beautiful expanse of gleaming metal with the moldings creating the right amount of contrast. The C-curved handle is accented by a decorated band, and there is the inscription PVM on the handle.

The contours of the mug showing rococo influence,

174. Teapot, silver; made by John Coney (1655–1722), Boston; early eighteenth century.

are delicately curved to set off the lively double scroll of the handle. Paul Revere's craftsmanship is here equal to his fame as dispatch-rider from Boston to Lexington. This mug, one of a pair, bears an engraved dedication in Latin, which tells us they were presented by a group of Harvard students of the Class of 1768 to their tutor, Stephen Scales, as tokens of affection.

John Coney was a contemporary of Edward Winslow, also a Boston silversmith. An excellent example of his work is this teapot with its domed lid, ring foot and duck-neck spout. There is a pleasing directness about the design. Though pear-shaped, the contour is close to the sphere, as if it hesitated to yield anything of its comfortable spread. The handle also is satisfied with a single C-curve, ending in horizontal sockets. The modest little spout clings to the pot as if not daring to strike out on its own. It is clear that the designer desires simplicity, and takes pleasure in uncomplicated shapes. Silversmithing and engraving were allied arts. Coney, who engraved this teapot with the Perkins coat of arms, also engraved the plates for the first paper money that Massachusetts printed for the colonies in 1690, as well as a seal for Harvard University.

175. Water Pitcher; attributed to Connecticut; nineteenth century.

176. Jar with Lid, redware; made in Portland, Maine; early nineteenth century.

177. Pottery Dog Ornament, yellowware; United States Potteries, Bennington, Vermont; mid-nineteenth century.

The water pitcher suggests rugged stability; it looks steadfast and straightforward. Even the incised bands of decoration emphasize the sober correctness of the design. The dark splashes in the glaze were probably applied with a sponge when the glaze was damp.

Our early potters were satisfied if the shape was simple and graceful and the glaze added color or luster. In the early nineteenth century there was as yet no elaboration; that occurred in the mid-century when potters became ambitious and began to draw inspiration from the more pretentious European models. This jar

achieves success through its finely mottled surface and the sparkling brilliance of its glaze. The base and upper rim were made not primarily for appearance, but to produce a solid bottom and a firm top. After the potter had cut the jar from his wheel he added the separate rim to assure a sturdy bottom.

The dog is an example of ceramic sculpture, illustrating Victorian love of overornamentation. Glaze containing color matter was spattered on, and the potter was so delighted with it that he was not troubled by the unrealistic mottling. Here too is the sentimental appeal

178. Jug, gray stoneware; attributed to Lewis Lehman & Co., New York City; 1859–1861.

179. Grotesque Jug, greenish stoneware; attributed to Connecticut.

180. Crock, tan stoneware; attributed to Caire Pottery, Poughkeepsie, New York; inscribed with purchaser's name, "F. A. Voorhee & Co. Kings[ton?] N.Y."; nineteenth century.

of the pet poodle so beloved by our grandparents.

The cobalt blue slip decorations of stoneware are particularly attractive in their spontaneous freshness. The brushwork is superior and the drawing of leaves, flowers, and birds is unbotanical. These decorations add to the interest of this ware; through constant repetition the artisans developed a fluent technique. This type of decoration is seen at its best in the leaves, tendrils, and flowers of the jug and crock. In the 1860's the shapes of the ware changed. The sides became straight and, along with this change, brushwork came to an end, stenciling taking its place.

Clay is universal and pottery is one of man's earliest achievements. Pottery more than any other craft unites man with his work. It is a parallel to the Biblical idea of creation out of mortal clay. The potter makes a pot as the Lord created man; he speaks of pots having a foot, shoulder, neck, lip, and other features. There is a close psychological relationship between man and clay.

Although distorted, this grotesque jug is appealing because it has style, for the features are related in shape. There may be here a reminiscence of African art. Some grotesque jugs were made by Negro slaves and others are potters' jests.

181. Flatiron Stand, cast iron; nineteenth century.

These flatiron stands reflect the spirit of early industrialism in this country. In many cases the designer used conventional motifs; but art alone was not sufficient, so he included something pertaining to the manufacturer, an advertising slogan, a trade name, or even a monogram. The practical requirements of the stand made it unnecessary to have a solid surface. Only enough metal was needed to give the iron a support and any openwork design, any combination of lines and shapes, would suffice.

Here the construction of the flatiron stand is consistent with the basic necessities. The designer started out with interlacing hearts framing the twisting "W." The manufacturer also worked his advertising into the design, and justifiably so. This trend toward advertising was inescapable, for the manufacturer had to sell his articles to as many housewives as he could reach. As any one flatiron stand is not too different from another, the producer tried to capture the customer by making the design attractive and by not allowing him to forget the maker's name.

182. Flatiron Stand, cast iron; nineteenth century.

This flatiron stand shows the Victorian spirit at its best. It has the scrolls, flowers, ribbons, and vase out of which grows a tree of life as the central motif. One would find it difficult to select themes which would be less appropriate from a purely intellectual point of view than flowers, ribbons, and vases as a support for a flat-iron. However justifiable it may seem to find fault with this type of design in theory, it cannot be denied that this particular result is attractive. It has a lush vitality, something of the character of tropical vegetation; it carries conviction, and it may come as a shock to many people that it was made in the U.S.A.

When ornamental cast iron first became popular, it would often be maligned by the older members of the household. They would remember the tough and sturdy wrought iron and look upon the fragile cast iron as a cheap substitute. Yet properly used in places where strength was not essential, the adaptability of cast iron to florid expression gave it a charm that explains its success.

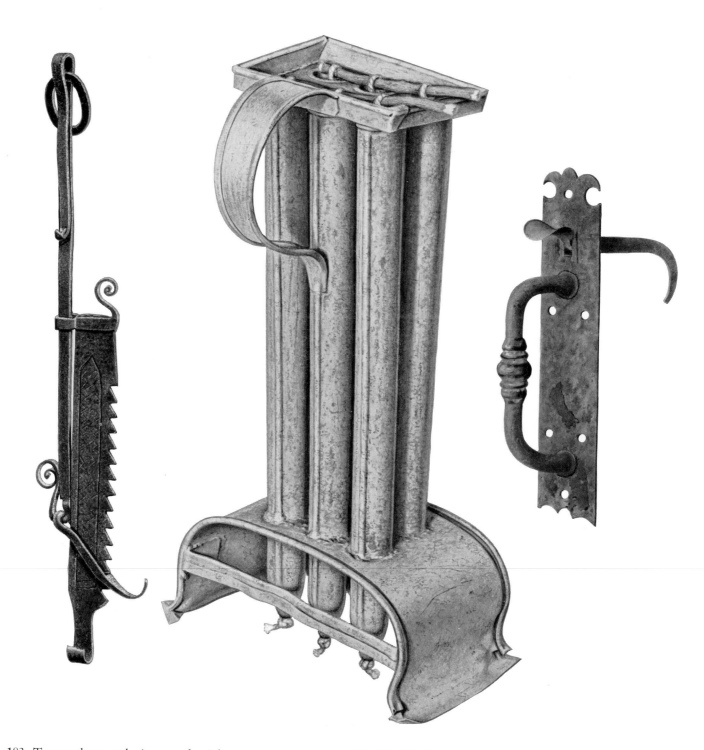

183. Trammel, wrought iron; early eighteenth century.
184. Candle Mold, tin; probably made in Pennsylvania; nineteenth century.

185. Norfolk Latch, iron with brass turning; made in Ohio; early nineteenth century.

Trammels served to suspend pots in the fireplace at different levels. They were widely used both here and in Europe. This one is comparatively simple. Though the freely-scrolled ends have not been abandoned, there is a lessening of the playful spirit that thrives on leisure but is not apt to be encouraged by a hardy pioneer life.

The candle mold tells us at a glance how candles were made. It is purely utilitarian yet extremely attractive, with its battery of six tapering cylinders and its curved base. This is one example of the many highly specialized utensils of the period.

The fleur-de-lis at the top of this Norfolk latch, so called because of its single escutcheon plate, is perhaps a local version of the nineteenth century Gothic revival.

The copper pan, on the opposite page, made for an open fireplace, needed legs to raise it above the coal or wood. Legs and handle are riveted on the body in an undisguised structural manner.

186. Pan, wrought sheet copper with iron handle and legs; latter part eighteenth century.

187. Tankard, wood; attributed to New England; probably latter part eighteenth century.

188. Door Latch; made by S. Baumann, blacksmith of Racine, Wisconsin; 1876.

189. Strainer, wood; early nineteenth century.

This tankard was hollowed out from a single piece of maple, more or less imitating a shape common to metal. The craftsman rounded the top and carved the heart-shaped design with loving care. Plates called trenchers, bowls, spoons, forks and many utensils were commonly made of wood, as silver and pewter for ordinary use were beyond the means of all but the well-to-do. In such utensils as cooking spoons and salad bowls, wood has lasted until our own day.

In early days when iron was scarce, latches were made of wood. The phrase "our latchstring is out," meaning "we are at home," originated because the latch-bar was raised from the outside by a string. Later a thumbpiece replaced the string. This Suffolk-type latch, with top and bottom plates, is made beautiful by its very simplicity. Blacksmiths did not sign their work, and much early hardware in this country came from England, but this example is known to be a native product.

The strainer is made from a single piece of maple, the bowl having been turned on a lathe. Holes were drilled to turn a dipper into a strainer. Being of wood, it had to be thick and solid. But the rim has been cut back to a slanted edge and the handle is neatly tapered for the sake of balance and to avoid clumsiness.

190. Dutch Bake Oven, cast iron; made in Ohio; mid-nine-teenth century.

191. Tailor's Stove, cast iron; first half nineteenth century.

192. Teakettle, tin; mid-nineteenth century.

The Dutch oven was a large iron pot, with a lid, used for baking or roasting. It hung from the crane over the fire or stood on three short legs amid the coals. It is not to be confused with the brick oven that was built into the side of the fireplace.

The cast-iron tailor's stove belonged to Andrew Johnson, Lincoln's successor as President, before he entered his political career. A tailor's apprentice at ten, he later worked at his trade in Greenville, Tennessee, where he used this stove. Though factory-made, there is elegance in the low-relief side panel. It shows the influence of the classic revival in its simplicity and reserve.

This teakettle is functional in form. The shape is the result of manufacturing reduced to its simplest terms,

depending largely on cutting and soldering, and avoiding hammering. This explains the straight lines in the sides, the funnel-shaped spout, the flat handle, and the slight curvature of the lid and top. This is already quantity production, the artisans working from wooden templates and molds.

Perhaps the best known large-scale embroidery that was made in this country is the Caswell Carpet, made by Zeruah Higley Guernsey, of Castleton, Vermont, for her parlor. She took at least two years to make it, beginning by shearing the wool from the backs of her father's sheep, and finishing it in 1835. The whole rug is twelve by thirteen and one-half feet, consisting of individual pieces, embroidered in chain stitch on a

193. Caswell Carpet (detail); made by Zeruah Higley Guernsey, Castleton, Vermont; completed in 1835.

coarse homespun ground and sewn together afterwards. The embroidered rugs came before the hooked rugs, and not many of them were made. (What is here shown is something over a quarter of the rug.)

Each small panel is a design, the natural form is simplified, the silhouette is emphasized, and the few subdued colors make for harmony. Certain panels are little gems, particularly the one of bride and groom, undoubtedly meant as a memorial to herself. Most of the rug is in the eighteenth century tradition; but the three panels with the blue cat and the kittens, in the lower right-hand corner, are pictorial in the taste of the nineteenth century.

Zeruah Guernsey married a Caswell and continued to live in Castleton, where she no doubt exhibited her rug to admiring friends. It is a masterpiece of folk art and is now in the American Wing of the Metropolitan Museum of Art.

194. Pitcher, aquamarine, hand-blown, South Jersey type; early nineteenth century.
195. Tumbler, aquamarine, mold-blown, South Jersey type; early nineteenth century.

10. Pitcher and Tumbler

It must always seem like a miracle that opaque substances like sand, soda, lime or lead can be mixed and fused by heat to produce transparent glass. When glass is fluid it is blown or cast into a mold; in another state it is rolled, or drawn out into a fine thread. Through the addition of metallic oxides, glass takes on most luminous and varied colors.

Before the nineteenth century all glass was blown from the end of a blowpipe by the breath of the glass blower. We still have blown glass today and the tools used in its manufacture have not changed greatly. Glass may be either free-blown, as in the above pitcher, or mold-blown as in the tumbler. Mold-blown glass is blown against the walls of a metal mold, often made in sections.

Glass is one of man's early discoveries, and its manufacture depended on a fund of information that was always jealously guarded. Glassmaking is an arduous task that requires skill and long training. The knowledge of making glass spread slowly, often only when glass blowers could be smuggled out of the country that employed them. Thus Venetian glass blowers were among the early arrivals at Jamestown, at a time when glass was rare even in England. Probably the first home-made glass in North America was the colored beads made by these artisans for trade with the Indians. However, the earliest glass that can be identified is of the eighteenth century.

Caspar Wistar, a Philadelphia buttonmaker, established the first important American glass factory in Salem County, New Jersey, in 1739. In this glasshouse, the main products were window and bottle glass. Pitchers and bowls were not produced commercially, but were blown during off hours for the glass blowers' own household use.

This so-called South Jersey glass makes the most of

the fact that molten glass can be freely manipulated. Partly blown pieces, often in bulbous shapes, were dipped back into the molten "metal" for an extra layer that was dragged into waves and "lily pads." These, as well as the threaded neck and crimped foot, all seen on the pitcher on the opposite page, are typical of South Jersey glass. We have here a folk-art manner that became the most potent influence in American glass.

Perhaps the most celebrated name in early American glass is that of the picturesque, German-born "Baron" Heinrich Wilhelm Stiegel, known as Henry William Stiegel. He arrived as a poor immigrant boy and started on the road to success when he married the daughter of one of Pennsylvania's prosperous ironmasters, manufacturer of the well known Pennsylvania German stoves. Eventually Stiegel assumed full control of the foundry.

From casting iron Stiegel branched out to manufacturing glass. While his glass business flourished he was a glamorous and splendid figure. He founded the town of Manheim, built a mansion, drove about in a coach drawn by six white horses, and had his entry into town heralded by a brass band, especially trained for such occasions. But his glass business failed shortly before the Revolution. It never recovered and Stiegel, though versatile and gifted in many ways, died in poverty.

Stiegel glass is distinguished for its elegance, fusing various European influences in an effort to equal the best European ware. In this, Stiegel was so successful that his glass is usually indistinguishable from the glass made by his European competitors. As far as is known, he was the first man in America to produce fine table and ornamental ware.

Artisans who had worked with Stiegel and others carried their techniques, particularly the use of the pattern-mold, to Pittsburgh and Ohio. It has therefore become customary to speak of Stiegel-type glass and of glass in the Ohio-Stiegel tradition. Certain colors, like cobalt blue and amethyst, are unique and such colored glass is often flint glass. In this the most brilliant of all glass, the sand is mixed with potash lead instead of soda lime. Stiegel claimed that he was the first to manufacture flint glass in this country.

Hand-blown glass was unchallenged until about 1826 and 1827 when Enoch Robinson, a carpenter at the New England Glass Company, and Deming Jarvis, a Bostonian of French Huguenot descent, made various pressing machines on which they took out patents. Instead of human breath, a mechanical plunger pressed the glass into an iron mold and stamped it with a pattern. Thus, the man who carved the wooden patterns for the molds became the real artisan of pressed glass. The new invention threatened the livelihood of the glass blowers and they became so enraged against Jarvis that for a time he had to hide in fear of his life. But as the owner of the Boston & Sandwich Glass Company at Sandwich on Cape Cod, he persevered to perfect the process and put it into practical use. Under his guidance the Sandwich factory became an outstanding success. From the standpoint of social welfare he conducted his business to bring security to his workers in spite of depressions. Through his concern for his workers, Jarvis gained their enthusiastic cooperation, and this of course helped his business.

Pressed glass aspired to surpass cut glass; the speed of the pressing machine was its great advantage. It could produce at a small cost an effect of high relief, that would have cost a fortune to produce by the old methods of cut glass. But pressed glass soon developed its own style, delicate in lacelike surface patterns, or massive and bold.

By 1845 virtually every American home had pressed glass, and by 1865 it had almost supplanted china in this country. Actually, pressed glass was made in many places and in numerous patterns so that today over a thousand designs have been identified, without considering differences of color. Today Sandwich glass means pressed glass. A type of glass that stood out as an industrial triumph of early America, is today, within a century of its manufacture, sought by collectors everywhere.

196. Cream Pitcher, mold-blown, Stiegel; probably 1769–1774.

197. Pitcher, South Jersey type; nineteenth century.

198. Mortar and Pestle; hand-blown in New Jersey; late eighteenth century.

199. Bowl, South Jersey type; hand-blown at Redwood, New York; 1833–1860.

The cream pitcher combines the South Jersey crimped handle with the diamond pattern of Venetian origin. These motifs were adopted by Stiegel and were used later by glass blowers who had migrated to Pittsburgh and Ohio.

A South Jersey influence is evident in the pitcher with the ample handle and crimped base. Its shape and smooth surface are effective, and it retains some of the vigor of the earlier bulbous-shaped pitchers.

The combination of colors in the mortar and pestle set is typical of window and bottle glass. The form is heavy and suitable for hard use. That such massive forms were used shows that the American glass blower was well aware of the wide range of designs possible in glass.

As far as we know, the lily pad or wave motif in glass design was developed in this country. In the bowl this free and irregular motif, more often found on globular forms, contrasts sharply with the severe cylindrical shape.

The sugar bowl, on the opposite page, is of that deep lustrous blue for which Stiegel was famous. Its shape shows

200. Sugar Bowl, mold-blown, over-all height six and one-half inches, Stiegel; probably 1769–1774.

201. Flask, enameled clear glass with metal cap, Stiegel-type; eighteenth century.

202. Bottle for Toilet Water, mold-blown, Stiegel; probably 1769–1774.

the restraint by which Stiegel glass differs from that of South Jersey. Each detail is well considered, like the delicately swirled ribbed finial which accents the shape and contrasts with the smooth surface of the lid. The pattern, the Venetian diamond design, was impressed on the glass in the mold. The blowing began in a small mold and, after the shape was withdrawn from the mold, the bottle was expanded to its full size. Sugar bowls of this type and size represent Stiegel glass at its best.

The flask, in shape and decoration, suggests German influence. Here we have the same charming freshness noted in Pennsylvania German crafts. It is typical of one of four groups of Stiegel glass made by artisans imported from all over Europe. The other groups show plain, engraved and modeled surfaces.

The so-called perfume bottle illustrates Stiegel's originality; the shape and the surface decoration, a "Daisy-in-a-Square" pattern with fluting below, are distinctive and believed to be his inventions. As far as is known, no other glasshouse, American or European, used this design.

203. Covered Goblet, engraved with the coat of arms of the city of Bremen, Germany; made by John Frederick Amelung in New Bremen, Maryland; 1788.

204. Salt Cellar, blue and milk glass, blown and flashed; perhaps by the Jersey Glass Company, Jersey City; first half nineteenth century.

205. Nursing Bottle, hand-blown; first half nineteenth century.

When this goblet was first discovered it was thought to be too fine for American manufacture. The inscription, "New Bremen Glass Manufactory, 1788, North America, State of Maryland," should have been clear enough, and today its American manufacture is no longer questioned. It may have been made by a worker who had fairly recently come from Germany, where such "presentation goblets" or drinking vessels for state occasions were traditional. It is an ambitious achievement, the finest of several such pieces that are known to be of American make. This goblet was made in a well known factory established by Amelung near Frederick, Maryland, in 1784. For various reasons this factory also failed, but Amelung glass is unique in several ways. As far as we know, only Amelung among eighteenth

century glassmakers has left us inscribed and dated examples of his work. In the quality of the glass and in the craftsmanship of the engraving, Amelung glass is of the best.

Flashed glass is made by superimposing a thin layer of glass of one color on top of glass of a different color, in this case milk glass. The shape of the salt cellar has a classic, almost architectural, character, and, like Stiegel, it is sophisticated and deliberate.

Compared to a modern nursing bottle this is hardly up to our present standards of hygiene. Even this however was an improvement on earlier types. The cork stopper on the top was probably the only way of filling the bottle, as the rest, from end to end, was glass.

206. Quart Decanter, olive green; Blown Three Mold type; Mt. Vernon Glass Works, Vernon, New York, first half nineteenth century.

207. Whisky Flask, olive amber, half-pint size; early nineteenth century.

The Blown Three Mold type, as in this decanter, is an American contribution that was no doubt inspired by the more expensive mold-blown English ware, with its wheel cut designs. In the designs used for mold-blown glass, American wood carvers achieved effects comparable to those of fashionable cut glass. As soon as glass blowers use molds, they surrender something of their own creativeness. The glass blower may still finish the shape but the carver who makes the wooden model for the metal mold creates the pattern. Conventional motifs like ribs and rosettes, the so-called "gadroons and sunbursts," are here impressed on heavy, coarse green glass.

American drinking habits in the early nineteenth century are believed to have hastened the development of our glass industry. The price of whisky was low, and competition keen; it was the bottle that sold the product. These flasks are vigorous in design. They show a relief that is higher than in other glassware. The patterns are historical, political, or of popular interest. The American eagle and George Washington adorned more flasks than any other design, but there is no end of popular subjects: Adams, Jackson, Lafayette, Jenny Lind, naval vessels, Masonic emblems, and many others, and each motif appears in many variations. The surface is uneven and coarse and the bottles are in various colors. This one with an urn containing fruit on one side and a cornucopia design on the other side was made at the glasshouse in Keene, New Hampshire, and Coventry, Connecticut. Liquor flasks were made in full size molds, of two sections.

208. Bitters Bottle, amber, pressed; S. T. Drake 1860 Plantation X Bitters.

209. Finger Bowl, deep amethyst; pressed at Boston & Sandwich Glass Company; first half nineteenth century.

210. Candlestick (one of a pair), vaseline yellow; pressed at Boston & Sandwich Glass Company; first half nineteenth century.

There is no resemblance between the bitters bottle and the liquor flask. Though bitters are also alcoholic, this fact was not admitted. The purchaser never thought of bitters having any connection with liquor; instead he was under the illusion that he was doing something for his health. One took bitters like a medicine, and it tasted bitter. That is why the health-giving herbs had to be stressed, and why the shape of the bottle suggested the woods, to soothe the mind of the purchaser and put him at ease that this was really only a tonic. Next to the name, the bottle proclaimed this deception. By making the bottle ornamental, it had a better chance of remain-ing unbroken longer, thereby continuing to advertise the beverage. The bitters industry became outstanding, and this helped the glass industry to its commercial success.

Pressed glass can be thick and massive, as in the finger bowl. Its richness is due in part to the fact that the light is refracted prismatically to produce attractive patterns.

Dolphin candlesticks were made in various colors, some with gilt decorations. Fragments of many types have been found on the rubbish heaps of the old Boston & Sandwich Glass Company.

211. Appliqué Picture, made by Eunice W. Cook in Vermont; nineteenth century.

11. The Linen Chest

Most household articles in early America were made by men and cared for by women, but the field of textiles and needlework belonged to women in so far as the work was done in the home. The crewel embroidery on linen or cotton twill, the woven coverlets and patchwork quilts that were put together with so much patience, are all the work of women. These are perhaps our most noteworthy types of needlework. Though there were other types, like the Moravian- and the French-embroidered bags and wedding gowns, it was the crewelwork, coverlets and quilts, so popular over a long period of time, that assumed a truly national character.

Crewel embroidery was used to decorate spreads and hangings for four-poster beds, valances for mantels and windows, chair covers, curtains, purses, dresses, shoes, and petticoats. Because of the design and color, crewel attains an artistry beyond mere seamstress's work. The designs of flowers and birds, deer and hounds, were fashioned or adapted by the women themselves.

The word "crewel" means a loosely twisted wool yarn. This type of needlework dates back to ancient Egypt, and there are notable examples of it throughout history. The famous Bayeux tapestries are crewelwork rather than tapestry, which is technically a kind of weaving. Our own crewelwork was inherited from Jacobean England, and in general character the designs perpetuate English patterns.

The "stem stitch," a large stitch on the surface and a shorter one on the back, was a favorite among the various stitches used. Knots were also used; the "French knot" frequently forms the center of crewel flowers.

Crewelwork remained popular until the 1830's, when it was replaced by "Berlin work," a commercial embroidery which offered wool yarns in a selection of brilliant colors to be used with ready-made patterns already stamped on the cloth for cross-stitching. It was used for covering chairs and sofas, screens and footstools. Embroidery lost its vitality and became mechanical, but around 1878 crewel came back into popularity, and the better design and high quality of earlier embroidery were revived.

Crewelwork applies decoration to a fabric which already exists, but weaving is a process that makes the cloth and the decoration at the same time. In weaving, the sturdier, lengthwise thread of cotton or linen, known as the warp, is crossed at right angles by the woof or weft thread of colored wool. The warp of early coverlets is all linen, or cotton and linen; later coverlets have an all-cotton warp. In plain weaving, the loom separates every other warp thread, making an opening, or "shed," through which the weft passes. Special loom devices called "harnesses" control the separation of the warp so that designs can be made. The more harnesses the more complex the pattern. Early American looms usually had but two or four harnesses, permitting only simple, geometric patterns.

In the early colonial period, cloth was produced at home. Later, weaving was done by traveling journeymen, the term "journey" meaning "a day's work." Then came the day of the weaving shop and the professional weaver from whom women ordered cloth, though they still furnished the yarn themselves. In 1810 there were still 10,586 looms in the Ohio country alone, and a majority of the coverlets in that state were still woven at home.

The earliest weave is the "overshot," in which the colored weft threads pass over the warp. This weave produced some of our finest designs in geometric patterns. A variation is "double cloth," in which there are two warp threads and two weft threads woven together wherever the patterns meet. Another type is the reversible, closely woven "Summer and Winter" weave. This style was introduced by the Pennsylvania Germans and developed particularly in Pennsylvania. It required intricate eight- or sixteen-harness looms and expert weavers. Because of its complexity, it was the first type to disappear.

The patterns, or "drafts," for the early geometric coverlets were largely traditional. Immigrant European weavers, including those from Scandinavia and Britain, had brought them over, and they were passed on from family to family and from town to town. As in folklore, variations were introduced by creative individuals. When written out, these drafts look like musical notations, and when woven they suggest the rhythm and pattern one feels in music.

In the late 1830's, the Jacquard loom was introduced. The new loom enabled the weaver to control each separate warp thread. Carried away by the possibilities of the new tool, the weavers let the quality of design deteriorate. Elaborate but weakly conceived patterns of birds, urns or floral shapes replaced the simple but more sensitive early designs.

Completely different in character and technique are the patchwork quilts. Though the technique of patchwork is old and inherited from Europe, it produced a particularly flourishing folk art in this country. Patchwork quilts may be pieced or appliquéd; some quilts combine both techniques. "Pieced" quilts consist of patches of cloth sewn together. "Appliqué" quilts are made by sewing smaller pieces of cloth on a piece of muslin. Usually one section of the quilt is done at a time, and these small sections and border strips are sewn together after the appliqué work is done.

In the pieced quilt, sewing skill counts for more than inventive design, and the result is necessarily geometric and mosaiclike. Appliqué, on the other hand, calls for imagination, and has produced the most appealing examples since it permits a freer design. Women created their own designs, but in quilt-making, as in weaving, there was a strong element of tradition.

Though very few existing quilts date back to Revolutionary times, it is believed that the usual method in the eighteenth century was piecing; appliqué probably came later. Early quilts were made from imported cottons, but from about 1840 on, the American-manufactured cotton prints used in dressmaking yielded a supply of scrap materials for quilt-making.

In the eighteenth and nineteenth centuries, when a girl was ready to announce her engagement, the young ladies of the neighborhood were invited to a quilting bee, where the dozen or so quilt tops she had made were backed and quilted. The quilting bee was thus an occasion for great festivity.

Many names were given to quilt designs, some poetic like "Birds in the Air" or "Snowball," and others prosaic like "Horse Shoe" or "Hit or Miss." Some fall into groups like "Ladies' Delight" and "Children's Delight" or "Bachelor's Puzzle" and "Missouri Puzzle." Others are historical like the "Union Quilt" or "Whig Rose." Over four hundred of these names have been discovered.

212. Petticoat Border (detail), crewel embroidery; eighteenth century.

213. Bed Valance (detail), crewel embroidery; probably made by a member
of the Boardman family, New Milford, Connecticut; eighteenth century.

Sometimes the same pattern had different names in different places. The same design is called "Bear's Paw" in Ohio, "Duck Feet in the Mud" on Long Island, "Hand of Friendship" in Pennsylvania, and "Best Friend" in South Carolina. The "Best Friend" was named after the locomotive of that name. The locomotive boiler blew up in 1831 when a fireman, who disliked the sound of escaping steam, sat on the safety valve. This was the first locomotive accident in America. After this, a new patch, violent in contrast and design, was added to the quilt pattern, which was then called "Explosion."

The colonial four-poster bed had curtains all about it to preserve heat and keep off drafts; there was a canopy over the top, a panel at the back, side curtains, and a bedspread. These curtains, a tradition inherited from ancient Europe, presented a splendid opportunity for crewelwork at a time when embroidery was part of a young lady's education. At private schools in Boston embroidery was taught along with other subjects. Advertisements like the following were not uncommon: "At the House of Mr. George Brownell in Wings-Lane Boston, is taught Writing, Cyphering, Dancing, Treble Violin, Flute, Spinnet, etc. Also English and French Quilting, Imbroidery, Flourishing, Plain Work, Marking in several sorts of Stitches, and several other works, where Scholars may board."

On this valance, dark colors accent the lightness of the forms, as in the large flower that unfolds with such elegance. Printed Indian cottons were often the source of the patterns.

214. Back Panel (detail), from a set of bed curtains, crewel embroidery; made by Mrs. Mary Bulman, York, Maine; 1745.

In 1745 Mrs. Bulman lost her husband in the battle against the French at Louisburg, Nova Scotia. We are told that she started to embroider this set to occupy her mind. The design of the bed curtains is so large and bold that a few rows of motifs suffice for the entire panel. Large surfaces may have inspired a largeness of design. Only women of some leisure could undertake such work, but even they were still busy overseeing their households. They may well have been intent on completing their needlework within a reasonable time, and small, intricate patterns requiring tedious labor would hardly have been suitable.

215. Purse, crewel embroidery; made by Mary Eaton, New-bury, New Hampshire; "April 3, 1764" stitched in the design.

216. Bedspread (detail), crewel embroidery; mid-eighteenth century.

217. Bedspread Border (detail), crewel embroidery; mid-eighteenth century.

Mary Eaton's purse shows such proficiency of design that one wonders if she copied or adapted an existing pattern. Some parts of the design may seem more orig-inal than others, but they still follow traditional crewel patterns. In this case we know the name of the maker, where she lived, and when she finished the work.

Design motifs of bedspreads, like this splendid bird, were fairly large. They were spaced in rows of three or four across the width of the bedspread to make a rich display of color. Even though these crewels have under-gone hard use, their fast colors are still fresh today.

The bedspread border is a trifle heavy and perhaps unimaginative in design, but the shapes and colors make it effective despite its lack of fluency.

218. Coverlet (detail), woven by Mehitable Harriman, near Hill, New Hampshire; eighteenth century.

The intricate pattern of this coverlet shows the creative instinct of the weaver. There is a sense of magnificence in the variety and inventiveness of the pattern. At the top, huge triple chevrons, like capital M's, contrast with quiet horizontal lines. The motifs are then varied from row to row to give an effect of great diversity.

In the overshot technique of weaving, the dark wool lies on the light warp, skipping a number of threads; hence the name "overshot." The heavy weft threads and thin warp produce an uneven surface so that there is a variation of texture as well as of pattern. The colors are modest, natural linen and indigo blue.

219. Coverlet (detail), linen "double cloth"; designed and woven by the Cumbie family in Alamo, Indiana; first half nineteenth century.

The pattern called "Nine Snowballs with Pine Tree Border" looks stately and severe when only a portion of the coverlet is seen. The pine tree border with its triple trunks against massed branches gives a rigid cool-ness, the silhouettes contrasting sharply with the light background. The "Snowball" motif, however, contributes liveliness to the whole design, so that the gay mingles with the sedate.

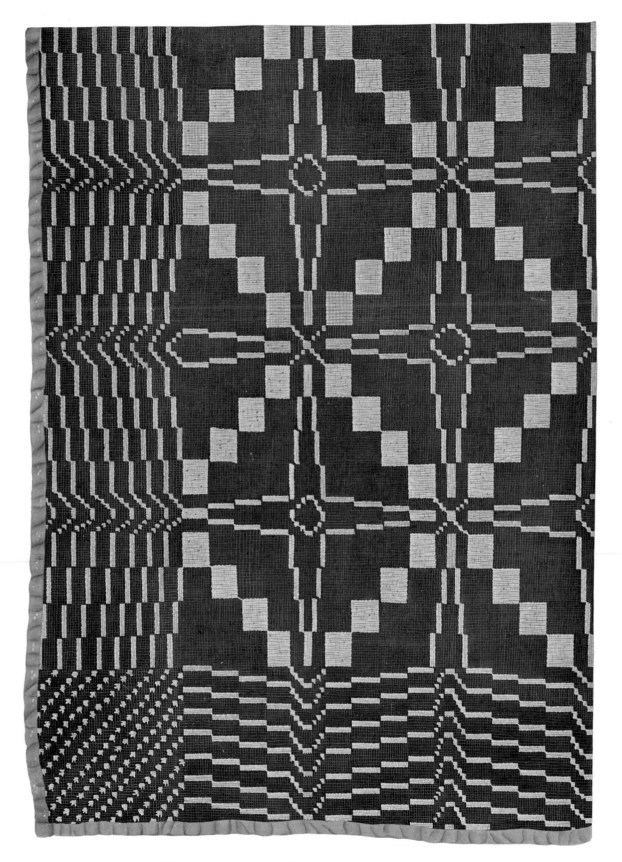

220. Coverlet, white and blue wool; nineteenth century.

The pattern here is distinguished by its clarity and simplicity. It is achieved by contrasts of dark blue and white which build up from small shapes to large. Studying the shapes, one becomes aware of their relationships, as if the smaller ones had been sliced off the larger; this gives unity to the whole design. The border also forms a contrast with the larger pattern, and there is a carefully thought-out progression of shapes and sizes. The coverlet has a rational appeal, and still it does not repel by being too mechanical. This is another example of "Double Weave," woven perhaps on a twelve-harness loom.

221. Coverlet, double cloth, blue and white wool and unbleached cotton;
woven in Indiana; nineteenth century.

This coverlet is an original adaptation of the well known "Boston Town" pattern, so commonly made on the Jacquard loom. But the design is without the tightness and hardness characteristic of coverlets of this group. It is also less elaborate than the usual Jacquard pattern. The weaver has really worked with each detail, so that the motifs unite in a well considered pattern. It is not just lifted from a pattern book, but is honestly inventive, particularly in the borders. The coverlet was woven in two widths of thirty-two inches each, and seamed down the center. The Jacquard loom permits the weaving of wider coverlets, but this weaver chose the width which best suited his purpose.

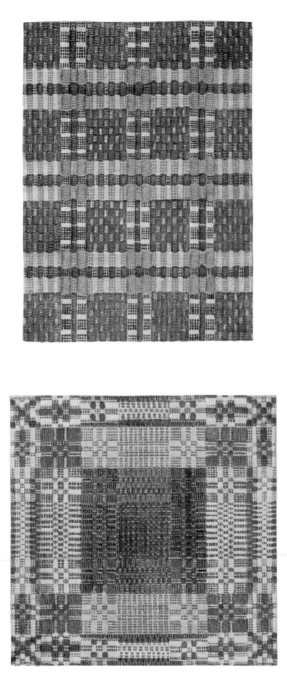

222. Coverlet (detail), woven near Mount Vernon, Indiana; about 1830.

223. Coverlet (detail), handwoven of wool, made by Liza Jane Weddell at Floyd, Virginia; about 1819.

224. Coverlet (detail), handwoven of wool, linen, and cotton by Samantha Charlotte Dudley, Roxbury, Massachusetts, or Kentucky; about 1830.

225. Coverlet (detail), wool and linen, handwoven by May Williams of Falmouth, Kentucky; about 1817.

The Indiana coverlet, made in the "overshot" technique, is simple in design but striking in color, using an orange and blue wool weft and a natural linen warp. The pattern of this weave consists of "skips" or "floats" of wool weft threads that lie loose on top of the linen warp. According to family records, all the materials were produced on the homestead.

In the second coverlet, the wool was dyed with indigo blue and sumac red, two of the most easily obtainable and popular colors in the early days. There was so much demand for this dyestuff that peddlers traveled over the country selling it. Full-width coverlets two yards

wide are woven in two strips and seamed, but the seam in the overshot can hardly be detected.

In the next pattern there is an extravagance in its delicate complexity, yet the design is based on a strict repetition of squares and rectangles, achieving variation through spacing, color, and texture contrasts. Although only blue, sumac, and tan are used, an effect of additional colors is achieved by the way the threads are overlaid in the weaving. The tans are varied by being woven with red and blue. As the tan thread is thinner than the wool, the underlying red and blue wool show through. The spacing of the tan is also varied to alter

226. Tablecloth, cotton homespun, probably made in Salem, Massachusetts; nineteenth century.

the intensity of color. This gives a richness of effect ranging from strong colors to soft neutrals.

The last pattern on the opposite page is a variation of the type known as "sunrise."

There is certainly nothing very original about the details that make up the pattern of this cotton homespun tablecloth. Dots, chevrons, and stripes are common motifs often used in folk art; by themselves they would not make a pattern distinguished. The attraction is in the total design and depends on the shape and space relations and the contrast of the light and dark areas. The horizontal lines that seem imbued with swift motion are pleasing against the solid array of rows of chevrons that spread a net across the width of the cloth. Color and texture also contribute something to the effect.

227. Quilt, appliqué; made in Virginia in 1853.

By the middle of the nineteenth century appliquéd patchwork had reached a high degree of elaboration. With the late 1870's colored bedspreads or counterpanes, as they were called, began to go out of fashion, although they were not purchased commercially until the appearance of the modern department store. The finest specimens were well cared for and used only on special occasions. The decoration is of two kinds: the appliqué and the quilting. The appliquéd central medallion and the quilt-block patterns of oak leaves form the major design; the stitched-in quilting designs of leaves and stars, which are barely visible in the background, form a subordinate pattern. Women's magazines, like *Godey's Lady's Book,* published quilting patterns.

228. Quilt, appliqué; made by Sarah Parell; first half nineteenth century.

This quilt attains great elegance, and yet it keeps its homemade look. It is extraordinarily rich because of its vigor of design, the boldness and fresh, striking contrast of dark against light; it is full of individual variation. It shows clearly that a person with taste and moderate skill can produce unusual results. In the combination of quilting and appliqué, the maker exploited the rich surface of the quilted area rather than the colorfulness of appliqué.

229. Quilt, appliqué; first half nineteenth century.

The design of pieced "Sunbursts" combines eight- and sixteen-pointed stars appliquéd on muslin, with a "Festoon and Bowknot" border. The design is trim and precise; you can almost see the scissors cutting the cotton prints. Gay colors, red, green, and a little yellow, on white muslin, add to its effect. Much of the elaboration is in the quilting in feather patterns. Quilting refers to the "free running-stitches or machine-stitches made through thickness of material with light-weight padding between." The soft and curvilinear background is in the form of a delicate relief that does not conflict with the spiked sunbursts and crisp border. The colors are well related to each other, and so are the designs of the quilt block.

230. Appliqué Bedspread, muslin background, calico figures; found in southeastern New York.

Although found in New York State, this bedspread is Pennsylvania German folk art, and must have originated in a region where there were German settlers. It is an ornamental bedcover without backing, padding, or quilting, made for appearance only. For warmth the Pennsylvania Germans used thick feather beds, which they covered with the appliquéd bedspreads for looks.

Scalloped edge, borders, and dots are quite in the folk-art tradition. The spread has great variety and charming color, using familiar motifs in sprightly patterns of flat color, constantly varied. The motifs seem reminiscent of village life; bird and tulip recur frequently and there are quail, flower pots, trees, deer, the master, his dog, and his farmhouse.

231. Quilt (detail), pieced and appliquéd, calico; made by Mary Bailey, Coweeta County, Georgia; early nineteenth century.

This quilt employs both the piecing and appliqué techniques. The star-shaped motif is pieced and then appliquéd on the white muslin. One variation of this star type quilt block, the "Star of Bethlehem," is constructed of diamond shaped patches.

The basic element of quilt making is the quilt block. There were two common ways of reducing the large block to smaller segments. The beginning of the quilt block was a square piece of cloth, which was folded over twice and cut to produce four small squares, or folded three times each way to produce nine small squares. These small squares could be cut further to get a diversity of shapes. Of these shapes, in either the four-patch or the nine-patch, an endless variety of patterns was possible. In the pieced quilt, all parts of the original square were retained and sewn together to equal a square.

232. Bedspread, tufted candlewick on muslin; nineteenth century.

233. Printed Kerchief, silk; made on Staten Island, New York; nineteenth century.

Candlewick was made by working thread over a roll to make knots. Sometimes the knots were left in loops and sometimes they were cut to appear tufted. Both techniques are seen on the border above.

This silk kerchief was block-printed by hand. First a large red area was blocked on a cream-colored ground, and then a second block was used for the black pattern. Hand-printed materials have no folk-art heritage com-parable to that of quilts or coverlets, for in colonial times prints were mostly imported. There were, how-ever, instances where printers and engravers also turned to printing linens, calicoes, and silks. According to a newspaper announcement of July 30, 1716, Francis Dewing, a New England engraver, "Engraveth and Printeth Copper Plates, Cuts neatly in Wood and Printeth Callicoes."

234. Armchair, pine; from near San Andreas, California; mid-nineteenth century. This chair expresses the needs of the farmhouse.

235. Empire chair, walnut; nineteenth century; the parlor chair of our grandmothers that remained fashionable up to the 1840's.

12. Furniture from Farmhouse and Mansion

In the early settlements on the Atlantic seaboard, before 1660, furniture was scarce. The Pilgrims brought few possessions with them, and any furniture they may have had was probably not in the latest English fashion. Though the well-to-do Puritans imported furniture, little of it has survived. It either perished in fires or wore out in the course of time. When the settlers made their own chairs and chests, they continued, as well as they remembered them, the traditions with which they had been familiar in rural England.

The history of American furniture begins with a familiar figure, John Alden, who was perhaps the first woodworker in the colonies. If any chest he made for Priscilla is still in existence, it remains unknown, for furniture was rarely signed.

In the seventeenth century American furniture was made by carpenters who were called joiners. In this first period from about 1630 to 1725 oak and other coarse-grained woods were used in rectangular and massive forms. Furniture was utilitarian, made for the living-room-kitchen, the center of family life. There were few chairs but many chests that also served as seats. The most elaborate chair was the wainscot chair, which was heavy and uncomfortable; furniture was not yet related to the curves of the human figure. But there were notable achievements among the chests, like those from Connecticut, the painted Guilford and carved Hartford chests, and those from around Hadley, Massachusetts. The gate-legged and butterfly tables, and a combination chair, table and chest, called the hutch table, became popular in colonial houses where space had to be saved, because these tables could be made smaller by turning the tops down.

Throughout this early period, the English influence is most important, and next to the English, the Dutch; but only in New Amsterdam was the Dutch influence felt directly.

By the beginning of the eighteenth century, the colonies had grown in wealth, and could indulge in furniture and fine cabinetwork. The houses were also larger and had rooms with paneled and plastered walls and larger windows.

This second period may be dated from about 1725 to 1790. The first part of the period is also known as the Dutch or Queen Anne style. With the reign of William of Orange and Mary (1688–1702), the Dutch influence had been introduced into England, and from there it was transplanted to the American colonies. One feature of this style is the cabriole leg with the club foot. Furniture now begins to show curves, the S-curve being dominant. This versatile line could be made flatter or more extreme, and was used in many ways. A number of variations can be traced in the chair splats, the cabriole leg, the top of the highboy, and the skirts of lowboys and chairs. In the chair the back, seat, and leg develop their own separate characters. Proportions become lighter, and carving is surface ornamentation, with the possible exception of the claw-and-ball foot, where the carving is structural.

This Dutch influence was followed by the so-called Chippendale, the English style that corresponds to the French rococo of Louis XV. It is named after a cabinet-maker and owner of a large shop in London. Chippendale's book on furniture design, *Gentleman and Cabinet Maker's Director* (1754), helped to spread his style in England and the colonies. During this Chippendale phase, from about 1760 on, American colonial furniture became outstanding in beauty and craftsmanship, equal to the best English work. It achieved its most florid expression in Philadelphia, particularly in the highboy with its scroll top and elaborate carving. There were many cabinetmakers in Philadelphia, among them William Savery and Benjamin Randolph, to whom specific pieces have been attributed.

Of equal significance is the block-front type of desk, usually associated with the Goddards and Townsends, two families of Quaker cabinetmakers of Newport, Rhode Island. The honor of having been the first to design block-front furniture has long been claimed for John Goddard, though it is difficult to assign the block front to a single person. The fine cabinetwork of several groups of men working in Philadelphia and New England, together with the production of Duncan Phyfe of New York, gave to American furniture its place in history. The highboy and block front particularly are American achievements.

In England, Chippendale was followed by Hepplewhite who had much in common with him. Hepplewhite is noted chiefly for his shield-back chair. He returned to the use of straight legs, either square or round. He also published a book on cabinetmaking which influenced both English and American styles.

The third period, the Federal (1790–1825), was the time of the classic revival. Our American furniture owes much to another English designer of the period, Thomas Sheraton, who was distinguished for the square-back chair and for inlay and veneering. All furniture now returns to straight lines, and takes on great delicacy and refinement. Where curves are retained, as on bracket feet and table tops, or on the bowed fronts of chests, they become long and sweeping. The decoration is in marquetry, consisting of inlay of contrasting woods set in a background of veneer. Our cabinetmakers simplified the Sheraton by suppressing the moldings and using straight edges; the American eagle in inlays and brasses supplanted the urns and floral decorations popular in London.

Scottish-born Duncan Phyfe, who worked largely for a wealthy clientele of the New York region, was the leading cabinetmaker. His designs, based on Sheraton, Directoire, English Regency and Empire inspiration, achieve individuality, but they cannot be said to be in a new style. He kept structural members thin, using the finest and strongest mahogany.

This type of furniture, also called period furniture, was made for the well-to-do town merchants. Visitors to New York, Philadelphia and Baltimore, in the days of the early Republic, were amazed at the elegant furnishings, even though the houses themselves hardly rivaled those of London.

After the first quarter of the nineteenth century, this delicate Sheraton style turned into heavy American Empire. Though his shop participated in various changes of taste, Phyfe held the mahogany and horsehair type of furniture in low esteem and referred to it as "butcher's furniture." But not all was of this kind. Lambert Hitchcock, among others, produced for middle-class homes chairs that deserved their popularity. They were painted black or green, gorgeously decorated with stenciled designs, and were called "Fancy Chairs." In the early days of his activity at Riverton, Connecticut, then known as Barkhamsted, rechristened Hitchcocksville, his factory turned out chairs unassembled for shipment to the South.

With the coming of the early Victorian period around 1840, curves, scrolls and cabriole legs, based on the French rococo, again became fashionable. John H. Belter, a New York cabinetmaker, illustrates this style in its more extravagant manner.

For furniture of a less pretentious expression, we must turn to the common chairs and chests, beds, tables and cupboards of the eighteenth century, the styles of which continued into the nineteenth century. This furniture, though not made of mahogany nor upholstered in satin, was in good taste. It was light in weight, simple in design. While this furniture often continued the traditions of the English or German, the Spanish or

236. Wardrobe or Kas, walnut; probably made in New York; early eighteenth century.

237. Gate-Legged Table, walnut, oval top, sixty-nine inches long when extended; made in Lewes, Delaware; late seventeenth century.

French, it emphasized function rather than style.

In the early eighteenth century, the Windsor chair was known as the Philadelphia chair. Though taken over from England, it achieved its greatest development in this country, where it became the most commonly used chair, remaining in favor until this very day. Windsor chairs were made of various kinds of woods, including ash, hickory and maple, and in various types of backs, U-shaped bow-back, comb-back and fan-back.

Purely utilitarian furniture, intended for farmhouse or kitchen, has given us some of the most satisfactory types. Basic materials and designs do not differ greatly in different sections of the country, but one can sometimes tell whether a piece was made in the North or

238. Lowboy, maple, Queen Anne; first half eighteenth century.

239. Desk Box, chip-carved, painted and stained, eighteen inches long; early eighteenth century.

South, and certainly whether the tradition is from New England or New Mexico. Much of our commercial furniture of the nineteenth century was poorly made and in bad taste. It is therefore comforting to realize that there were porch rockers in Iowa or chests in Texas that we can admire today.

The Dutch "kas" (English "case"), a wardrobe or clothes cupboard, is characteristic of Europe where closets are uncommon; the Dutch introduced it to New York. This one has massive pilasters and panels, and top moldings which form an elaborate cornice. Its three sec-

tions, chest, cabinet and cornice, are held in place by large taper dowels.

American gate-legged tables follow the English type. They have square, round, rectangular or oval tops with drop-leaf ends, and two swinging legs that fold under to save space. The use of a hand tool produces minor variations that give individuality to the carving.

The lowboy or dressing table is light, graceful and consistent in design. Vigorous curves in the structure of the piece break up the boxlike shape, for the S-curve appears in skirt and leg.

240. Hartford Chest, with two drawers, quartered oak and pine; made in Hartford County, Connecticut; late seventeenth century.

The slant-top desk box on the previous page was used on a table before the writing desk had evolved. Chip-carving in V-shaped notches forming rosettes, stars and hearts is common to folk art, and survived especially on the Frisian Islands, north of Holland. It is therefore not surprising that the style was popular with Dutch settlers.

By adding drawers to a chest, the chest of drawers developed. A chest on a framework became a piece of

furniture halfway between chest and highboy. It was sometimes decorated by means of "japanning" in imitation of Oriental lacquer, using paint, whiting, metal leaf and powder.

This Connecticut chest uses carving and combines carved asters or sunflowers and tulips with applied split spindles and bosses painted black in imitation of ebony. Some fifty chests are known, a local development of Hartford County, that vary only in details.

241. Wing Chair, walnut and maple; made in New England; early eighteenth century.

The high back and wings of the "easy-chair" served as a protection against drafts. Its slim lines are strikingly effective, and the firm upholstery was comfortable enough for those accustomed to loose cushions laid on wooden seats. Turned stretchers survive from the seventeenth century, but the carved leg with the intermediate Spanish foot, that later becomes the cabriole leg, is in the spirit of the eighteenth century. East Indian floral motifs are block-printed on the cotton covering.

242. Highboy, curly maple, Queen Anne; probably made in Connecticut; first half eighteenth century.

This high chest in the Queen Anne style is an early version of the highboy, which is a modern term. It has the structure of the highboy of the Chippendale period, but it is more restrained in decoration. This is noted in the simple, almost straight, cabriole legs with club feet, in the flame finials, the rising sun pattern of the top and lower drawers, and the moldings of the scroll-top. Compared to the full opulence of the Philadelphia highboy, this earlier type seems almost thin and meager. All of the drawers overlap. Straight lines control the curves, particularly the skirt with its drop pendants. What it lacks in carving, it makes up for in the beauty of the wood, in the brass keyhole plates, and above all in its wholly satisfying reticence.

The Windsor chair with writing-arm, a drawer for sand and quills, and a pull-out slide for a candle, is a native development unknown in England. Shawls could be hung on the comb back to keep off drafts, and a lamp

243. Windsor Chair, various woods; probably made in New England; mid-eighteenth century.

244. Side Chair, mahogany, Chippendale; made in Philadelphia; about 1765.

on the upturned ear. The legs of American Windsors are more slanting than those of English Windsors. The seat was made in one piece of green wood so that when the wood dried it contracted, gripping the spindles more firmly than any glue could do. There were Windsor chairs at Mount Vernon in George Washington's day, they were used by the First and the Second Continental Congress in Philadelphia, and it is said that Thomas Jefferson wrote the Declaration of Independence in a Windsor chair with a writing-arm, built according to his design.

The chair, like the tea table, represents the most sump-

tuous Philadelphia furniture made just before the Revolution. The back splat, which was plain in the Queen Anne period, is here perforated and carved, yet it does not seem frail. There is a delicate flower pattern in the uprights, and the carved cabriole leg with its claw-and-ball foot looks sturdy. The whole back is one consistent design, particularly successful in its rhythmic flow of curves.

The desk on the next page with its slanting top is a fine example of the block-front type of furniture. It is vigorous and delicate in design and ingenious in its twenty-eight small drawers, arranged in tiers, one re-

245. Block-Front Desk, cherry, Chippendale; made by Benjamin Burnam, probably in Connecticut; dated 1769.

246. Chair, chestnut and cherry, painted, Sheraton; made in New York City; early nineteenth century.

247. Settee, mahogany, oak and cherry, Chippendale; made in the upholstery shop of Joseph Cox, New York City; 1757–1760.

cessed above the other. The lower drawers were cut from wood sufficiently thick to allow for both the raised and depressed surfaces. On the front that is here visible, the designer gets his elaboration through delicately fluted stiles. A finely molded base merges on the front into richly carved claw-and-ball feet. An inscription reads, "This desk was made in the year 1769 by Benjm. Burnam that sarvfed his time in Felledlfey."

After the Revolution, American designers found that the Chippendale manner had become obsolete in England, and that Hepplewhite and Sheraton had become the fashion. In this Sheraton chair we have a return to straight lines and geometric shapes. The free way in which flowers grow out of a slender vase suggests the provincial adaptation of a Sheraton motif. A more sensi-

tive designer would probably have stressed severity or freedom, making one or the other the dominant note of his design.

In the design of the settee the emphasis is on the large, simple curves of the back that contrast with the short scrolls of the ends. The lines of the upholstered frame are virtually in the same style as the earlier wing chair, for old traditional designs that had proved satisfactory frequently outlived the period with which they were first identified.

A graceful slenderness was typical of the period to which Duncan Phyfe belongs. It also appears in attenuated columns and in the high-waisted skirt of the Empire dress. We have the same emphasis on continuity of line in the armchair, where the line of the back con-

248. Armchair, mahogany; made in workshop of Duncan Phyfe, New York City; early nineteenth century.

249. Sofa Table, mahogany; made by Duncan Phyfe (1768–1854), New York City; early nineteenth century.

250. Chest of Drawers, mahogany veneer with satinwood inlay, Hepplewhite; made in New York; 1796–1803.

tinues without interruption into the back leg and seat. In the Chippendale or Hepplewhite, curves are allowed a freer play; here they are held to a greater reserve. Side chairs made by Duncan Phyfe originally sold for $22.

Duncan Phyfe made tables for many uses, but structurally there are only three kinds: those supported on the four corners, in the center, or at the ends, as in this drop-leaf sofa table. To lighten the appearance, the stretcher is slightly curved at top and bottom. The reeded edge of the top emphasizes the unity of design, as reeding also appears on the under structure. Brass drawer pulls and paw feet add a note of vigor which is

in keeping with the slightly heavy character of the design. This is one of the rarer pieces attributed to Duncan Phyfe's shop.

The bow-front chest of drawers, with inlaid eagles and brass handles, is an American adaptation of an English style, the curve of the long bracket foot and apron being typically Hepplewhite. This is an example of the American custom of eliminating moldings and carving for the sake of inlay. The beautifully mottled satinwood luster enhances the attractiveness of the design. The sixteen stars in the inlay date the piece around 1800.

251. Side Chair, wood, painted black and stenciled; made by Hitchcock, Alford & Co. (1829–1843), Riverton, Connecticut.
252. Side Chair, burl walnut, Victorian; nineteenth century.

253. Shaving Stand, mahogany; made in Wilmington, Delaware; first half nineteenth century.

In general design the Hitchcock chairs follow the American Empire style. The decorations of fruits and flowers in color, and in bronze or gold powder have retained their luster. Stenciling supplanted the more expensive earlier method of hand-painting that had been popular on chairs since the late eighteenth century. The same artisans worked for various manufacturers; identical designs have been found on chairs bearing the labels of different makers. Hitchcock chairs were not only well made and pleasing to look at, they were also most reasonable in price, retailing as low as $1.50.

In the Victorian chair with the needlepoint seat, the curved Empire legs combine with a Queen Anne type of back splat. The more graceful curves of the earlier chairs here take on a suggestion of strength and utility.

The motifs are all adapted from past styles, and the machine-carved crest glued to the top rail is unrelated to the rest. Nevertheless, its lack of originality is not so important as the fact that such chairs were comfortable and durable. Here is an expression of forthright utility; not all furniture of the Victorian era was debased in taste.

Something of the simplicity of the eighteenth century remains in the design of the shaving stand, but it is without the earlier grace, and the proportions tend toward the heaviness of the Empire period.

The lyre-shaped wall clock is a variant of the banjo clock, patented in 1802 by Simon Willard, younger brother of Benjamin, of the well known Massachusetts clockmakers. It was Benjamin who advertised clocks

254. Wall Clock, mahogany, three feet long; made in Boston; first half nineteenth century.

255. Shelf Clock; made by Eli and Samuel Terry, Connecticut; first half nineteenth century.

256. Armchair, rosewood, Victorian; made by John Henry Belter (active 1844–1865), New York City.

that "play a new tune every day of the week and on Sunday a psalm tune." Cases like this have a long shaft to allow the pendulum to swing, and a small head to encase the brass works. The banjo shape happened to be appropriate, and its simplicity fitted in with the prevailing classic taste. Even though one shape is piled on top of another, the total effect is sober.

The case of the shelf clock, delicate yet sturdy, is in the best late eighteenth century tradition. Eli Terry, famous American clockmaker of Connecticut, produced the first shelf clock. He made four thousand wooden-works clocks on one order and sold them without the case through peddlers. Among his apprentices was Seth

Thomas, the founder of another branch of Connecticut clockmakers that turned a local craft into a large business.

The rosewood chair, from a parlor set, represents the height of Victorian splendor. Restless curves emphasize decoration for its own sake, but the design, based on the French rococo, is consistent. Leaves, flowers and grapes were carved out of thin layers of rosewood, glued together and steamed to achieve the desired curves. The curved backs were also covered with rosewood veneer. Even though this furniture was primarily for display, it was well constructed. Belter claimed it could be tossed out of a window without suffering damage.

257. Four-poster Bed, white oak; made near Gay Hill, Texas; 1842.

258. Armchair, rawhide seat; made in San Antonio, Texas; first half nineteenth century.

259. Chair, pecan frame, rawhide seat; made by B. Schweer-Balsen, Quihi, Texas; 1846–1850.

260. Chest, cypress with wrought-iron lock and hinges; made in Yorktown, Texas; probably about 1860.

The heroes of the Revolution still slept in four-poster beds draped to keep out the cold. But in the first quarter of the nineteenth century high posts went out of fashion. In this bed from Texas, they were retained because they were used for hanging mosquito netting. The heavy posts and the straight line of the headboard suggest the late Empire, its curved ends and ball feet recall an earlier colonial manner. Bed, chairs and chest were made by provincial artisans in rural Texas.

This type of armchair with its high seat and flat projecting arms has a general European background, but is also Spanish and, therefore, Mexican. The chair comes from San Antonio, a region of Spanish culture, and the high back posts are in the local tradition.

The side chair was made by an Alsatian settler; the rawhide seat is indigenous to a cattle country. A German peasant influence is suggested in the notched ends of the uprights. Such utilitarian pieces still reflect various European traditions. Differences are recognizable only in the general shapes because the aim to simplify for the sake of economy did away with elaborations.

The beauty of the bed-chest or utility cabinet is in the grain of the wood, left unpainted and unfinished. The chest is also in the German tradition.

The seat table is an adaptation of the early American hutch table, with its tilting top, combination chest, bench and table. The hutch table, however, was usually smaller, having only a seat instead of a bench. Like

261. Seat Table, walnut; made in Burlington, Iowa; about 1860.

262. Ladder-Back Chair, oak (?), seat of twisted corn husks; made by Arthur Pimar, Alachua County, Florida; mid-nineteenth century.

263. Rocking Chair, combination of woods; made in Pennsylvania; nineteenth century.

264. Bible Box, pine, made in Pennsylvania near Carlisle; eighteenth century.

other tilt-top tables, it was designed to save space. The grain of the wood is one of its attractions.

The ladder-back chair, with low cornhusk seat, stood in the kitchen. It was used by the grandmother when she prepared vegetables, with pans set out on the floor around her. This type of chair is also associated with the old unpainted puncheon kitchen floors, sprinkled with white sand for protection against ashes and grease from the open hearth. Chairs with straight horizontal slats are probably as old as the more pretentious creations of professional artisans.

Rocking chairs originated in this country and became very popular. According to tradition, Benjamin Franklin invented the idea of putting rockers on his favorite chair. Those that date before 1800 are often found to have been converted from straight chairs. A combination of woods is common in chairs, each wood being selected to serve the requirements of a particular part. This chair shows a Windsor influence in splay and spindles. It is functional and comfortable, and shows a minimum of decoration.

This Bible box, with its slanting top and drawer beneath for pens and paper, is a piece of furniture which comes nearest the modern writing desk. As the wood, protected from the weather, gradually ages, it takes on a patina in the soft satiny finish. The box is about fifteen inches high and over sixteen inches wide.

265. Corner Cupboard, walnut; believed to have been made in Ste. Genevieve, Missouri; nineteenth century.

266. Cupboard or Open-Shelved Dresser, white pine and poplar, Pennsylvania German; made in Pennsylvania.

Historic Ste. Genevieve on the Mississippi River was settled by the French in the eighteenth century and received an influx of German settlers in the nineteenth century. This type of cupboard with rectangular panels is different from those of New England; it follows a tradition common to the Mississippi valley. In moldings and feet it reveals a simplification of the period manner, adapted by some frontier craftsman.

The dresser also has an Old World ancestry. In place of the elegance of a professional craftsman it shows the bolder manner of the village carpenter. The scalloped contours are the florid lines of folk art. Such open cupboards perpetuated the European tradition of displaying attractive pottery for its decorative effect. The indented profile, the butterfly hinges and the guardrails are in the Pennsylvania German tradition.

FOR PROFIT AND PLEASURE

267. Eagle, painted wood, Pennsylvania German; attributed to Wilhelm Schimmel; second half nineteenth century.

13. Whittling and Wood Carving

Whittling is one of the simplest of all crafts. Even carving takes a few chisels, but to whittle one needs only a jackknife. Probably every boy at one time or another has made something out of wood with his pocketknife. In early America, when most people lived on farms or in small towns, whittling was a national pastime. A farmer made a toy for his son, or a lumberjack with leisure on his hands recaptured the skills of his boyhood. The village store had its whittlers, even if they produced no more than shavings off the boxes they sat on. People whittled as we doodle while we talk on the telephone; cutting away on a piece of wood was not merely a display of skill, it was a needed outlet for the emotions and an exercise of the imagination. Whittling on occasion might help one over a tense moment when one had to keep one's wits. A painting by Mount, entitled "Coming to the Point," shows two horse traders,

both shrewd Yankees. Each works away with his knife at a stick, as he plays for time before the final decision.

Among the many who used their knives haphazardly there were some who were actually creative. These talented individuals produced the whittled horses, eagles and various kinds of animals, including a few human figures, that here and there have come to light. Such creations are usually small; often they are the work of amateurs, who made no pretensions to art. A sailor went in for scrimshaw work by engraving a tusk, and a westerner shaped a block of wood into a charging buffalo. Eventually such pieces may have been given away or traded off for something useful, or on occasion sold for necessities. Some of these pieces had no apparent purpose; others were made for an occasion and usually not intended for sale.

In the hard life of the frontier there was no place for

painting. Even where there was a desire for creative expression, artists' materials were lacking. But wood, at least, was plentiful, and in periods of enforced idleness, as in the rainy season or during the winter months, a man could always whittle.

In some instances the work shows professional competence. Among those who came to America were wood carvers from the Alpine countries, from Bavaria, the Black Forest, and other regions where wood carving was a tradition. The craftsman who depended on carving for his livelihood did not remain idle when not working at his craft. If his regular work was scarce, he carved whatever came to hand.

Artisans have always taken to the road. They traveled from one town to another, and the more adventuresome they were the more they wandered. Usually they remained anonymous, but occasionally the identity of individuals has been preserved. The names of Schimmel and Mounts of Pennsylvania have been handed down to us. According to tradition they were itinerants who depended on their skill with the knife to see them through from one shop or tavern to another, exchanging their carved birds and animals for bed and board.

What is known to have been preserved of such folk art is but a small portion of what once existed. Certainly these objects reflect various persons and many conditions, from the naive work of one who may have produced but a single piece, to the work of an accomplished artist who worked while on holiday.

The chicken shown below is cut from cypress-root, built up in several sections. It dates from the years 1810 to 1815, and is said to have been carved by a Negro slave of Jean Lafitte, the notorious chief of the Barataria Bay pirates.

268. Chicken, wood; first quarter nineteenth century.

269. Eagle, wood, Pennsylvania German; attributed to Aaron Mounts; second half nineteenth century.

270. Poodle Dog, pine, painted; made in Pennsylvania, probably by Aaron Mounts; second half nineteenth century.

271. Decoy, carved and painted pine; mid-nineteenth century.

Schimmel traveled through the Shenandoah Valley after the Civil War, and pieces attributed to him have been acquired in Carlisle, Pennsylvania. Such carvings were used as ornaments by the Pennsylvania German people. The eagle at the head of this chapter shows real spontaneity. The carving is nervous and impetuous in its broad, loose treatment. The use of red, black, and yellow color has been explained by the fact that he and Mounts both did their carving in various blacksmiths' and wagoners' shops, and used the paint that was at hand in such places. Old-timers of Cumberland County some years ago still retained from their youth memories of Schimmel as a picturesque old character, of whom the children were afraid.

Mounts was a friend of Schimmel, and the story goes that he was encouraged to try his hand at carving by watching Schimmel. Although both carved the same subjects, such as eagles, squirrels, and dogs, Mounts here reveals a manner of his own. His style is painstaking and precise, and he makes the feathers into an ornamental pattern. This is characteristic of the naive carver who gives us the general character of the living model and then emphasizes what lends itself to a decorative treatment. He produces smooth, flowing outlines and stylized patterns as in the bird and poodle dog.

Decoys were made by the Indians, from whom the early settlers learned the art. The method of stuffing skins was supplanted by carving and painting wooden forms to float on the water in imitation of live birds. The drake shown above represents the American merganser, and is believed to have been carved about 1850 by Mark Griffin, a decoy-maker of Gardiners Island, New York.

272. Head, hard wood; carved in California; nineteenth century.

There is bitter sadness in this impressive face, with its slightly distorted mouth and half-closed eyes. According to tradition, it reflects the artist's impressions of a hanging, but realism is here modified, and there is an effect of calm. It is so competent that we must surmise that the man who carved this distinguished head was an experienced craftsman. Probably never painted, the wood with time has taken on a dark, bronze hue.

The piece originated in the days of the California Gold Rush. It was discovered in a nearly abandoned old mining town in the Mother Lode region of the state, where it was an ornament in a saloon. When miners came upon meagre days those who had other ways of earning a living fell back on their professional skills.

273. Decoy, painted wood, Hudsonian Godwit; nineteenth century.

274. Horse, wood; made in Kingston, New York.

In this instance the bird is sawed and chiseled out of a thick board. This type of decoy was stuck in the ground, rather than floated on the water.

This toy horse is larger than the usual whittled object, and big enough for a two-year-old to ride. It was made by a carpenter, who so overemphasized structural forms and straight lines that it is obvious he was more used to boards and posts than to living things. The legs are doweled on to the body, like the legs of a chair. Though this piece offers only a faint suggestion of a horse, it still creates a pleasing visual impression, with the sleek, smooth shapes of neck and head. The carver treated wood with a loving care that carries over to the observer and must also have delighted the children. Its lack of realism is not important.

275. "Log Hauling," wood; made in Eau Claire, Wisconsin; nineteenth century.

276. "Whaling Scene," scrimshaw engraving on whale tooth; made in New Bedford, Massachusetts; nineteenth century.

This group, three feet long, was carved by a lumberjack who had considerable talent. The sled, yoke, and chain are implements with which he was well acquainted, and the details are done with accuracy. Although the animals are treated with less realism, the artist succeeds in giving a good impression of the big, patient beasts of burden. The teamster has definite racial characteristics, perhaps suggestive of a Slavic type. The use of oxen as draft animals was common in the pioneering days, as a carry-over of European customs.

There is a spiritual kinship between what the sailor engraved with his knife and what the woodsman carved with his. Both were lonely men away from home, who felt a need to absorb themselves in a creative task. The rough surface of the tooth had to be made smooth and polished by long, tedious work before it was ready for engraving. The craftsman shows his skill in the clever treatment of the men in the little dories, whose actions are unmistakable even though the figures are small. The drawing of the ship and the indication of the choppy sea show that this artist probably had drawn nautical scenes all his life. He knows his ships as well as the story of whaling, and he describes both with artistry.

277. Charging Buffalo, soft wood; made in northern Iowa; second half nineteenth century.

278. Oxen and Cart, carved of pine near Stoughton, Wisconsin; nineteenth century.

The carver of the buffalo took liberties with proportions, making his beast more agile than is characteristic of the cumbersome buffalo. His conception does not seem to have been based entirely on firsthand experience with the living animal, and his imagination may have fused other images with his main theme. Yet the action is clearly that of the buffalo, creating a successful impression of movement and vigor. The artist must have been an experienced craftsman, stressing decorative line, flowing curves and smooth, rounded shapes.

The miniature oxcart is believed to have been carved by an early settler in imitation of the primitive oxcart in general use in the sixties and seventies. We do not

realize how universal was the use of oxen in this country. The ox was sure-footed and had great strength for pulling loads. These solid disc wheels were used in the primitive frontier regions before the wheelwrights were available. To couple two animals together to draw the load, the yoke was used and is still used today. It consists of a curved piece of timber with four holes into which two bows are inserted. These are slipped over the animals' necks and fastened with a wooden key. The hauling chain is fastened to a wrought-iron ring attached to the underside of the bow. The yoke was made of ash or hickory; the bows of hickory or sweet walnut.

279. "Cycle of Life," carved of elmwood by Pierre Joseph Landry (1770–1843), at Iberville Parish, Louisiana; 1834.

This elaborate piece of carving, over two feet in diameter, was made by Landry, an early settler who came to Louisiana from Nantes, France. After a strenuous life, as an old man he became an invalid. On his plantation he settled down to wood carving to keep himself occupied. This topic of the ages of man has a broad basis in art and literature. The combination of foliage and figures makes one think of Gothic choir stalls, and the falling figure may also go back to medieval art. Perhaps the artist depended upon a book illustration as a guide.

The ten separate incidents may be interpreted as follows. Beginning at the bottom and proceeding in a clockwise direction, we have: (1) Birth; (2) Childhood, a boy stalking a bird; (3) Youth, a shepherd with his flute; (4) Courtship, a man pursuing a maiden; (5) Man at his peak, with the implements of learning, labor and the mechanical arts carved at the base; (6) Middle age; (7) Man's decline, holding an empty acorn; (8) Death, the reaper carved on the base; (9) Worshiper by the tomb; (10) Mourners at a mausoleum.

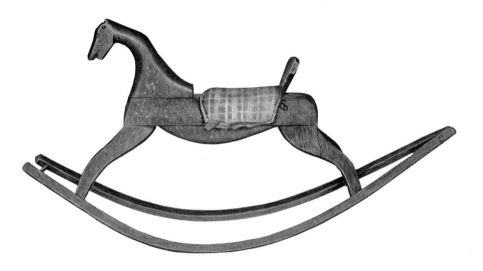

280. Rocking Horse, wood; nineteenth century.

14. Playthings

We enjoy looking back at the playthings of our childhood, even if we cannot easily recall the pleasant fantasies that once surrounded them. Children need toys, and when they were lacking, as in the days of the Puritans, shells and pebbles, and leaves and sticks were used instead. There were no playthings available then, but by the end of the seventeenth century English toys were in demand in the colonies. Few of them have been preserved, because toys disappear when worn and old-fashioned. The more elaborate dolls' houses have survived, and may now be seen in museums. But not all miniature replicas of furniture and dishes were toys, some were curios made for display in adult households.

The costume dolls that milliners and dressmakers imported several times a year to keep abreast of the latest styles took the place of living models, and were not intended as playthings. The elegant lady-doll of the late Victorian era is the successor to the fashion doll of an earlier period. She was often fitted out with an ample wardrobe and was of course made for young girls to play with. This type of the late nineteenth century doll was very handsome, as manufacturers strove to beautify the features. We still have the expression "doll-like beauty" to describe a kind of feminine attractiveness that strikes us as artificial. The true baby doll in which the head is modeled in convincing imitation of a real infant was unknown till the twentieth century.

For most toys, wood long remained the common ma-terial. When tin came into use for household utensils, toy miniatures were made from the scraps, and were sold off the peddler's wagon out of Berlin, Connecticut. Then came the pewter toys that were popular during the time of the Revolution, paper cut dolls in the mid-nineteenth century, and cast-iron toys, particularly stoves, in the 1870's.

Toys tend to copy contemporary life, and change with the fashions. Foreign-made toys cannot always be readily distinguished from domestic ones, but we may be reasonably certain that the ones illustrated are American-made, of the fairly recent past.

Toys were made by artisans, incidentally, as an addi-tion to their craft, and often only for the immediate use of their own families. When toys were first pro-duced in quantity they were still manufactured as a sideline and used as premiums to stimulate sales of other goods. There were few American toy factories before 1875, and until 1900 most of our toys came from Germany. Villages like Berchtesgaden, with century-old traditions of toymaking as a folk art, are not found in this country.

The rocking horse might have been made by a car-penter, and is perhaps a simplified version of a more elaborate model. The sleek, elongated lines resulting from its economical construction are particularly grati-fying to contemporary taste.

281. Doll, "Camela," cloth body, papier-mâché head, kid hands and shoes, calico dress and embroidered cotton underwear; from South Haven, Michigan; about 1855.

282. Doll, "Mollie Bentley," muslin, calico skirt, and gingham apron; from Lancaster County, Pennsylvania; about 1886.

Dolls with papier-mâché heads were imported in the early nineteenth century. These were mounted on canvas, linen, or kid bodies stuffed with sawdust. They had wooden arms and legs, and they looked stiff. China heads from Austria and Germany came next, and they were followed by wax heads from England. The older papier-mâché heads were continued along with the new types. Linen pantalets were in fashion from 1818 to 1858, so this doll would probably not be of a later date.

"Mollie Bentley" is to all appearances homemade. Her hair is of blue fringed serge; she has no hands, but feet with feather-stitched shoes; eyes, mouth, and cheeks are embroidered in red. Her dress is made up of a variety of scraps, and is complete as to stockings and underwear. The scraps here used demonstrate two popular kinds of cotton dress goods known throughout the nineteenth century. The overskirt is made of calico, a plain, woven cotton cloth printed with a figured pattern on one side. It derives its name from Calicut, India, where cotton textiles were first printed. Gingham is a light or medium weight cotton fabric woven of dyed yarn, often in stripes, checks, or plaids. It goes back to the early days of the Republic, its name being either of Malay or French origin, if the latter, from the town of Guingamp in Brittany.

283. Train, cast iron; designed in Rye, New York; inscribed "Patented May 25, 1880."

284. Top, wood, carved and painted; first half nineteenth century.

285. Model of a Stagecoach, wood; nineteenth century.

The sturdily constructed little train approximates the type of locomotive current at the time the toy was patented. Toys sold in America were not necessarily made here, but in this case the cowcatcher probably stamps the design as a native product.

This top was wound up with a string in the familiar fashion, but otherwise it differs from more recent types. It has holes to make it whistle and is carved with a human head and made to look like a little lady in a hooped skirt. Until our day man desired to minimize the importance of things mechanical, because they came uncomfortably close to human performance. One way was to give the mechanical principle a playful

expression in the form of a toy; another was to give it human form. In this top the two are combined.

The Overland Stage may be a homemade toy, but it could also have been made for the purpose of display in a store window. It is of a fairly recent date. The Overland Line furnished its hazardous transportation through the West when Indian tribes were still roving the territory between the Missouri River and the Rocky Mountains. Congress authorized this transcontinental stage line in 1857, and service began in 1858, a decade before the completion of the first transcontinental railroad (1869).

286. Cornhusk Doll; made about 1880.

287. Quaker Doll, papier-mâché head and padded; made about 1865.

288. Rag Doll; made about 1830.

Cornhusk dolls were originally made by the early settlers as children's playthings. They were either invented by them or copied from the Indians. This doll is a product of civilization, an interpretation of the costume of a Victorian lady. She wears a fashionable dress tailored with professional skill. The panniered skirt with full back and the basque with the little cape are characteristic of the eighties. Careful attention is given to the elegant blue trimming, the flowers, buttons and ruffles. The bow with which the bonnet is tied and the little parasol add the finishing touches.

This Quaker doll is well worn; it is evident that she was not only admired but actually played with. She wears a Quaker bonnet, and is Quaker in spirit, if we consider the thrifty way in which she is constructed. Her papier-mâché head was perhaps the chief item of expense; she had no limbs and padding takes the place of her body.

In the doll with the figured calico dress we have an example of a homemade toy, put together from scraps of material. The body is of stuffed cotton, the features are painted, the hands are of kid, and the head is covered with brown satin to suggest hair. Perhaps only her black leather shoes were purchased in a store. Though the cloth doll is one of the oldest known types, it was not produced commercially in this country until late in the nineteenth century.

289. Roller Skates; mid-nineteenth century.

290. Hobby Goat, wood, carved and painted; nineteenth century.

291. Doll, pine; made in New Hampshire.

Early roller skates were patterned after ice skates, with wheels substituted for the steel blade. This design, though satisfactory for ice, did not prove adaptable for roller skating. Such skates, now obsolete, must have proved tiring to the skater, who had to keep moving and could stop only with difficulty.

This carved hobby goat seems obviously to have been made in imitation of a carrousel horse, but is very much smaller. Presumably the original was mounted on a base, perhaps with rockers. The carving is realistic, but the trappings have a gay, festive character.

Attributed to a Swiss craftsman who settled in New Hampshire, this doll, a sturdy little country girl with thick, heavy braids, has a distinctly European flavor. Here we see the hand of an expert carver in the good proportions and the careful detail.

Mechanical toys were often favored by parents, but questioned by those who had studied children at play. It seems that for a while they were entertaining, but children soon tired of a toy that did all the performing, thereby robbing the child of his initiative. Toy banks, now eagerly sought after by collectors, were once manu-

292. Mechanical Toy Bank, "Speaking Dog," cast iron; made in the Stevens Foundry, Cromwell, Connecticut; patented 1885.

293. Mechanical Toy Bank, "Teddy and the Bear," cast iron; made in the Stevens Foundry, Cromwell, Connecticut. 294. Locomotive, tin and cast iron painted; nineteenth century.

factured by the thousands, even as late as the 1920's. Novelty, bright color, and human interest were stressed. In this example, upon pressing a plunger, the lid of the seat opens to receive the coin placed in the girl's paddle and made to drop as her arm rises. At the same time, the dog opens his mouth and wags his tail.

The "Teddy and the Bear" bank is operated in the

following manner: the coin is placed in the gun; when the lever is pressed, Teddy Roosevelt shoots the coin into a hole in the tree trunk, and the head of the bear springs up. This subject is based on an actual event. On one of Theodore Roosevelt's hunting expeditions in Mississippi (in what used to be a small place called Smedes) he indignantly refused to shoot a bear cub. The

295. Toy Horse, pine carved and painted; Pennsylvania German.

296. Knitted Doll, wool, made in California; nineteenth century.

297. Harlequin Dancing Figure, wood, papier-mâché head and collar, made in Pennsylvania; about 1800.

well known cartoonist, the late Clifford Berryman, was present and the following day in a cartoon created "Teddy Bear." The idea caught on with the public and was exploited by manufacturers. The Teddy Bear came into vogue as a toy and is still popular the world over.

This type of horse with its small head, thick neck, and rotund body reflects an old-world tradition of folk art. In the simplified posture, the pattern of dots, and the strong decorative feeling, there is no emphasis on realism. Its plump compact form is like a Christmas cookie. The horse is about one foot high, and was found in Carlisle, Pennsylvania.

This knitted doll was made in California and shows the influence of old Mexico. Knitted of woolen thread and stuffed, this somewhat exotic type might be soldier, cavalier, or a purely imaginative character.

The Harlequin is of French origin. Such figures, that could be manipulated by pulling strings, were popular with adults in the late eighteenth century. Harlequin is a famous character of the Italian theater.

298. Marionette, "Simon Legree," wood carved and painted, cotton shirt and wool trousers, California; nineteenth century.

This man with his chequered trousers and elegant mustache is a prettified version of the forceful character of Harriet Beecher Stowe's *Uncle Tom's Cabin*. In this figure there was no attempt at characterization, in contrast to the grotesque figure of "Punch." Marionettes were attached to strings held by the operator above the scene in such a way that the figure could be made to move and execute lively gestures to the accompaniment of a dialogue.

299. Hand Puppet, "Punch," wood head and hands; dressed in clothes of velvet, wool, cotton, and corduroy, tan leather shoes; about 1870.

Punch, the husband of Judy, is one of the chief characters in the old English puppet play, once beloved by children and adults. Puppet shows, often attached to circuses or dog shows, traveled far and wide through America. Performances were given at country fairs and carnivals, in theater halls, churches, or in barns illuminated by flares and candles; settlers and Indians often formed the audience. "Punch and Judy" was slapstick comedy, with much abuse and many hard knocks. The

300. Black Mammy Doll; nineteenth century.

two main characters traditionally had the broad mouth and hooked nose shown here. This particular puppet is manipulated by a stick which extends into the head and is held in the hand of the operator.

The Mammy doll exists for the attractive clothes she wears. She has a cloth body, stuffed with sawdust, a composition head, and wooden limbs. She cannot stand up. She wears a bright gingham dress and a bandanna wrapped about her head; her apron is percale and her petticoats are of wool and cotton. There were such character dolls in the eighteenth and nineteenth centuries, and the vogue is even further developed in our own day.

301. Carrousel Horse, wood; made in the late eighties of the nineteenth century.

15. Circuses and Carrousels

The traveling circus tent with canvas top may be said to have begun in this country in 1824, when John Robinson took three wagons, five horses, and a tent across the Alleghenies. Before the century ended the American Circus had become "the greatest show on earth" and embarked on a spectacular five-year tour through Europe. In the early days a circus meant acrobats and horseback riders performing in theaters, or behind side-canvases open to the sky. Another, independent business was the wild-animal show called the menagerie. It got its start when an enterprising ship's captain took the risk of importing some wild animals for purposes of public exhibition. As the circus grew, it added minstrels, dancing and an occasional Negro song. The menagerie, too, enlarged its stock of animals. By the middle of the century circus and menagerie combined, forming the three-ring circus.

In the days before the railroads, the circus traveled by wagon, the manager in a buggy and the slow moving elephants out in front. Starting at an early morning hour, under torch light, the caravan often had to seek its way along poorly marked country roads. Days before, a man on horseback had preceded the show, placarding the barns along the way with his posters. When the tent was pitched on the outskirts of the town, the clown would attract a crowd and lead it to the tent.

Later the big parade announced the circus by the blare of the steam calliope, "that could be heard five miles." The gaily decorated wagons drawn by matched teams of fine horses, the general bustle and excitement made the coming of the circus into something of a holiday, for the whole town turned out to gape at the splendor.

Until recently the carrousel was the mainstay at fairs and carnivals, and it is still seen today. The "show horses" that stood on the outside were hand-carved like the stately animal above. The early carrousel horse was fastened to the platform in a stationary pose.

302. Dancing Girl, wood; carved in relief for a Sparks circus wagon, about 1900.

Circus wagons were spectacular. They were elaborately carved and painted in shining white, in gilt, and in color. Seen against drab city streets they stood out in dazzling splendor. This dancing girl once joined hands with a partner, and formed the chief decoration on the side of a wagon. The carving was executed in Milwaukee; the wagon could have been built in Baraboo,

Wisconsin, for many years a wintering place for circuses.

Comparatively little circus carving has been preserved. On wagons in use, old figures were recarved to fit new purposes. Wagons no longer in use were left out in the open for years; they became unsightly and eventually were burned to get them out of the way.

303. Figure, wood; carved in relief and painted in New York City for a Barnum and Bailey circus wagon; presumably by John Sebastian, designer, and Peter Breit, master-carver; period 1880-1903.

304. Lion Head, wood; carved in relief for a circus wagon; about 1890. Produced by the Parker Carnival Supply Company, Leavenworth, Kansas.

A carved figure for a circus wagon was not made for the delight of the sophisticated or the approval of critics. It was seen but briefly and then as part of the total picture of the parade. This one combines a wealth of sculpturesque motifs loosely put together. The way the drapery is gathered goes back to historical examples of sculpture, but it is done so freely that it may well be said that John Sebastian designed his own figures. He inherited his business from his father Jacob, who had learned wood carving in France. Soon after the middle of the nineteenth century he established himself in the carriage business in New York City. Most of the circus wagons that can still be attributed to this concern were made in the eighties and nineties when John Sebastian was in charge.

Basically circus decoration had no style of its own; it depended on craftsmen who were drawn into circus work from other fields. Some may have had experience in architectural carving, and adapted their work to fit the circus wagon. This fragment was made by the Parker Carnival Supply Company.

305. Ornamental Head, wood; carved in relief; about 1890. Produced by the Parker Carnival Supply Company, Leavenworth, Kansas.

306. Figure, "Medieval Lady," wood; carved for a Barnum and Bailey circus wagon, by the Sebastian Wagon Company; about 1890.

The wolf's head, "a mask," is also presumably from a carrousel or a circus wagon. It is an adaptation from historic ornament. The nineteenth century was eclectic in its taste and the circus craftsmen followed this general trend. But the freer spirit of the circus may also have affected the carver, for circus work never seems archaeological.

Figures carved in relief were for the sides, those in the round for the corners of the wagon. The medieval dress suggests that the wagon featured a medieval subject. Though the circus was gay, it permitted a serious expression if the subject required it. Hence the carver made this figure austerely dignified. Circus carving did not waste its efforts on undue refinement which would certainly have been lost. On the other hand it meant to impress by appearing rich and opulent. As a result we get boldness combined with enough literal detail to satisfy popular tastes. Samuel Robb of New York, known for his figureheads, may have been responsible for this figure as he is known to have worked for the Sebastian Wagon Company.

307. Circus Wagon, "The Golden Age of Chivalry"; designed by George Lawrence of the Sebastian Wagon Company; 1887–1889.

As a change from the dreary monotony of small town life, the circus was truly welcomed. Extravagant advertising had prepared the public to expect the "grandest and greatest." The most picturesque figure of the American circus, P. T. Barnum, pledged his honor that "probably not since the creation of the world, has there been a combination of exhibitions of such stupendous nature that would bear any comparison with ours . . ."

In another instance a circus offered "a ten-thousand dollar premium for the most beautiful woman in the world." It was made clear that "it was distinctly understood that the most beautiful woman in the world was not to be shown under canvas, but that she was merely to impersonate Lalla Rookh (the beautiful Eastern princess) in a grand Oriental-fair street pageant." This wagon, too, was designed for the parade. A young woman, beautifully gowned, occupied a seat on the dragon's back. Ordinarily wagons had relief figures in

three-quarter life-size, but this one is exceptional. It has a monster "two-headed dragon protecting womanhood" placed on top. The dragon heads were inspired by a sea monster from an engraving by the well known Italian artist Mantegna. No doubt this particular motif was selected because it best expressed what the designer had in mind. The claws are those of an eagle, and the artist added bat's wings, along with the tail from an old discarded figure of a devil, presumably from another wagon. Most wagons were trap wagons for tents, benches, and other equipment. Externally they were carved to represent an historical event or some subject of general appeal. This is one of the few circus wagons still almost in its original condition. Many have perished and others have been altered in appearance. Originally a float, this one was later made into a wagon for Barnum and Bailey. When wagons became too large for city traffic they had to be discontinued.

308. Carrousel Rooster; wood, made in St. Johnsbury, Vermont; nineteenth century.

This youthful rooster has a stride like an ostrich. The carver made the most of the grand feathered tail, and the rhythmic lines throughout; the curves flow together in an attractive fashion. The rooster is about four and a half feet high, about the right size for a little boy or girl. It belongs to that stage in the development of the carrousel when it was hoped that novelty would attract trade. It was soon discovered, however, that the

309. Bear's Head, carved walnut, from Nantucket; about 1884.

310. Carrousel Horse, wood; nineteenth century.

children invariably chose the horses and particularly the dappled kind. After that, the strange menagerie, including bears, reindeers, and giraffes, was abandoned, and every merry-go-round since has been content with the horse, and made sure to have a quantity of dappled ones.

The artist who carved this head certainly worked from memory. The system of ridges and furrows is a convention created by the carver to suggest fur. It stands for a rough texture, but otherwise has no visual resemblance to reality. Since it comes from Nantucket, one wonders if this head may not represent the fanciful creation of some ship's carpenter.

This horse was probably made in North Tonawanda, New York, where the improved American carrousel

originated in the early eighties. Instead of the animals being fastened to poles connected with a rotating center they stood on a platform that ran on tracks. The extended legs indicate that the horse rested on a metal rod which gave it an up-and-down movement. Eventually carvers achieved convincing horses with the movement and anatomy of a live animal, but these early examples are still quite conventional. The artist instead developed the ornamental features, trappings, and saddle covers. The mane flying in the wind, the extended nostrils, and the open mouth suggest the spirited thoroughbred. In his eagerness to express animation the artist verges on travesty but at the same time achieves attractive patterns. To us this is a funny little horse that is still pleasing to look at.

311. Seated Lion, wood, carved in relief for a Sparks circus wagon; about 1900.

312. Carrousel Giraffe, wood, carved and painted, from Riverside, Rhode Island; about 1888.

The extravagance of the circus parade, and the vigorous, forceful carving of each figure shows clearly that the designer was above all striving to gain attention. Carving, color, and gilt are part of the general spectacle which was to impress the crowds that lined the streets on circus days. This thoughtful expression of the lion, almost saddened and perhaps slightly embittered, makes one wonder of whom the carver was thinking when he carved this head. Serious rather than wild, man and animal have merged in the imagination of the designer. Nor is the soft, bulging carving appropriate for the lean strength of the King of Beasts. The artist did not study a lion from life but humanized his subject instead. This lion also belonged to the same wagon which had the

Dancing Girl and a figure of Pan. He is about two and one half feet high and with a partner flanked the central panel. Because lions belonged to the circus, a carved lion appears with a dancer and with Pan, the personification of music. But the lion is chiefly decoration, and it mattered less how he fitted into the allegory.

This animal was meant to be a giraffe, but to judge from the hind legs the carver had not entirely overcome the idea of a horse. By the time he reaches the front legs, the animal begins to resemble a giraffe, but the head makes one think of a camel. This well nourished animal was meant for a carrousel and not the Museum of Natural History; it is folk art, not taxidermy.

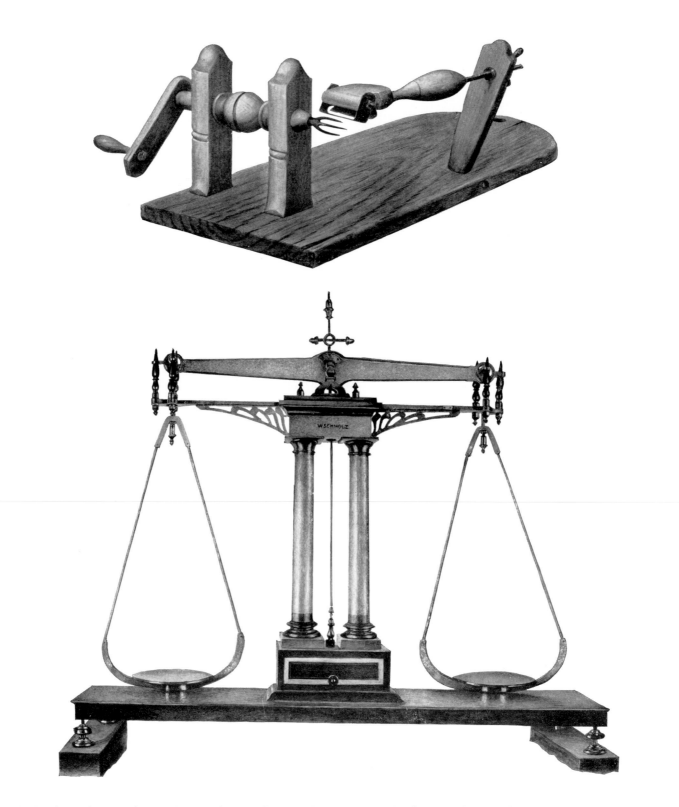

313. Apple Peeler, maple wood on a chestnut base; eighteenth or nineteenth century.

314. Scales for Weighing Gold, bronze and brass; made by W. Schmolz in San Francisco; nineteenth century.

16. Gadgets and Mechanical Devices

Our early settlers on the Atlantic seaboard brought with them a knowledge of materials and the techniques and skills of England. The handicrafts had achieved their highest development in Europe, and for two centuries they were continued in this country, where they furnished the people with the necessities of life.

Even after the Industrial Revolution got its start in England, during the last third of the eighteenth century, it was not immediately transplanted to the colonies. The mill towns of New England developed in the early decades of the nineteenth century, and by the time of the Civil War the small shop with its hand tools was already being replaced by machines. In a new country with great natural resources, there was more work to do than men could do unaided. The necessity of overcoming a chronic shortage of labor through mechanical means stimulated the inventive genius everywhere.

To lighten work in the home, new mechanical appliances were produced. A whole group of inventions were aimed to speed up the preparation of fruit for canning or drying. Innumerable apple parers and cherry stoners were offered to the public. Some homemade ones even date from the eighteenth century. As early as 1803 there was a patented apple parer that worked by turning a crank. Other models had wheels, gears and belts for greater speed.

Formerly the spinning wheel had been almost the only labor-saving device for the home. In appearance and operation it influenced the design of these first American domestic machines. The long traditions of woodworking carry over into the early wooden appliances. They are often well made, like the apple parer illustrated on the opposite page, and show an appreciation of simple, functional forms. In the second half of the nineteenth century cast iron became the usual material for all such gadgets.

Various devices were produced to grind meat, coffee and spices, to chop vegetables and to sift flour. Numerous manufacturers turned out washing machines and clothes wringers. Between 1805 and 1809 there were only fifteen different types of patented washing machines, but before 1883 the number had increased to over seventeen hundred. Many were cumbersome and never became widely used. In the late sixties the *American Agriculturist* tried out annually half a dozen or more. Among the machines so tested there was only one which the "help" would use willingly.

Based essentially on straight lines and simple geometric shapes, machines carry within them possibilities of a beauty of their own. But this was not immediately recognized. The new devices were quite inappropriately decorated with gilt, scrolls and even fluted columns to make them presentable for the front part of the house. After their utilitarian character had been partly disguised under an ornamental exterior, they were tolerated amidst Victorian furnishings.

There was a passion for all sorts of gadgets, and it almost seemed the more complicated they were the better they were liked. As long as it was a machine, it did not have to be practical. No contraption was too elaborate for the enthusiastic inventor. A new patent often started numerous modifications without necessarily involving a new principle. Stores, and even post offices and banks, at times profited from this flood of inventions.

Often the invention became standard equipment and a necessity for a certain business. Scales for the weighing of the gold that was brought to the bank in the mining days of the West are among the fine precision instruments of the period. The pair of scales shown here is over four feet high and was found in Nevada.

A spirit of freedom had encouraged diversity in matters of religious beliefs and social creeds. This same liberty persuaded others to seek the pot of gold at the end of the rainbow through some new invention that could survive the Patent Office. All these products of a machine age were a necessary preparation for our own power age with machines that at times seem to have reached a final goal of perfection.

315. Coffee Mill, wrought iron; late eighteenth century.
316. Cherry Stoner, cast iron; nineteenth century.

317. Clothes Wringer, wood with iron parts; second half nineteenth century.

In this coffee mill the coffee beans were forced between the wheel and the sides of the hopper that were roughened by chisel cuts to provide a grinding surface. A thumbscrew regulated the coarseness or fineness of the grind. The whole grinder was made by one craftsman from start to finish before the era of mass production of interchangeable parts. Its primitive appearance is somewhat due to the fact that the parts are heavier than necessary. As the beans were freshly ground for each serving, the hopper did not have to be very large.

In this type of cherry stoner, pulp and seeds are separated by the action of curved ribs on a rotary disk. The text of the patents, taken out in the 1860's, tells specifically how this type of cherry stoner worked. A craft tradition is still reflected in this mechanical tool. Though

it no doubt was efficient, its appearance owes something to furniture. This is still a small table with curved legs and curved top on which the mechanism has been mounted.

Various labor-saving household devices seem to have been popular chiefly because superior makes were not yet available. Even this method of forcing clothes between the corrugated surfaces of two wooden cylinders was preferred to wringing clothes by hand.

The stamp canceling machine on the opposite page, once used in a Maryland Post Office, is operated by pushing down and subsequently releasing the handle. One wonders how this particular mechanism would save time by eliminating useless motion. The spirit of progress was determined on improvements through

318. Stamp Canceling Machine, wood; made in Maryland; nineteenth century.

319. Fly Catcher, wood and metal; patented by George Gilbert, Westville, Connecticut, 1856.

320. Bootjack, cast iron; nineteenth century.

mechanical inventions, even where the result hardly warranted the effort.

According to the "specifications and claims" for the fly catcher, a bait like molasses was applied to a revolving cylinder "to attract flies, and while they are feeding the revolving motion of the cylinder carries them quietly into a dark chamber, from which they will naturally pass up through a screen, into a light chamber which is enclosed by wire gauze, and will thus be securely caged, to be dealt with at pleasure." A slide at the back opens and flies can be driven down to a back chamber below, by shaking, "and then shut up so close, without air or light that they will soon die."

Utility forms at times show surprising originality.

They are less subject to historical influence, and feel no obligation to follow a style. This bootjack is a fantastic combination of insect and quadruped, with the body of an insect and the feet of a turtle. Bootjacks have not disappeared entirely, though modern living conditions have restricted their use. The kind of shoe we wear is not entirely a matter of fashion; shoes reflect dirt roads or paved streets, ox carts or automobiles. High boots served as protection against mud and rain; they had to be pried off when wet, and the bootjack was a necessity. The heel of one foot was clamped into the prongs of the bootjack while the other foot held the bootjack down. One boot was pulled off with the aid of the other foot.

321. Pepper Mill, mahogany; nineteenth century.

322. Sewing Machine, cast iron; made by B. Atwater in Connecticut; patented 1857.

Formerly spices were purchased whole and ground as used. Because only small quantities were needed, they were made fresh and neither spice nor coffee mills had to be large. As the use of metal advanced only gradually, many items were still made of wood. Here only the interior parts are of metal; the body itself is wood turned on a lathe. The fact that wood was pleasant to touch no doubt favored it for handles and containers, where metal would have offered no advantage. The first half of the nineteenth century greatly increased the use of wood in this country. The outgoing crafts and the incoming industries put wood to more varied uses than ever had been the case before. Wood served in the early industrial machinery. In clocks not only the cases were made of wood, but the working parts as well; gears were finely cut out of hard wood with a surprising degree of precision.

Of early domestic machines, the sewing machine was by far the most important. Though the first patent for a leather-stitching machine was taken out in England, the sewing machine was invented and perfected in the United States. The mechanical parts of this model are inconspicuous compared to the casing. The fluted post with its vaselike finial and the ornate base satisfy a love for ornamentation.

But that is perhaps not the whole explanation. A frank display of utility still seemed ugly to the Victorians just as in all preceding centuries the machine had seemed like an effrontery to man and his vanity. The underlying reason for this was the thought that a machine, a dead mechanism, could rival the works of man who supposedly stood at the apex of creation. Though an age-old prejudice against machines was being overcome, they were still offensive to artistic sensibilities. The lion feet and the scrolled edges made the sewing machine more like a piece of furniture, as if it still belonged to the safe and comfortable age of the handicrafts.

323. Mariner's Compass; used on the Great Lakes; made in New York by R. L. Shaw; about 1870.

What is attractive to the eye about this compass is the card on which the points are marked in the manner of an eight-pointed star. With its subdivision the circular card represents a design severe and functional, rather than ornate. Additions of a purely decorative type have been eliminated almost entirely, except for the elaboration of the North point. For a scientific device entirely practical and used by men outside the home, decoration is here dispensed with even at this early date.

324. Police Rattle, oak; nineteenth century.

325. Static Electric Generator, built by Joseph Coles, in Colestown, New Jersey; eighteenth century.

Before there were gongs, bells, and sirens to announce the arrival of patrol wagon, fire engine, and ambulance, hand rattles served everywhere, on land and sea. Well constructed, of hard wood, and designed to give the hand a firm grip, they could not help being attractive. The principle is the same as our own New Year's Eve noise makers, in which a revolving blade of wood snaps against a ratchet.

This electric machine consists of a glass bottle mounted on supports and in contact with a flap. In this case the flap is a piece of velvet. By turning the handle the glass cylinder is revolved. Glass being a nonconductor, a positive charge of electricity is held on its surface until discharged through use of a prime conductor.

As the prime conductor was invented in 1741, this bottle generator must be of the period 1741 to 1760, when the bottle was supplanted by a plate machine. All such electric machines were experimental. They were used for therapeutic purposes up to our own period, but otherwise the practical advantages were slight. Their real importance consists in the fact that they laid the foundation for a popular acceptance of the idea that electricity was a force worth investigating. These generators prepared the way for subsequent developments in the field of electricity. The knowledge of static electricity goes back to Thales of Miletus, who around 600 B.C. observed that yellow amber, when rubbed, would attract small particles. The Greek name

326. Gramophone, wood with tin horn and rubber bands; designed by Emile Berliner, made by the United States Gramophone Company, Washington, D. C.; 1887.

327. Ice Cream Freezer, made of cedar with an iron handle, in Dover, Delaware; about 1860.

for amber, *electron,* gave us electricity. The bottle here used was most suitable for electrical machines on account of the amount of silica contained in the glass.

The Gramophone was the basis of all disc phonographs. Sound waves were transmitted through a stylus and recorded on a glass disc coated with lamp black. From this, a corresponding hard rubber disc was made which was used for the reproduction of sound. This is still the principle underlying modern disc-playing recording devices. The disc was moved by a wheel turned by hand. Here the working parts are still in plain view. It is an uncompromisingly functional piece of machinery which is truly modern in its approach.

In this ice cream freezer, ice mixed with salt was

packed in the usual way in the wooden box surrounding the inner container. This container was rotated by turning the handle. This comparatively small freezer could have held hardly more than a quart; the largest dimension of the wooden box is about fifteen inches. It is believed that ice cream was introduced to this country in Philadelphia during the period of the Revolutionary War. The New York *Gazette* of May 10, 1777, carries an advertisement of a confectioner, Philip Lenzi, that citizens and "guests" could get ice cream at his establishment every day. The guests were the red uniformed British staff officers of General Howe, who were occupying New York City at the time.

328. Rush and Candle Holder, wrought iron; eighteenth century.

329. Kerosene Lamp, glass and brass; late nineteenth century.

17. Rushlight to Kerosene Lamp

Electric light is so much taken for granted today that it is hard to imagine what life after sundown must have been like in colonial days. The illumination then in use was what had been passed from one generation to another through the centuries. Candlewood cut from the heart of the pitchpine was burned in the corner of the fireplace, or rushlights, dipped in grease, were clamped in tongs that extended from an iron stand. The stand here illustrated also has a bracket for candles.

We think of candles as primitive, but our forefathers saved them for special occasions. The waxy berry of the bayberry bush so common along the coast provided candles that burned with a pleasant odor, but spermaceti candles gave a brighter light. They were made from the fatty substance found in the head of the sperm whale. After cattle became plentiful, tallow was used for candles.

The small iron open-wick lamps that came over in the *Mayflower* were no more advanced than those used by the Assyrians five thousand years before. In basic shape all lamps were remarkably alike; a loose wick was laid into an open saucerlike container. It was not until the late eighteenth century that a new era of invention was able to produce a bright light without smoke.

The first improvement took place when some unknown inventor provided a channel for the open wick. The wick channel developed into a closed tube, then into a separate spout that held the wick in an inclined position. This type of "Betty" lamp was found in every home throughout the eighteenth century. Since it burned whale oil, it was odorous; it smoked and its light was hardly more than a glow. This was because the thick wick kept oxygen away from the center of the flame. But with the invention of the narrow, ribbonlike wick, the flame could reach the center as well as the outside of the wick; most of the free carbon was consumed and smoke was reduced.

The lamp in general use before the Civil War was the American whale-oil lamp. It had a wick held in a vertical position and a distinctive burner. This burner became general after 1818 and 1825, when the New England and the Boston & Sandwich glass companies put out glass lamps in quantities. This type of lamp became so popular that it was imitated in tin, pewter, and brass. It gave a good light; one needed only to trim the wick.

It is not clear where or when the principle of the burner was established. The idea of using two tubes close together to create an updraft has been attributed to Benjamin Franklin. It has been suggested that he could have placed a cork burner supporting a wick tube on top of a bottle like a stopper and shown it to his friend and neighbor, Wistar, who is known to have made glass lamps.

In 1834 John Porter made a new burning fluid by combining purified oil of turpentine and alcohol. You can recognize a fluid lamp by the burner which has two thin tubes pointing outward to produce two separate flames. Burning fluid was highly inflammable and each wick duct had its own metal extinguisher attached by a chain, as it was considered dangerous to blow out a fluid lamp. Purified turpentine without the alcohol was called camphene, though the terms were used indiscriminately.

A widely used, efficient lamp appeared after 1860, when kerosene came into use. This was the student lamp with the oil tank to one side to eliminate shadows. Every kerosene lamp had a glass chimney. At this late stage of development, the student lamp is functional in form and without ornamental features.

Lamps designed on the same principle had much in common, no matter how they might differ in purely ornamental exteriors. A tendency toward simplicity in design and perhaps a more general use of the central burner whale-oil lamp are American characteristics.

330. Lantern, perforated tin, probably made in New England; eighteenth to nineteenth century.

331. Betty Lamp, wrought iron, with wick support, lid, hanger, and wick pick; early nineteenth century.

332. Slut Lamp, wrought iron; early type.

Traditionally this type of tin lantern is named after Paul Revere. When lighted, the perforations form a delicate pattern of light against dark. We do not know what the lantern was—"one if by land and two if by sea"—that hung in the tower of North Church. It has been pointed out that a perforated lantern gives but a feeble light that might not have been visible from "the opposite shore." Still, on a dark night, even a small light is visible for miles. But its use by Paul Revere is doubtful.

In this wrought-iron Betty lamp, the loose wick was held up by a channel set back from the opening so that the drippings would be caught by the receptacle. This type of lamp, with its lid, is an improvement over the open type. It could be suspended, or the pointed hook inserted between the stones of a fireplace or the logs of a cabin. The staple was used to keep the wick free from carbon.

This grease, or "slut," lamp of the early frontier

333. Sconce, sheet tin; from Maine; eighteenth century.
334. Candlestick, pewter; from Ohio; nineteenth century.

335. Candlestick, Snuffer and Wick Trimmer, brass; probably imported from England; nineteenth century.

period represents the most primitive type of lamp. The word "slut" refers to the wick and is defined as a "piece of rag dipped in lard or fat and used as a light." It is supplied with bear or other animal fat and a twisted rag wick which emerged from the spout. In the earliest days lamps of this type were probably wrought from bog iron, made from the ore collected from local bogs and swamps.

Sheet tin was put to many uses, as it could be shaped easily. In the eighteenth century, candlesticks and sconces were commonly of tin, even in public buildings,

as in the courthouse of the small town of Bridgeton, Maine. The tooled reflector and the crimped edge of the candle socket show good taste in ornamentation.

The pewter candlestick belongs to the last quarter of the pewter century, the period from 1750 to 1850. Elaborate shapes in coffee pots, whale-oil lamps and candlesticks dominate this eclectic era. Pewter plates had been largely replaced by china, and the period of industrialization had begun, yet in this candlestick the manner of the earlier period is continued without sacrifice of good design.

336. "Ipswich" Betty Lamp, tin; eighteenth to nineteenth century.

337. Betty Lamp and Stand, tin, from Pennsylvania; mid-eighteenth century.

The simple dishlike brass candlestick on the preceding page adheres to a traditional shape. An ample bowl affords space for a wick trimmer, and the snuffer is given its special place at the end of the handle.

Betty lamps, fitted with lids and wick ducts, were better than the open type lamp. They could be suspended or placed safely on a "tidy top" or stand with the deep base filled with sand. It has been said that this improvement was responsible for the name, possibly derived from the German *besser,* that led to "better" and "betty" (old English "beet" or "bete"). According to another theory, the French *petit,* meaning small, be-

came "petty" or "betty." The "Ipswich" Betty lamp was named after the Massachusetts town where it was first made.

In another style, the Betty lamp was attached to a stand, so that the lamp could be adjusted to different heights. The stand was weighted at the bottom, and is under two feet high. This one is from Pennsylvania, but the same type was also used in England.

The whale-oil lamp on the opposite page perpetuates the basic shape of the candlestick. It is made to be set on a table, but it is a modern lamp. It has a vertical burner and the oil font is completely enclosed. These

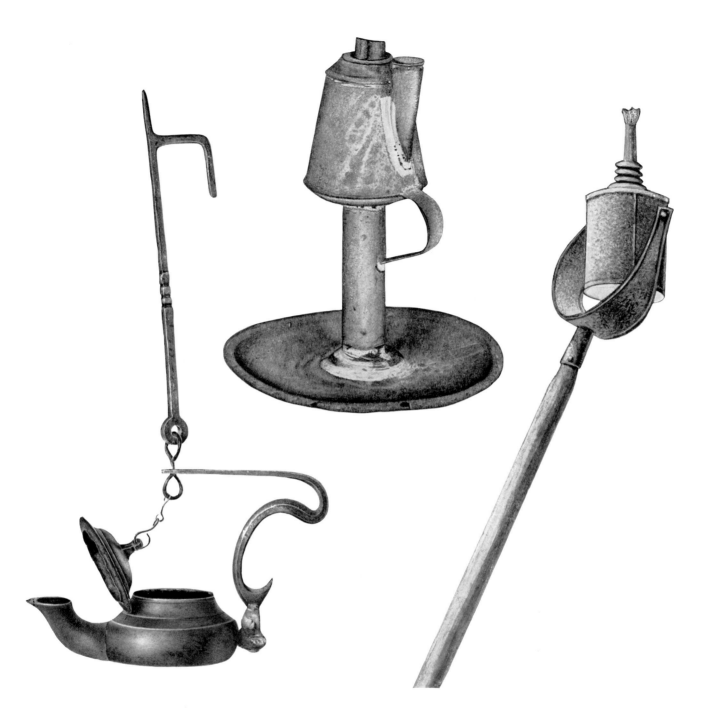

338. Whale-Oil Lamp, tin with brass double burner; nineteenth century.

339. Betty Lamp, cast brass; late eighteenth century.

340. Election Torch, tin, made in Nauvoo, Illinois; about 1860.

two factors constitute a major break with all preceding lamps. It gave a good light, was clean and well adapted for use indoors. Abraham Lincoln used one like it during the early days when he studied law in his home outside Springfield. In the first part of the nineteenth century, whale-oil lamps tended to replace the Betty type of movable hanging lamp.

The ornate type of brass Betty lamp is closer to European models. It is well made, and its elegant shape betrays its classical tradition; yet for all its artistic quality, it is a primitive lamp. Its wick duct is here separated from the oil font, but it is still only a spout lamp.

The election torch is really a lard-oil lamp made of a tin can, that has been fitted with a burner and mounted through a tin swivel on a long pole. This particular one was carried in Lincoln's campaign. Members of political organizations, the "Lincoln Club" and the "Wide Awake Club," paraded at election time carrying from thirty to forty torches in the procession. The town of Nauvoo, where this torch was made, is in Hancock County, Illinois, on the banks of the Mississippi River. It derives a historic interest from the fact that it was settled by the Mormons in the early forties of the last century.

341. Carriage Lamp, brass and tin with etched glass; nineteenth century.

342. Lamp, pressed glass and brass top with two camphene burners; 1853.

343. Whale-Oil Lamp, used at sea, japanned tin; nineteenth century.

This type of carriage lamp was in common use during the nineteenth century. Its rectangular frame, here still primitive in design, is combined with a circular ventilator and vertical shaft to hold the candle. This lamp belonged to Jefferson Davis, president of the Confederacy, and therefore dates from the Civil War period.

Small lamps called "tavern" or "sparking" lamps were common in inns where they were handed to guests to light the way to their rooms. Used in the home, when the flame burned out it was a signal to the suitor that it was time for him to leave. The two long, thin burning tubes indicate that this lamp was made for burning fluid, including camphene. Though it gave a bright flame, it was highly explosive. For that reason the burning tubes were long and heavy wicks were used to keep the flame well away from the oil.

The oil font in a marine lamp is freely suspended, so that the lamp maintains a level position irrespective of the ship's motion. This one was taken from an old ship, the *South America,* which the United States Government bought in 1861.

The small glass lamp on the opposite page is another example of the tavern type of lamp. This single-burner lamp was used for whale oil.

344. Small Whale-Oil Lamp, blown flint glass with a single-wick, cork-disk tin burner; attributed to Boston & Sandwich Glass Company; first half nineteenth century.

345. Lard-Oil Lamp, sheet tin; found in New Jersey; nineteenth century.

346. Camphene Lamp, pressed glass; period 1830–1859.

Lard-oil lamps, less common than whale-oil or fluid lamps, required a wide, flat wick. For a period in the middle of the nineteenth century the heavier lard oil was in favor. For many years it was used in lighthouses, and, after the Civil War, in the Navy for economy and efficiency.

In the 1830's, burning fluid came on the market, requiring long, thin tubes and heavy wicks. The screw cap, metal top was used to prevent evaporation. Earlier fluid lamps of glass have elongated, bell-shaped bowls of blown glass joined to a pressed glass base. Glass lamps were made by various factories in large numbers. As the glass was not marked by the firm name, it is difficult to assign a particular lamp to its place of manufacture. The designs show much variation, but this type of design is related to candlesticks and vases. Three sections can be distinguished: base, shaft or knop, and oil font, candle socket or vase top. After 1859, when the discovery of petroleum brought on the kerosene lamp, the oil font took on a globular shape.

347. Dress, imported brocaded silk; made in Boston; about 1770.

348. Woman's Shoes, brocaded silk; made in Baltimore; about 1758.

18. A Century of Costume

The everyday dresses that our great-grandmothers wore have disappeared almost completely. What has been preserved is the fashionable, costly gown that was treasured by the wearer and passed on to her descendants.

Only from paintings and documents do we know what the earlier colonial costume was like, as few of the examples now existing go back before the Revolution. Seventeenth century costume was characterized by durability and simplicity, due to the rigors of life in a new country and to some extent to religious convictions. The Puritans, for instance, put curbs on furbelows and trimmings. Buttons they considered "vanities"; they used instead hooks and eyes.

But as time went on, the leather worn by the early settlers was replaced by woolens. The sumptuary laws, probably not always strictly enforced, were relaxed, and as the frontiers moved westward, the fashions in American cities became practically those of western Europe. Fashionable women dressed in Boston, New York and Philadelphia much as they might in London. Costume was more affected by occupation and by income than by geography.

The costumes here illustrated belong to the period from just before the founding of the Republic to the end of the nineteenth century.

The flaring skirts of the eighteenth century were but a graceful variation of the bulging curves of the preceding period. Characteristic are the tightly-laced bodice and the full skirt. The dress on the opposite page is of a splendid brocade enriched with a large floral pattern. It is lavish in the use of costly material, but its love of

display is without loss of dignity. The slippers shown at the top of the page are in the same general style and could be a part of the costume. As yet one shoe is like the other; not until the early nineteenth century were shoes made to fit the right and left foot.

Immediately after the Revolution our fashions were more extravagant than those of either France or England. The exuberant spirit of the early Republic is reflected in the fine materials put into feminine costume. Paris was the fashion center, and the Napoleonic period produced the long, clinging gowns of the neoclassic revival just as it produced Empire furniture and classic architecture. The whole nineteenth century was retrospective in costume and decoration, seeking its inspiration in the past.

Empire dress was followed by early Victorian, a revival of eighteenth century ideas, and straight lines were once more replaced by curves. Toward the end of the century, skirts again became voluminous and shoulder effects broadened. But the trend was counteracted by the liberating influence of the suffrage movement. This striving for equal rights for women in the political and social spheres is reflected in more sensible dress. The influence of sports and athletics made women's dress comfortable and better suited to a broadened scope of activity.

Style trends were profoundly affected by two developments, the invention of the sewing machine and the appearance of paper patterns. From Ellen Butterick's idea of a paper pattern for a child's suit came the patterns for women's dresses that revolutionized the art of dressmaking. When every housewife could make her

353. Dress, cotton print; from New Jersey; about 1840.

354. Comb, horn with pressed and painted decorations; about 1840.

355. Earring, tortoise shell and gold; nineteenth century.

used but chastened to fit the ideas of a later century.

The shoe on the preceding page still bears the label of a Broadway retailer, but it may well have been patterned after a French design. The earlier high heel and extreme curve have been abandoned in favor of a low heel and a straight line. Slipper ribbons wrapped around the ankle probably were to imitate ladies' sandals of antiquity.

Victorian dress, like Victorian furniture, goes back to eighteenth century curves, but such reversions of style are never complete. The new is not exactly like the

old, and the periods can be distinguished. Elements from other periods are introduced, as here the puffed sleeves of 1840 recall the shoulder puffs of 1580. In the pattern of the material, the spirit of eighteenth century gaiety has been lost. The colors are dull, and browns predominate, symbolizing the cities which were becoming brown from factory smoke.

Ornamentation in connection with dress diminished in the course of the nineteenth century, but accessories continued in favor. Ornamental combs were used with hairpins to keep long braids in clusters on top of the

356. Coin Purse, crocheted of twisted silk with applied steel beads; from Lockport, New York; about 1850.

357. Lady's Slipper, needlework on canvas; probably from New York; 1844.

358. Dress, plaid taffeta, from New Orleans, Louisiana; 1845.

head, and the combs were matched with tortoise-shell earrings.

The coin purse is another proof that not everything Victorian was in poor taste. Steel, instead of glass, even for the manufacture of beads, is characteristic of the industrial era when steel began to come into its own as the metal of the century.

The house slipper illustrates one of the many uses of embroidery in the nineteenth century. This example was made by one friend for another, for the inscription reads: "Mary E. Post to Mary King, September 17, 1844."

The Victorian fashion favored fullness of dress, as we see in the dress from New Jersey, on the opposite page. In the above dress from the South, of about the same period, the high waist Empire fashion still prevails. Its simplicity and lack of emphasis on any extreme trend of the fashion of the period makes this design attractive, even a century after its day. "Taffeta is a smooth, glossy silk fabric in plain weave, alike on both sides" (M. B. Picken, *The Language of Fashion*).

359. Woman's Wrapper, China silk; made in Boston; about 1880.

360. Sunbonnet, gingham; from Utah; 1892.

361. Man's Shoe, leather with wood sole; made in Monterey, California; early nineteenth century.

The wrapper was made for informal, casual wear in the house, which explains its ample, loose fit. The central panel suggests a colonial influence and its comparative simplicity is a hint of a modern trend.

Bonnets of washable cotton were common in the 1890's, when women wore them out of doors around the house and garden. This style of head covering is as typically American as blue overalls for men.

This pair of wooden shoes was made by an Indian for wear on a ranch. But in this California shoe only the sole is wood. The uppers are of leather, which was abundant in the Southwest. They seem primitive but must have been better for wear than any heavy one-piece wooden shoe could have been. We have here a stage between sandal and shoe, where the uppers are of solid leather instead of straps only.

362. Woman's Shoe, black kid with fabric top; 1885–1895.
363. Clog, ash sole, leather toe and heel piece; eighteenth century.

364. Sealskin Cap; probably made in New York; about 1850.
365. Two-Piece Dress, boned, silk trimmed in velvet; about 1895.

Shoes of the nineties were commonly of the high-buttoned, all leather type. This one has a fabric top and a blunt toe, representing a trend toward comfort and away from the elegance of the pointed toe. The heel, too, is suitable for walking and outdoor wear. In those days the obliging shoe clerk would strip off the buttons on a new pair of shoes and replace them with patented buttons that stayed on better.

A clog is an early form of overshoe, and this one is well made and not at all clumsy. Although women did little walking in the eighteenth century, overshoes were necessary since there were few roads and an abundance of mud.

The use of furs, particularly in men's caps and hats, goes back to early days in American history. Sealskin caps are as native to this country as gingham bonnets.

The nineteenth century was eclectic as well as forward looking. The extreme styles of the day, as shown

366. Woman's Gymnasium Suit; 1895.

in the two-piece dress on the preceding page, with its "wasp" waist, bustle, and "leg-of-mutton" sleeves, together with a growing interest in sports for women, helped to bring about a movement for dress reform.

The trend toward common sense in women's clothes is illustrated in this gymnasium suit. To the modern eye this may look clumsy and impractical, but its plainness and obvious striving for comfort and ease of movement stand out in contrast to the tight-laced dress of regular wear. Bloomers, roomy and worn with stockings, were at least an improvement on long skirts and petticoats.

367. Wall Painting (detail), stencil and freehand work; made by an itinerant decorator in Washington, Connecticut; 1772–1779.

19. Symbols of a Nation

It is characteristic of the human mind to think in symbols, and we do so unconsciously. We have our personal symbols, and others we share with people the world over. The season of spring means youth; light stands for virtue; and darkness symbolizes evil and misfortune.

Before there was a United States, the American Indian served as the symbol of this continent. After independence had been won and the foundations of a new government laid, emblems of a patriotic character, like the flag and the American eagle, were adopted as national symbols.

The flag of the United States evolved out of various devices and ensigns. The resolution of the Continental Congress of 1777 adopted the flag in which the thirteen stars expressed the unity of the states. The stars are referred to as a "constellation," which meant the constellation Lyra, known as the harmony or unity group. In this, our first national flag, the stars were placed in a circle because a circle seemed more beautiful than the irregular group of the Lyra constellation.

The American eagle became a patriotic emblem after it had been adopted by Congress in 1782 for the Great Seal of the United States. After Washington's inauguration and particularly after the close of the War of 1812, the eagle was used extensively in the arts. The eagle was chosen probably because of its association with classical antiquity, for the new republic belonged to the era of the classical revival; new institutions, like the Senate, were often modeled on those of the old Roman Republic. Emblematic eagles had been used before in the colonies, as for example the one reproduced above, but the American bald-headed species was specifically designated as the eagle of the Great Seal. Bald here means white, because this eagle has white head and tail feathers.

Liberty acquired a particular importance because it symbolized the American dream. Jefferson wrote in the Declaration of Independence, "life, liberty and the pursuit of happiness," and "the blessings of liberty to ourselves and our posterity" are mentioned in the Preamble to the Constitution. Freedom is a jealously guarded right that we affirm in our everyday speech when we use such words as "This is a free country." "Liberty" appears as a profile head on coins and was made into statues, weathervanes, and inn signs; Columbia, as a symbol for the United States, was used in the same way.

These particular emblems of unity and freedom are more than heraldic devices; as expressions of our fundamental ideals, they have always been deeply revered. In times when patriotic feeling was intense, these emblems were freely used in the arts throughout the nation.

Justice is dear to mankind everywhere, and we have always associated justice with freedom. A wooden figure of justice, with bandaged eyes and holding the balanced scales, was often seen on our early courthouses.

Before the days of photography, portraiture was the only means of preserving a likeness. Comparatively few people had the good fortune to see Washington face to face, but many were eager to see what their great President looked like.

The works of the leading painters and sculptors served as models for innumerable craftsmen who carved, drew and painted these emblems, varying and adapting them to the materials of their crafts. Eagles, shields bearing the flag, Columbia, the Liberty Cap, Washington, Jefferson, and Franklin were universally popular.

A patriotic motif does not necessarily identify an object as having been made in this country. Pictures of George Washington amidst stars and stripes were applied to earthenware jugs made in Liverpool, England. When wares like these, and others made to capture the American market, appeared in this country, they found eager buyers.

Today these motifs are part of our artistic heritage. They are easily recognized and rich in pleasant associations so that they can be modified in subtle ways without losing their identity.

In addition to this small group of specifically American motifs, we have in our folk and popular arts a treasure of native material, much of which has not yet been discovered by our designers. This does not mean that we should copy the ideas of the past as if we wished to restore what cannot be revived in any literal manner. But modern artists who have become familiar with the art of early America may well profit from this contact. Let them infuse one with the other for a greater enrichment of the present.

368. Ship's Ornament, carved by John Bellamy at Kittery Point, Maine; late nineteenth century.

369. Coverlet (detail); woven on a Jacquard loom by Harry Tyler, in Butterville, Jefferson County, New York; in 1853.

Bellamy carved a number of ship's ornaments, like the one on the opposite page. Here he worked from a wooden pattern, indicating that he produced this eagle in quantity. It is also known that Bellamy presented this particular ship's carving to his friends, and they are still owned locally in Kittery Point, where Bellamy had his shop. His largest eagle, with a wing spread of over eighteen feet, is the well known figurehead carved for the U.S.S. *Lancaster* when the vessel was reconditioned at the Portsmouth Navy Yard in the early 1880's. Another group includes small eagles carved in the round. Bellamy is best known for his eagles, in which he worked out a well defined style, more marked than in his carving of other patriotic motifs.

When George Washington triumphantly toured the thirteen states in 1789, transparent painted eagles appeared on windowpanes everywhere, with lighted candles behind them. Soon the eagle became the most popular motif in American decorative art. Here it is used in heraldic fashion with the patriotic slogan, *"E Pluribus Unum,"* denoting one nation formed of many parts. Harry Tyler is known for his rugs and coverlets, which he produced as a professional weaver from 1834 to 1858. Tyler received the thread from his clients, after he had instructed them how to spin the wool and how much would be needed.

370. Andrew Jackson, figurehead, carved in the Boston Navy Yard; about 1834.

This gaunt figure of Andrew Jackson, seventh President, carved for the *Constitution* about 1834, is a striking work. The carver, Laban S. Beecher, represented Jackson in contemporary dress in a determined, upright pose. He tried to make the cloak look like drapery, for he is not altogether happy with the unaccustomed difficulties of modern dress. A President could not be turned into a typical figurehead. The carver was impressed by the austerity of his model, and the folds had to be turned into dignified drapery, undisturbed by ocean breezes.

371. Sign, made for Richard Angell's tavern in Providence, Rhode Island; 1808.

This figurehead is wood sculpture with its grim, portraitlike head. Hat and roll are hardly more than minor interruptions that interfere but little with the essential simplicity of the uncomplicated pose.

A good deal of feeling was aroused at the time this vessel was lying at anchor in Boston harbor. On a dark night an incensed naval officer rowed out to the vessel and managed to saw off Jackson's head, which he then carried in triumph through the streets of Boston. This act was the culmination of a widespread resentment against having Jackson, an Army man, so closely associated with a vessel held dear by all followers of the Navy. Eventually a new head was carved to repair the damage.

The artist who created this tavern sign probably had in mind the American eagle from the Great Seal. This he fused with the symbol from the seal of Rhode Island, for in place of the customary arrows, the eagle holds an anchor. The artist was experienced in lettering, which he handled with professional aptitude. In addition, he showed a good feeling for design in the placing of the eagle, as well as in the forceful manner in which he developed the silhouette.

372. George Washington, carved plaque; thirty-eight by fifty-six inches; by Samuel McIntire of Salem, Massachusetts; early nineteenth century.

No other American has been so revered and so often represented in art as the first president. During his lifetime, twenty-seven different painters and sculptors immortalized his likeness. Gilbert Stuart heads the list, with about one hundred portraits. The painter, Charles Willson Peale, his two sons and daughter, pursued their hero with determination. On one occasion all four gathered around in a semicircle to sketch the President. Houdon, who came over from France, is the best known of the sculptors. His bust of Washington can be seen today at Mount Vernon where it was modeled from life in 1785. Folk artists were also engaged in this worthy endeavor to popularize Washington on a wider scale. McIntire occupies a place between the academic sculptor and the folk artist.

On October 29, 1789, Washington visited Salem and addressed the townspeople from the Courthouse balcony. McIntire, seated at a window near-by, made a sketch of him. The carved plaque is a painstaking delineation from the point of view of the craftsman. The uniform in its ornamental delicacy receives as much attention as the features. For years the plaque was part of a gateway to Salem's common.

The type of eagle at the top of the opposite page we associate today with Bellamy, though there were others who carved eagles, as well as those who imitated him after he had established a vogue. Whoever the carver may have been, this eagle shows a good deal of spirit.

373. Eagle, carved and gilded; late nineteenth century.
374. Headboard of a Bed, walnut, carved; from Wilmington, Delaware; 1810.

There is much freedom in the disposition of the wings, though the contour of the pennant is halting and uncertain, without the easy, graceful curvature characteristic of Bellamy. Perhaps the nearest approach to Bellamy is in the carving of the beak.

Since the eagle was the popular motif of the day, the bird on this headboard no doubt was also meant to represent an eagle. Nevertheless, neither the proportions nor the general character shows any striking resemblance to an eagle; the head could be taken for a parrot. It is a remarkable design, particularly successful in the way the artist has accepted the challenge of the shaped contour of the headboard and worked it into the curved wings of the bird. Symmetry is suggested but not carried out in any mechanical way. The artist shows taste in the way he has simplified the details and treated the surface of the bird decoratively using the grained surface of the wood in the headboard itself. This still shows something of the easy grace of the eighteenth century, combined with a more severe treatment characteristic of the Empire manner, which was just getting started. There is here an appreciation for surfaces and textures, in the way in which the rock on which the bird is perched is handled. In place of the usual sharp crags meant to suggest the eagle's stony home, this carver subdued and softened contrasts to bring realism into harmony with the unobtrusive background of the headboard.

375. Sign for the Bissell Tavern, made in East Windsor, Connecticut, in 1777; repainted in 1801.

Collectors have been active in Connecticut, which may account for the fact that many of the tavern signs that have been preserved come from this State. The artistic level of this sign is high, both in the shape of the wooden panel and in the design itself. The motifs are those of late colonial architecture.

We must remember that below the level of the leading portrait painters there was no sharp division in what a painter might be called upon to do. The itinerant artist who painted a portrait might also make a sign if necessity required it. Even well known artists began as craftsmen to earn enough to study the art of painting.

The cap here represented is known as the "Liberty Cap" and gets its name from an old Roman tradition that a freed slave was permitted to wear a blue cap as a symbol of his freedom. Sixteen stars are painted on the border, because in 1801, when the sign was repainted, there were sixteen states in the Union.

John and Simeon Skillin were the leading wood carvers of their day. When John Skillin died suddenly on

376. Justice, wood, about six feet high; probably from the Skillins' workshop
in Boston; about 1800.

January 28, 1800, William Bentley of Salem wrote of
him in his "Diary" as "an eminent carver in Boston."
It was Simeon Skillin who carved the Mercury on the
Boston Post Office (see No. 135). Today the Skillins
rank with William Rush of Philadelphia as the first
sculptors of the early Republic. The reason for the attribution of this figure to the Skillins may be found in its
resemblance to other known works by them. Here are
the slender proportions, with the drooping shoulders
and the ends of the skirt blown against the ankle as if
by a wind coming from behind. The spiral-shaped
drapery over the breasts is also a characteristic detail
which occurs elsewhere in the work of these carvers.
According to tradition, the actual carving was done in
a shop on Front Street, in Worcester, Massachusetts,
and the statue was put up on the cupola of the New
Worcester Court House some years after this building
had been erected in 1803.

377. Eagle on a Cannon, wood, covered with gesso and gilded; early nineteenth century.

The eagle here is in an attitude of defiance, prepared to stand its ground. This is an interpretation of a new country, proud and sensitive of its strength. Older, more static symbols, like the spread eagle, are here modified to fit a spirit of lively self-confidence. The cannon suggests that this ornament occupied a place where a martial topic was appropriate in some architectural connection on land or sea. The design is imaginative, but of a basic simplicity, and the bottom indicates that it rested on a flat support.

There are three kinds of military drums: the snare drum of the infantry, the bass drum, and the brass or copper kettledrum used by the cavalry. Few drums from the Revolutionary War are in existence; but Civil War drums, like the one on the opposite page, are common. The most conspicuous part of the drums was the colors, the American eagle holding the shield beneath a sunburst and a banderole. Usually half of the banderole was delivered uninscribed to allow room for the regimental designation. Drums were made of pine or spruce, or as in this case mahogany, with hard wood hoops and calfskin head and bottom. When not in use, the ears, the leather flaps used to give tension to the head, were pulled down in order to release the tension. The drum is one of the four instruments used in the military band for field music; the fife, trumpet, and bugle are the other three. Aside from their use in marching, to beat time, drums were also used for signals. We associate the Civil War drums with the drummer boys, who were known to have joined the colors at the early age of twelve years. During battle they took their station near the commander in order to be at hand for orders to signal retreat, charge, or assembly.

The 9th Regiment of Vermont Volunteers, to whom this drum belonged, was the first regiment organized under the President's summons for help to protect the national capital.

378. Civil War Drum, from the 9th Regiment, Vermont Volunteers, U.S. Infantry; about 1860.

LIST OF ILLUSTRATIONS

In almost every case, the location of the original is given as of the date when the artist made the rendering.

9. From Parlor to Pantry

12. Furniture from Farmhouse and Mansion

13. Whittling and Wood Carving

14. Playthings

19. Symbols of a Nation

SUBJECT LIST

This list covers the entire collection of water-color renderings and photographs in the Index of American Design at the National Gallery of Art. The illustrations reproduced in this volume represent a selection of the renderings.

A

accordions

advertisements of branding irons

adzes

afghans

AGRICULTURAL EQUIPMENT: *see* beehives, bells, carts, combs, corn jobbers and planters, cradles, cultivators, harrows, hayforks, IMPLEMENTS, nose pieces for weaning calves, ox stocks, plows, potato planters, snubbers for bulls, yokes

altarpieces

altars

Amana, Iowa

anchor links and trip hooks

anchors

andirons

animals: *incl.* carrousel, circus wagon, figurine, garden, toy

apple peelers

aprons

arches

ARCHITECTURAL DECORATION: *see* arches, balconies, balustrades, banisters, brackets, bricks, buildings, capitals, conductor heads, corbels, cornices, cresting, doors, doorways, downspouts, drain tiles, fences, finials, fireplaces, gargoyles, gateposts, gates, gratings, grilles, keystones, lintels, lunettes, mantels, newel posts, niches, panels, park shelters, pillars, RELIGIOUS ARTICLES, sills, snow breakers, spandrels, staircases, transoms, windows

ARMS AND ARMOR: *see* army kits, bags, breast plates, bullet molds, bullet pouches, bullets, burgonets, canteens, crossbows, daggers, drums, guns, holsters, insignia, patch boxes, pistols, powder flasks and horns, racks, revolvers, rifles, sabers, scabbards, swords, tomahawks

army kits

asparagus bunchers

augers

axes: *incl.* firemen's

B

babies' clothing: *see* bibs, bootees, christening caps and robes

backdrops

bags: *incl.* ammunition, mail, money, saddle

balconies

ballot boxes

balustrades

bandboxes

bandwagons: *see also* carrousels, circus animals

banisters

banjos

banknotes

banks (toy)

barber poles

baritone horns

bark peelers

barometers

barrels

basins: *see also* fonts

baskets: *incl.* bee, bread, cake, cap, clothespin, fruit, key, market, miniature, sewing, traveling

basques

bathtubs

beadwork

beakers

beds: *incl.* day, double, folding, four-poster, three-quarter, trundle

beehives

bell jars

bellows

bells: *incl.* church, cow, dinner, door, locomotive, sheep, ship, sleigh, streetcar, wagon. *See also* chimes

belts: *incl.* firemen's

benches: *incl.* carpenter's, church, dough trough, garden, jeweler's, saddler's, shoemaker's, tailor's, wagon, woodcarver's

bibs

bicycles

billetheads

bird cages

birds: *see also* eagles, TOYS

biscuit boards

Bishop Hill, Illinois

blacksmith's equipment: *incl.* bellows, flatters, hammers, hot cutters, knives, markers, measuring wheels, punches, tongs

blankets: *see also* afghans, coverlets, quilts

blouses

bodices

boleros

bologna stuffers

bolts

bone

bonnets: *see also* hats, hoods, snoods, veils

book covers and markers

bookcases

books: *incl.* music

boot forms

bootees

bootjacks

boots

bottle corkers

bottles: *incl.* barber's, liquor, medicine, nursing, toilet

boundary markers

bouquet holders

bow pieces

bowls: *incl.* baptismal, butter, chopping, dough, finger, mixing, punch, salad

boxes: *incl.* band, Bible, bootjack, bread, bride's, butter, candle, collar and cuff, comb, desk, drawing instrument, epaulette, game, glove, hat, jewelry, knife, lunch, mail, match, medicine, money, music, patch, pillow, poker chip, powder, razor, sew-

ing, shadow, silverware, snuff, spice, strawberry, strong, sugar, tea, tinder, tobacco, toilet, tool, trinket
brace bits
bracelets
brackets: *incl.* architectural, drapery, lamp, mirror, shelf
brailing pins (lumberman's)
branding irons: *see also* advertisements of branding irons
brands
braziers
breast plates
bricks
bridles
bristle removers
broilers
brooches
brooms
brush cutters
brushes
buckboards
buckets: *incl.* fire
buckles: *incl.* belt, knee, shoe
buggies: *incl.* doll
buildings: *incl.* barns, churches, dormitories, elevated stations, exteriors, houses, interiors, laundries, refectories
built-in furniture
bullet molds
bullet pouches
bullets
bureaus
burgonets
bustles
butler's tables
butter boxes and dishes
butter firkins and tubs
butter molds
butter paddles, scoops and workers
buttonhole cutters
buttonhooks
buttons

C

cabinets: *incl.* egg, medicine
caddies: *incl.* tea
calendars
calipers
campaign banners
canceling machines
candelabra
candle holders, pendants and sconces
candle makers and molds
candlestick drapery
candlesticks
canes: *see also* walking sticks
canisters
cans
canteens
Cape Cod lighters
capes: *see also* dolmans
capitals
carafes
card holders
carpet stretchers
carpetbags
carpets
carriages: *incl.* baby, doll, horse-drawn
carriers: *incl.* bundle, liquor
carrousel animals and figures: *see also* bandwagons, circus ani-

mals
cartouches
carts: *incl.* ox
carving: *incl.* bone, stone, wood
cascarons
cases: *incl.* card, cartridge, comb, document, dressing, knitting needle, lancet, match, needle, portrait, sewing, spectacle, thimble, watch
cash registers
casks
casters
ceiling decorations
celery holders
cellarets
ceramics: *incl.* bow ware, china, earthenware, lusterware, majolica, Parian ware, porcelain, redware, sgraffito, slip decoration, stoneware, whiteware
certificates: *incl.* baptismal, birth, christening, discharge, marriage
chains
chair seats
chairs: *incl.* arm, barber, billiard, camp, children's, church, commode, corner, dental, folding, garden, high, ox-cart, rocking, sewing, side, swivel, wing, writing
chalices
chalkware
chandeliers
chaps
chatelaines
cheese draining boards
cheese presses
chemises
chest protectors
chests: *incl.* blanket, medicine, money, sea, sugar, wine
chests of drawers
chests-on-chests
chimes: *see also* bells
china closets
chisels
chocolate pots
choppers: *incl.* meat
christening caps and robes
churns
cider presses
cigar lighters
cigar-store figures
cinches
circus animals, figures and wagons. *See also* bandwagons, carrousels
clamp jacks
clamps
clappers
cleavers
clevises
cloaks
clocks: *incl.* banjo, marine, shelf, steeple, tall, thirty-hour, wall. *See also* sundials, watches
clogs
clothes wringers
clothespins
coaches
coal scuttles
coasters
coats
coats of arms
coffee grinders and roasters
coffeepots
colanders

collars
combs: for flax, horses, people, stripping grass
commode forms
compasses: *incl.* dry card, hand, ship's, surveyor's
compotes
conductor heads: *see also* downspouts, rain gutter stirrups
confessionals
convict boots
cookie cutters
corbels
cork compressors
corn jobbers and planters
cornices
corsets
COSTUME: *see* aprons, ARMS AND ARMOR, babies' clothing, basques, belts, blouses, bodices, boleros, bonnets, boots,
bouquet holders, buckles, bustles, buttons, capes, chemises, chest
protectors, cloaks, clogs, coats, collars, combs, corsets, cravats,
cuffs, dolls', dolmans, drawers, dresses, dressing gowns, eyeglasses, fans, fichus, gaiters, garters, gloves, gymnasium suits,
hair ornaments, handbags, handkerchiefs, hats, hoods, hoops,
jackets, JEWELRY, mantillas, mittens, mitts, muffs, neckerchiefs, neckties, nightcaps, nightgowns, pantalets, pants,
parasols, pattens, pelisses, petticoats, pocketbooks, pockets,
reticules, riding habits, sabots, scarves, shawls, shirts, shoes,
skirts, slippers, snoods, spats, stockings, stocks, suits, suspenders, tippets, trains, trousers, uniforms, veils, vestments,
vests, waistcoats, waists, wallets, wrappers
coverlets
cradles: *incl.* babies', grain
cranberry pickers
cravats
creamers
cresting
crimpers for pastry
crocks: *see also* jars
crossbows
crosses
crowns
crucifixes
cruets
cuff links
cuffs
cultivators
cup holders
cup plates
cupboards: *incl.* corner, court, press, wall. *See also* cabinets,
wardrobes
cups: *incl.* caudle, communion, egg, invalid's, loving, mustache,
spot, wetting
curb bits
curtain tassels: *see also* curtains, draperies, tiebacks
curtains: *see also* curtain tassels, draperies, tiebacks
cushions
cuspidor holders
cuspidors
cutlery kits
cutters: *incl.* brush, cabbage, cookie, dowel, shingle, spoke,
sugar, thread or screw, tobacco

D

daggers
daguerreotypes
dashers
deadeyes
decanters
deck eyes

DECORATION AND ORNAMENT: *see* animals, ARCHI-
TECTURAL DECORATION, backdrops, bell jars, birds,
book covers and markers, candlestick drapery, cartouches,
cascarons, ceiling decorations, coats of arms, COSTUME,
daguerreotypes, eagles, embroidery, figures, figurines, FIRE-
PLACE EQUIPMENT, fish, fountains, *Fraktur,* frames,
lace, masks, mosaics, mourning embroideries, numerals,
paintings, panels, pictures, plaques, reliefs, RELIGIOUS
ARTICLES, scrimshaw, seals, ship models, SHIP'S DECO-
RATION, signs, stove plates and urns, TEXTILES, tiles,
wall paintings, wallpaper, weathervanes, whirligigs, witch
balls, wreaths
decoys
demijohns
desks: *incl.* accounting, lap, school, writing
dies
dippers
dishes: *incl.* alms, pickle
documents: *see also* certificates
doilies
doll carriages, clothes and furniture
dolls: *incl.* children's, fashion, witchcraft
dolmans: *see also* capes
door handles
door knockers
doors
doorstops
doorways
dough bins, mixers and troughs
dowel cutters
downspouts: *see also* conductor heads, rain gutter stirrups
drain tiles
draperies: *see also* curtain tassels, curtains, tiebacks
drawer pulls
drawers (underwear)
drawknives
dressers
dresses
dressing gowns
dressing tables
drills
drums
dulcimers
dumb irons
Dutch ovens

E

eagles
earrings
Economites (Pennsylvania)
egg beaters, boilers and roasters
election posters
electric generators
elevated stations
ember carriers
embroidery: *incl.* crewel, cross-stitch, eyelet, featherstitch, needlepoint. *See also* chair seats
epaulettes
ewers
eye shades
eyeglasses

F

fans
farm equipment: *see* AGRICULTURAL EQUIPMENT
fences

fichus
fifes
figureheads
figures: *incl.* allegorical, cigar-store, circus, classical, figurines, garden, historical, hitching post, merry-go-round, military, religious, shop, tavern
figurines
files
filters
finger bowls
finials
fire engines
FIRE EXTINCTION: *incl.* extinguishers, helmets, hydrants, trumpets. *See also* axes, belts, buckets, fire engines, fire marks, hats, hose holders and reels, pumps, shirts, torches
fire marks
FIREPLACE EQUIPMENT: *incl.* fire grate covers, firebacks, fireplace fenders and grates, fireplace sets, fire screens. *See also* andirons, bellows, Cape Cod lighters, coal scuttles, ember carriers, fireplaces, jacks, kettle rings and tilters, pokers, pole screens, shovels, spits, tongs, trammels
fireplaces
first-aid kits (lumberman's)
fish
fish net menders
fish spears
flagons: *incl.* communion
flags
flails
flambeau: *see also* torches
flasks
flatiron stands
flatirons
flint strikers
flour bins and sifters
flower pots and stands
flowers
flutes
flycatchers
fonts: *incl.* baptismal, holy-water
foot baths and tubs
foot scrapers
footstools
forceps (dental)
forks: *incl.* hay, pitch, table
fountains: *incl.* drinking, garden
Fraktur
frames: *incl.* mirror, picture
frows
fruit presses and slicers
funnels
FURNISHINGS: *see* afghans, bird cages, blankets, calendars, card holders, carpets, chair seats, clocks, coverlets, curtain tassels, curtains, cushions, cuspidor holders, cuspidors, DECORATION AND ORNAMENT, doorstops, draperies, figurines, FIREPLACE EQUIPMENT, flower pots and stands, flowers, frames, FURNITURE, handkerchief cases, HOUSEHOLD EQUIPMENT, lamp shades, lamps, LIGHTING DEVICES, lithographs, MECHANICAL DEVICES, MUSICAL INSTRUMENTS, paintings, photograph albums, pictures, pillow cases, pillow sham holders, pillows, quilt covers, quilts, racks, rugs, safes, samplers, shadow boxes, SMOKING EQUIPMENT, stoves, TABLEWARE, tiebacks, towels, urns, valances, vases, wall pockets, watch holders, wine chests and coolers, WRITING MATERIALS
FURNITURE: *see* beds, benches, bookcases, built-in furniture, bureaus, butler's tables, cabinets, cellarets, chairs, chests, chests of drawers, chests-on-chests, china closets, cradles, cupboards, desks, dolls', dressers, footstools, FURNISHINGS, highboys, love seats, lowboys, mirrors, ottomans, secretaries, settees, settles, shelves, sideboards, smoking lounges, sofas, stands, stools, tables, tailoresses' counters, wardrobes, washstands, window seats

G

gaiters
gangboards
garden designs: *see also* LANDSCAPE GARDENING
garden furniture and ornaments: *see also* LANDSCAPE GARDENING
gargoyles
garters
gateposts
gates
gauges
gavels
gesso
gilding
glass: *incl.* free-blown, mold-blown, pressed; Amelung, Sandwich, South Jersey, Stiegel, etc.
glasses
globes
gloves
goblets
grain cradles and scoops
Gramophones
grape crushers
graters: *incl.* nutmeg
gratings
grave markers: *see also* tombs, tombstones
gravy boats
griddlecake turners
griddles
gridirons
grilles
grills
grinders: *incl.* coffee, meat, potato, sausage, spice
guns
gymnasium suits

H

hair ornaments: *incl.* brooches, combs, pins, ribbons, wreaths
halyard bands and blocks
hammers: *incl.* blacksmith's
handbags
handcuffs
handholds (for horse racing)
handkerchief cases
handkerchiefs
HARDWARE: *see* bolts, brackets, clevises, deadeyes, deck eyes, door handles, door knockers, drawer pulls, hasps, hinges, hooks, hound's bands, IMPLEMENTS, keyhole plates, keys, latches, locks, nails, rain gutter stirrups, SHIP'S DECORATION AND EQUIPMENT, shutter fasteners, whip sockets
harp pianos
harps
harrows
hasps
hatboxes
hatchets
hats: *incl.* firemen's. *See also* bonnets, hoods, snoods, veils
hawsing beetles and irons
hayforks
hearses

hide stretchers
highboys
hinges
hitching posts
hobbles
hobby horses
hoes
holsters
hoods: *see also* bonnets, hats, snoods, veils
hooks: *incl.* anchor trip, apple, bucket, button, ceiling, grappling, log-loading, meat, pot, rug, sled-starting, weaving
hoops
horse collars
horseshoes
hose holders and reels
hound's bands (for wagons)
HOUSEHOLD EQUIPMENT: *see* apple peelers, barometers, barrels, basins, baskets, bathtubs, beakers, bells, biscuit boards, bootjacks, bottles, bowls, boxes, braziers, broilers, brooms, brushes, buckets, butter boxes and molds, caddies, canisters, cans, carafes, cases, casks, cheese draining boards, choppers, churns, clothes wringers, clothespins, coasters, coffee grinders and roasters, coffeepots, colanders, compotes, cookie cutters, crimpers for pastry, crocks, cup holders, cups, cutlery kits, dashers, DECORATION AND ORNAMENT, demijohns, dippers, dough bins, Dutch ovens, egg beaters, ewers, filters, FIREPLACE EQUIPMENT, flatiron stands, flatirons, flint strikers, flour bins and sifters, foot baths, foot scrapers, fruit slicers, funnels, FURNISHINGS, FURNITURE, grape crushers, graters, griddlecake turners, griddles, gridirons, grills, grinders, ice-cream freezers, IMPLEMENTS, inhalers, irons, jars, jugs, kegs, kettles, ladles, lavabos, lids, LIGHT-ING DEVICES, mangles, mashers, match holders, measuring utensils, MECHANICAL DEVICES, molds, mortars and pestles, muffin pans, mugs, nutcrackers, ovens, pails, pan sliders, pans, pastry squeezers, pie markers, piggins, pitchers, pitters, popcorn poppers, pots, presses, roach traps, rolling pins, rug beaters, salvers, saucepans, sauerkraut stompers, sausage stuffers, scissors, scouring boards, SEWING EQUIP-MENT, skewers, skillets, skimmers, spatulas, spiders, SPIN-NING EQUIPMENT, springerle boards, stove lid lifters, strainers, sugar chests and tubs, TABLEWARE, tankards, teakettles, teapots, thermometers, tinderboxes, toasters, Toby jugs, trivets, tubs, wafer irons, waffle irons, warmers, wash-boards, washing machines, water coolers and heaters, water-ing cans
humidors
hurricane shades

I

ice-cream freezers
IMPLEMENTS: *see* adzes, AGRICULTURAL EQUIP-MENT, asparagus bunchers, augers, axes, bark peelers, bo-logna stuffers, bottle corkers, brace bits, brailing pins, brand-ing irons, bristle removers, brush cutters, buttonhooks, cali-pers, carpet stretchers, chisels, clamps, cleavers, commode forms, cork compressors, cranberry pickers, cutters, dies, drawknives, drills, files, FIREPLACE EQUIPMENT, fish net menders, fish spears, flails, forceps, forks, frows, gauges, grain cradles and scoops, hammers, hatchets, hide stretchers, hoes, hooks, HOUSEHOLD EQUIPMENT, irons, jacks, knife sharpeners, knives, lancets, lathes, leather guide markers, levels, log load tighteners, MECHANICAL DEVICES, peaveys, picks, pikes, pill coaters, pinkers, pitchforks, planes, plumb lines, printer's measures, printing blocks and stamps, pumps, rakes, razors, reamers, saws, scoops, scrapers, screens, SEWING EQUIPMENT, shears, SHIP'S DECORATION

AND EQUIPMENT, shovels, sickles, spades, spokeshaves, sugar-industry, tar pots, tongs, tooth extractors, turpentine dip irons, tweezers, wire-making machines, wrenches
inhalers
inkstands and inkwells
insignia
irons: *incl.* curling, flat, fluting, wafer; for plastering, for solder-ing
ironwork

J

jackets
jacks: *incl.* clamp, clock, wagon
japanned tin
jars: *incl.* honey, slop, tobacco. *See also* crocks
JEWELRY: *see* bracelets, brooches, buckles, chains, chatelaines, crosses, cuff links, earrings, lockets, necklaces, pins, rings, watch chains, watches
jugs

K

kegs
keno
kettle rings and tilters
kettles
keyhole plates
keys
keystones
knapsacks
knife sharpeners
knitting needle holders
knitting shields
knives: *incl.* blacksmith's

L

lace
ladles
lamp shades
lamps: *incl.* Argand, astral, Betty, baker's oven, bull's-eye, bunker, camp, camphene, candle, carriage, garden, grease, hurricane, kerosene, miner's, peg, petticoat, sinumbra, spark, spirit, spout, street, student, wall, whale-oil. *See also* LIGHT-ING DEVICES
lancets
LANDSCAPE GARDENING: *see* animals, fences, figures, fountains, FURNITURE, garden designs, sundials, urns, water nozzles
lanterns: *incl.* candle, hotel, kerosene, Paul Revere, policeman's, railroad, ship, street
lasts (shoe)
latches
lathes
lavabos
leather guide markers
lecterns
leg irons
letter openers
levels
lids
LIGHTING DEVICES: *see* brackets, candelabra, candle hold-ers and makers, candlesticks, chandeliers, hurricane shades, lamps, lanterns, rush holders, sconces, snuffers, torches, wick trimmers
lintels
lithographs

lockets
locks
log load tighteners
looms: *incl.* tape
lottery wheels
love seats
lowboys
LUGGAGE: *see* baskets, boxes, carpetbags, knapsacks, satchels,
   trunks
lunch boxes
lunettes

M

mail bags and boxes
mangles
manicure sets
mannequin shoes
mannequins (hat models)
mantels
mantillas
mantles
marionettes
martingales
mashers: *incl.* corn, grape, potato
masks
mast sheaths
match holders
measuring utensils
MECHANICAL DEVICES: *see* canceling machines, cash registers, compasses, electric generators, flycatchers, Gramophones,
   HOUSEHOLD EQUIPMENT, IMPLEMENTS, keno,
   lottery wheels, mouse and rat traps, music boxes, scales,
   SHIP'S DECORATION AND EQUIPMENT, stereopticons,
   stereoscopes, ticket punches, TOYS, washing machines
medicine cabinets
melodeons
metal: *incl.* brass, britannia metal, bronze, copper, gold, iron,
   lead, pewter, silver, steel, tin, zinc
milk pails and tubs
millstones
mirrors
missal stands
mittens
mitts
molds: *incl.* aspic, bonnet, bullet, butter, cake, candle, cheese,
   cookie, ice-cream, jelly, maple sugar, pudding, spoon
money bags and vests
mortars and pestles
mosaics
mourning embroideries
mouse traps
muffin pans
muffs
mugs: *incl.* beer, shaving, Toby. *See also* noggins
music boxes
MUSICAL INSTRUMENTS: *see* accordions, banjos, baritone
   horns, drums, dulcimers, fifes, flutes, harp pianos, harps,
   melodeons, organs, pianos, psalmodicons, recorders, violins
mustard pots

N

nails
napkin rings
napkins
Nauvoo, Illinois
neckerchiefs

necklaces
neckties
newel posts
niches
nightcaps
nightgowns
ninepins
noggins: *see also* mugs
nose pieces (for weaning calves)
numerals
nutcrackers

O

octants
organs: *incl.* church, cottage, gem roller, pipe
ottomans
ovens: *incl.* Dutch, Franklin, roasting
ox carts
ox stocks

P

paddle-wheel covers
pails: *incl.* milk. *See also* piggins
paintings: *incl.* landscape, portrait, religious. *See also* pictures,
   tavern signs, wall paintings
pan sliders
panels
pans: *incl.* frying, roasting
pantalets
pants
paper
paper clips and cutters
paper weights
papier-mâché
parasols
park shelters
party emblems
pastry squeezers
patch boxes
pattens
peaveys
pelisses
pencils
Pennsylvania German
pens
petticoats
pews
pewter
photograph albums
pianos
pickle dishes
picks
pictures: *see also* DECORATION AND ORNAMENT, lithographs, paintings, spirit writings
pie markers
piggins: *see also* pails
pikes
pill coaters
pillars
pillow cases
pillow sham holders
pillows
pincushions
pinkers
pins
pipe stands

pipes
pistols
pitchers: *incl.* cream, syrup
pitchforks
pitters: *incl.* cherry
planes
plaques
plaster
plates: *incl.* communion, cup
plows
plumb lines
pocketbooks
pockets
pokers
pole screens
police belts and clubs
pony robes
popcorn poppers
porringers
portraits
potato planters
pothooks
pots: *incl.* flower, mustard
powder flasks and horns
presses: *incl.* cheese, cider, fruit
printer's measures, presses and rollers
printing blocks and stamps
psalmodicons
pulpits
pumps: *incl.* firemen's
punch bowls
puppets

Q

quilt covers
quilts: *incl.* appliqué, patchwork, tufted

R

racks: *incl.* book, clock, clothes, comb and brush, drying, gun, hall, hanging, hat, magazine, mirror, newspaper, spool, spoon, towel
railings: *see also* balconies, balustrades, banisters, fences
rain gutter stirrups: *see also* conductor heads, downspouts
rakes: *incl.* hay
rat traps
rattles: *incl.* babies', police, watchmen's
razors
reamers
recorders
reels: *incl.* clock
reliefs
RELIGIOUS ARTICLES: *see* altarpieces, altars, basins, bells, benches, chalices, chimes, clappers, confessionals, crosses, crowns, crucifixes, dishes, flagons, fonts, grave markers, lecterns, missal stands, organs, paintings, pews, plates, pulpits, railings, reredos, rosaries, shrines, stands, tabernacles, tombs, tombstones, trays, vestments
reredos
reticules
revolvers
riding habits
rifles
rings
roach traps
rocking horses
rolling pins

rosaries
rug beaters
rugs: *incl.* braided, hooked, woven
rush holders

S

sabers
sabots
saddle bags
SADDLERY: *see* bridles, cinches, curb bits, handholds, hobbles, horse collars, horseshoes, martingales, pony robes, saddle bags, saddles, spurs, stirrups, whips
saddles: *incl.* pack, side
safes: *incl.* kitchen, letter, match
salad bowls
saltcellars
salvers
samplers
sand shakers
satchels: *incl.* boot, hand
saucepans
saucers
sauerkraut stompers
sausage stuffers
saws: *incl.* bone saw, bucksaw, butcher's, coopersmith's, hacksaw, sawknife, whipsaw
scabbards
scales
scarves
scissors
sconces
scoops: *incl.* butter, grain, sugar
scouring boards
scrapers: *incl.* dough trough, foot, oven, turpentine
screens (lead miner's)
scrimshaw
seals: *incl.* letter, school, state
secretaries
settees
settles
SEWING EQUIPMENT: *incl.* birds, emeries, kits, machines, sailors' horns, spool holders. *See also* baskets, boxes, buttonhole cutters, cabinets, cases, pincushions, pins, scissors, shears, stands, tables, thimbles, thread holders
shadow boxes
Shaker
shaving horses
shaving mugs
shaving stands
shawls
shears
shelves
ship models
SHIP'S DECORATION AND EQUIPMENT: *see* anchor links and trip hooks, anchors, bells, billetheads, bow pieces, compasses, dumb irons, figureheads, gangboards, halyard bands and blocks, hawsing beetles and irons, mast sheaths, octants, paddle-wheel covers, spreaders, stern pieces, trail boards
shirts: *incl.* firemen's
SHOEMAKER'S EQUIPMENT: *see* benches, boot forms, lasts, shoeshine foot rests
shoes
shoeshine foot rests
shovels
shrines
shutter fasteners

shuttles
sickles
sideboards
signs: *incl.* inn, shop, tavern. *See also* barberpoles, figures
sills
silver
skates
skewers
skillets
skimmers
skirts
slave collars
sled starting hooks
sleds: *incl.* children's, dog
sleighs
slippers
SMOKING EQUIPMENT: *see* boxes, cigar lighters, humidors, jars, pipe stands, pipes, tobacco cutters
smoking lounges
snoods: *see also* bonnets, hats, hoods, veils
snow breakers
snowshoes
snubbers (for bulls)
snuff boxes
snuffers
sofas
soldering irons
spades
spandrels
Spanish Southwest
spats
spatulas
spiders (flapjack)
SPINNING EQUIPMENT: *incl.* cards, combs, reels, sticks, swifts, wheels
spirit writings (drawings)
spits
splint holders
splints
spokeshaves (cooper's)
spoons: *incl.* baby, folding, funeral, marrow, salt, souvenir, sugar, tea
spreaders (for schooner rigging)
springerle boards
spurs
stage coaches
staircases
stands: *incl.* bedside, candle, flower, incense burner, ink, music, pipe, prayer, reading, roasting, sewing, shaving, snuffer, umbrella, vase, wash
stenciling
stepping stones
stereopticons
stereoscopes
stern pieces
stirrups
stockings
stocks (neckwear)
stone
stools: *incl.* foot
stove lid lifters
stove plates and urns
stoves: *incl.* box, cannon, charcoal, Franklin, jamb, portable, tailor's
strainers: *incl.* cheese, lemon, punch, starch, sugar
sugar bowls
sugar chests and tubs
sugar industry implements

suits
sundials
survey marks
suspenders
swifts (for skeining yarn)
swords
syrup pitchers and pots

T

tabernacles (altar)
tablecovers
tables: *incl.* bedside, butterfly, candle, card, chair, communion, console, dining, drawing, dressing, drop-leaf, game, gate-legged, hutch, ironing, kitchen, occasional, pier, refectory, serving, sewing, side, silver, sofa, tailor's, tavern, tea, tip-top, trestle, work
TABLEWARE: *see* casters, celery holders, chocolate pots, creamers, cruets, cups, decanters, dishes, doilies, forks, glasses, goblets, gravy boats, HOUSEHOLD EQUIPMENT, knives, napkin rings, napkins, pitchers, plates, porringers, saltcellars, saucers, spoons, sugar bowls, tablecovers, teapots, tongs, trays, tumblers, tureens, urns
tailoresses' counters
tankards
tar pots
tavern signs
tea caddies
teakettles
teapots
TEXTILES: *incl.* appliqué, broadcloth, brocade, candlewick, chalis, chintz, crocheting, homespun, Jacquard, knitting, linen, muslin, netting, prints, satin, silk, taffeta, velvet, wool
thermometers
thimbles
thread cutters
thread holders and winds
ticket punches
tiebacks: *see also* curtain tassels, curtains, draperies
tiles
tinderboxes
tippets
toasters
tobacco cutters
Toby jugs and mugs
toleware
tomahawks
tombs: *see also* grave markers, tombstones
tombstones: *see also* grave markers, tombs
tongs: *incl.* fireplace, grape pomice, sugar
tool kits
tools: *see* IMPLEMENTS
tooth extractors
toothpicks
torches: *incl.* election, firemen's, "jacking," lead miner's, lumber camp, parade. *See also* flambeaux
towel racks
towels
TOYS: *incl.* boats, fire engines, mechanical, musical, Noah's arks, soldiers, trains. *See also* animals, banks, birds, carts, coaches, doll carriages, dolls, marionettes, puppets, rocking horses, skates, sleds, wagons, whistles
trail boards
trains (court)
trammels
transoms
trays: *incl.* altar, dough, pin
trivets

trousers
trunks
tubs: *incl.* bath, foot, milk, sugar
tumblers
tureens
turpentine dip irons, hacks, and scrapers
tweezers

U

uniforms: *see also* ARMS AND ARMOR, epaulettes
urns: *incl.* coffee, garden, hot water, stove, tea
utensils: *see* IMPLEMENTS

V

valances
valentines
vases
VEHICLES: *see* bandwagons, bicycles, buckboards, buggies, carriages, carts, coaches, hearses, sleighs, stage coaches, TOYS, wagons, wheelbarrows
veils: *see also* bonnets, hats, hoods, snoods
vestments: *incl.* chasubles, maniples, stoles
vests
violins

W

wafer irons
waffle irons
wagons: *incl.* circus, Conestoga, farm, toy
waistcoats
waists
walking sticks: *see also* canes
wall paintings
wall pockets
wallets
wallpaper
wardrobes
warmers: *incl.* bed, foot, hand, milk, plate, pocket
washboards

washing machines
washstands
watch chains, fobs and keys
watch holders
watches
water coolers and heaters
water nozzles, pipes and spouts
watering cans
weathervanes: *see also* whirligigs
weaving: *see also* looms, shuttles, SPINNING EQUIPMENT
wheelbarrows
whip sockets
whips
whirligigs: *see also* weathervanes
whistles: *incl.* toy, water
wick trimmers
wig blocks
windlasses
windmill counterbalances
window seats
windows
wine chests
wine coolers
wire-making machines (jeweler's)
witch balls
witchcraft dolls
wood
wrappers
wreaths: *incl.* bridal, cemetery, framed, hair
wrenches
WRITING MATERIALS: *incl.* inkstands and inkwells, letter openers, paper clips, paper cutters and weights, pencils, pens, sand shakers, seals

Y

yokes

Z

Zoar, Ohio

SELECTED BIBLIOGRAPHY

ADAMS, JAMES T., *The Epic of America*, 1941. ALLEN, EDWARD B., *Early American Wall Paintings*, 1926. ALSTON, J. W., *Hints to Young Practitioners*, 1804. ANDREWS, EDWARD D., *Community Industries of the Shakers*, 1932; "The Kentucky Shakers," *Antiques*, Nov., 1947. ANDREWS, EDWARD D. AND FAITH, *Shaker Furniture*, 1937; "The Furniture of an American Religious Sect," *Antiques*, Apr., 1929; "An Interpretation of Shaker Furniture," *Antiques*, Jan., 1933. ANON.: *American Fire Marks: The Insurance Company of North America Collection*, 1933; *Art Recreations*, 1860; *Glass*, The Metropolitan Museum of Art, 1936; *Illustrations of Iron Architecture*, 1865; *Life in America*, The Metropolitan Museum of Art, 1939; *New York Clipper*, Mar. 26 and Apr. 9, 1881; *Publications of the Rhode Island Historical Society*, New Series, vols. 5–6, 1897–1898; "Tobacconists Figures by the W.P.A. Art Program," Index of American Design MS., 1937; *Worcester Historical Society Proceedings*, vol. 8. ASHLEY, EDGAR L., "Spanish Blonde Lace," *Antiques*, Aug., 1922. AUER, MAY H., "Variety in Old Apple Parers," *Antiques*, Aug., 1942. AVERY, C. LOUISE, *Early American Silver*, 1930. BAKER, JOEL C., *Revised Roster of The Vermont Volunteers (1861–1865)*, 1892. BANCROFT, HUBERT H., *California Pastoral (History of the Pacific States*, vol. 29), 1888. BARBER, EDWIN A., *Tulip Ware of the Pennsylvania German Potters*, 1903; *The Pottery and Porcelain of the United States*, 1909. BARBER, JOEL, *Wild Fowl Decoys*, 1934. BARBER, LAURENCE L., "Massachusetts Shelf Clocks," *Antiques*, July, 1937. BEAR, DONALD (see HOUGLAND). BIGELOW, FRANCIS H., *Historic Silver of the Colonies and its Makers*, 1917. BEMENT, ALON, "Is There an American Design?" *Antiques*, Jan., 1942. BENTLEY, WILLIAM, *The Diary of William Bentley*, vol. 2 (1793–1802), 1907. BORNEMAN, HENRY S., *Pennsylvania German Illuminated Manuscripts*, 1937. BOYD, E., *Saints and Saint Makers of New Mexico*, 1946. BRACKETT, R. W., *A History of the Ranchos of San Diego County, California*, 1939. BRAZER, ESTHER S., "The Tinsmiths of Stevens Plains," *Antiques*, June and Sept., 1939; *Early American Decoration*, 1940; "The Early Boston Japanners," *Antiques*, May, 1943 (see also FRASER). BREITENBACH, EDGAR (see WILDER), *Santos*, 1943. BROWN, ALEXANDER C., "Paddle Box Decorations of American Sound Steamboats," *American Neptune*, vol. 3, No. 1, 1943. BROWN, MARY L., "John Welch, Carver," *Antiques*, Jan., 1926. BRYAN, JOHN A., "Molded Iron in the Middle West," *Antiques*, Feb., 1943. CAHILL, HOLGER, *American Primitives*, 1930; *New Horizons in American Art*, Museum of Modern Art, 1936; *Emblems of Unity and Freedom*, illustrated catalogue, Metropolitan Museum of Art. CAHILL, HOLGER, AND ELINOR ROBINSON, *American Folk Sculpture*, 1931. CHAPMAN, ETTA T., "The Tyler Coverlets," *Antiques*, Mar., 1928. CHIPPENDALE, THOMAS, *The Gentleman and Cabinetmaker's Director*, 1762. CIGRAND, BERNARD J., *Story of the Great Seal of the United States or History of American Emblems*, 1892; "Flag of the United States," in *Encyclopedia Americana*, vol. 11, 1940. CLARK, ARTHUR H., *The Clipper Ship Era*, 1910. CLARK, VICTOR S., *History of Manufacture in the United States, 1607–1860*, 1929. CLEMENT, ARTHUR W., *Our Pioneer Potters*, 1947. COMSTOCK, HELEN, "Federal Furniture:

An American Style," *Antiques*, Mar., 1943. CORNELIUS, CHARLES O., *Furniture Masterpieces of Duncan Phyfe*, 1925; *Early American Furniture*, 1926 (see also HALSEY). COSTELLO, AUGUSTINE E., *Our Firemen*, 1887. COUSINS, FRANK, AND PHIL M. RILEY, *The Wood-Carver of Salem: Samuel McIntire, His Life and Work*, 1916. CRANE, PRISCILLA C., "The Boston and Sandwich Glass Company," *Antiques*, Apr., 1925. DALAND, EDWARD L., "Engraved Types of Scrimshaw," *Antiques*, Oct., 1935. DAVIS, GHERARDI, *Regimental Colors in the War of the Revolution*, 1907. DILLIN, JOHN G. W., *The Kentucky Rifle*, 1946. DOW, GEORGE F., *Arts and Crafts in New England, 1704–1775*, 1927. DOWNS, JOSEPH, "American Japanned Furniture," *Bulletin of Metropolitan Mus.*, Mar., 1933; "New York State Furniture," *Bull. of Metro. Mus.*, Feb., 1934; "A Gift of New York Furniture," *Bull. of Metro. Mus.*, May, 1942; "John Henry Belter and Company," *Antiques*, Sept., 1948. DRAKE, SAMUEL A., *Old Landmarks and Historic Personages of Boston*, 1900. DREPPERD, CARL W., "Origins of Pennsylvania Folk Art," *Antiques*, Feb., 1940; "What Is Primitive and What Is Not?" *Antiques*, May, 1942; "Art Instruction Books for the People," *Antiques*, June, 1942; "The Decline and Fall of Adam," *Antiques*, Mar., 1943. DUNSHEE, KENNETH H., *Enjine! Enjine!* 1939. DUNTON, WILLIAM R., JR., *Old Quilts*, 1946. DYER, WALTER A., "Early Pottery of New England," *Antiques*, Jan., 1922; *The American Bureau, Primitive to Chippendale*, 1928. EARLE, ALICE M., *Two Centuries of Costume in America*, 1903; *Home Life in Colonial Days*, 1937. EATON, ALLEN H., *Immigrant Gifts to American Life*, 1932; *Handicrafts of the Southern Highlands*, 1937; *Handicrafts of New England*, 1949. ENGELHARDT, FR. ZEPHYRIN, O.F.M., *Santa Barbara Mission*, 1923; *San Fernando Rey*, 1927; *San Gabriel*, 1927; *San Buen Ventura*, 1930. ENSKO, STEPHEN G. C., *American Silversmiths and Their Marks III*, 1948. ERVING, HENRY W., *The Hartford Chest*, 1934. FARNSWORTH, SIDNEY, *Illumination*, 1923. FAWCETT, CLARA HALLARD, *Dolls: A Guide for Collectors*, 1947. FEDERAL WRITERS' PROJECT, American Guide Series: *Maine*, 1937; *Vermont*, 1937; *Iowa*, 1938; *New Hampshire*, 1938; *Texas*, 1940; *Missouri*, 1941. FIELDING, MANTLE (see MORGAN). FINLEY, RUTH E., *Old Patchwork Quilts*, 1929. FLOWER, MILTON E., "Schimmel the Wood Carver," *Antiques*, Oct., 1943. FOCILLON, HENRI, Introduction to *Art Populaire*, vol. 1, 1931. FORD, ALICE, *Pictorial Folkart, New England to California*, 1949. FOX, D. R. (see KROUT). FRARY, I. T., "Stagecoach Luggage," *Antiques*, Aug., 1940. FREEMAN, RUTH AND LARRY, *Cavalcade of Toys*, 1942. FRASER, ESTHER S. (see also BRAZER), "The Golden Age of Stencilling," *Antiques*, Apr., 1922; "Painted Furniture in America (1817–1835)," *Antiques*, Sept., 1924; "Painted Furniture in America (1835–1845)," *Antiques*, Jan., 1925; "Pennsylvania Bride Boxes and Dower Chests," *Antiques*, July and Aug., 1925; "Pennsylvania German Dower Chests," *Antiques*, Feb., Apr., and June, 1927; "The American Rocking-Chair," *Antiques*, Feb., 1928; "Zachariah Brackett Stevens," *Antiques*, Mar., 1936. FREY, H. C., *The Conestoga Wagon, Lancaster County Historical Society, Historical Papers and Addresses*, Lancaster, Pa., 1930. GARDNER, ALBERT T. E., *Yankee Stonecutters*,

1945. GILLINGHAM, HARROLD E., *The Fascinating Fire-Mark*, 1923. GOULD, MARY E., "Early New England Woodenware," *Antiques,* Feb., 1937; *Early American Wooden Ware*, 1942. GRANCSAY, STEPHEN V., *American Engraved Powder Horns*, 1946. GREEN, SAMUEL M., "Edbury Hatch: Down-East Carver," *Magazine of Art*, Dec., 1948. GREENWOOD, ISAAC J., *The Circus*, 1898. GRÖBER, KARL, *Children's Toys of Bygone Days*, 1928 (transl. by Philip Hereford). HALL, CARRIE A., AND ROSE G. KRETSINGER, *The Romance of the Patchwork Quilt in America*, 1935. HALL, ELIZA C., *A Book of Hand-Woven Coverlets*, 1931. HALM, PHILIPP M., "The Peasant Furniture of Southern Germany," *Antiques*, Jan., 1929. HALSEY, R. T. H., AND CHARLES O. CORNELIUS, *A Handbook of the American Wing* (Metropolitan Museum of Art), rev. ed., 1942. HALSEY, R. T. H., AND ELIZABETH TOWER, *The Homes of Our Ancestors*, 1937. HARLOW, ALVIN F., *Old Towpaths*, 1926. HAYDEN, ARTHUR, *Furniture Designs of Chippendale, Hepplewhite and Sheraton*, 1938. HAYWARD, ARTHUR H., *Colonial Lighting*, 1927; "Lard-Oil Lamps," *Antiques*, Nov., 1938. HERTZ, LOUIS H., *Mechanical Toy Banks*, 1947. HIGLEY, MARY G., "The Caswell Carpet," *Antiques*, June, 1926. HILL, HAMILTON A., *History of the Old South Church*, 1890. HILL, HARRY S., *The Conestoga Wagon*, 1930. HIPKISS, EDWIN J., *Eighteenth-Century American Arts*, 1941. HOLME, C. GEOFFREY, *Children's Toys of Yesterday*, 1932. HONEY, W. B., *Glass*, 1946. HOUGH, WALTER, "Collection of Heating and Lighting Utensils in the United States," *Bulletin 141* of the National Museum, 1928. HOUGLAND, WILLARD, AND DONALD BEAR (Foreword), *Santos: A Primitive American Art*, 1946. HOWE, FLORENCE T., "Carved Wood Circus-Wagon Figures," *Antiques*, Aug., 1947. HULBERT, A. B., *The Paths of Inland Commerce*, 1918. HUMPHREYS, GREGOR N., "Foreign Influences in American Glass," *Antiques*, Sept., 1928 (see also NORMAN-WILCOX). HUNTER, FREDERICK W., *Stiegel Glass*, 1914. JACKSON, JOSEPH, *Encyclopedia of Philadelphia*, 1932. JACOBSON, MARGARET E., "The Painted Record of a Community Experiment," *Journal of Illinois State Historical Society*, June, 1941. JESSUP, LAWRENCE F., "The Tobacconists' Tribe of Treen," *Antiques*, Sept., 1930. KARLINGER, HANS, *Deutsche Volkskunst*, 1938. KARR, LOUISE, "Paintings on Velvet," *Antiques*, Sept., 1931. KAUFFMAN, HENRY, *Pennsylvania Dutch*, 1946. KERFOOT, J. B., *American Pewter*, 1924. KETTELL, RUSSELL H., *Pine Furniture of Early New England*, 1929. KEYES, HOMER E., "Two Windsor Chairs," *Antiques*, Oct., 1923; "Once More the Betty Lamp," *Antiques*, Mar., 1925; "Sandwich Models," *Antiques*, Mar., 1927; "Paul Revere's Lantern," *Antiques*, Dec., 1930; "Perplexities in Pottery" and "Title-Hunting Americana," *Antiques*, Feb., 1933; "Concerning an Unfrocked Eagle," *Antiques*, July, 1933; "Some Clues in the Amelung Quest," *Antiques*, Sept., 1934; "Bellamy's Style and Its Imitators," *Antiques*, Mar., 1935; "The Individuality of Connecticut Furniture," *Antiques*, Sept., 1935. KIMBALL, FISKE, "Some Carved Figures by Samuel McIntire," *Bulletin* of the Metropolitan Museum, Aug., 1923; "Joseph Wright and the Portraits of Washington: Paintings and Engravings," *Antiques*, May, 1929; "Joseph Wright and the Portraits of Washington: Sculpture," *Antiques*, Jan., 1930; *Mr. Samuel McIntire, Carver, the Architect of Salem*, 1940. KIMBALL, MARIE, "The Furnishing of Monticello," *Antiques*, Nov. and Dec., 1927. KING, ELIZABETH, *Quilting*, 1934. KNITTLE, RHEA M., *Early American Glass*, 1937. KOUWENHOVEN, JOHN A., *Made in America*, 1948. KRETSINGER, ROSE G. (see HALL, CARRIE A.). KROEBER, A. L., *Handbook of the Indians of California*, 1925. KROUT, JOHN A., AND DIXON R. FOX, *The Completion of Independence*, 1944. LANDIS, D. H., "Pennsylvania Decorated Boxes," *Antiques*, May, 1935. LARKIN, OLIVER W., *Art and Life in America*, 1949. LAWALL, CHARLES H., *The Curious Lore of Drugs and Medicines*, 1927. LEE, RUTH W., *Early American Pressed Glass*, 1933; *Sandwich Glass*, 1947. LESTER, KATHERINE M., *Historic Costume*, 1942. LEWITTES, ESTHER, "A Cotton Travelogue," *Antiques*, Dec.,

1939. LICHTEN, FRANCES, *Folk Art in Rural Pennsylvania*, 1946. LIPMAN, JEAN, "The Study of Folk Art," *Art in America*, Oct., 1945; "Two Nautical Shop Signs," *American Antiques Journal*, Jan., 1947; "Mermaids in Folk Art," *Antiques*, Mar., 1948; *American Folk Art*, 1948. LITTLE, FRANCES, *Early American Textiles*, 1931. LOCKWOOD, LUKE V., *A Collection of English Furniture of the XVII and XVIII Centuries*, 1907; *Colonial Furniture in America*, 1926. LONG, EVAN W. (see WATKINS, LURA W.). LUTHER, CLAIR F., "The Hadley Chest," *Antiques*, Oct., 1928; *The Hadley Chest*, 1935. LYNES, WILSON, "Slat-Back Chairs of New England and the Middle-Atlantic States," *Antiques*, Dec., 1933, and Mar., 1934. LYON, IRVING P., "Origin of the Rocking Chair," *Antiques*, Apr., 1928. MCCLELLAN, ELIZABETH, *History of American Costume, 1607–1870*, 1937. MCCLELLAND, NANCY, *Duncan Phyfe and the English Regency*, 1939. MCKEARIN, GEORGE S. AND HELEN, *American Glass*, 1941. MACLAY, ALFRED B., *Early American Bottles and Flasks*, 1945. MARCEAU, HENRI, *John Rush*, 1937. MELCHER, MARGUERITE F., *The Shaker Adventure*, 1941. MERCER, HENRY C., *The Survival of the Medieval Art of Illuminative Writing Among Pennsylvania Germans*, 1897; *The Bible in Iron*, 1914; *Ancient Carpenters' Tools*, 1929. MIKKELSEN, MICHAEL A., *The Bishop Hill Colony*, 1892. MILLER, CATHARINE R., "Some Hand Woven Coverlets," *Antiques*, Feb., 1925. MILLER, EDGAR G., JR., *American Antique Furniture*, 1937. MINITER, EDITH, "When Tree Ware Was 'The Ware,'" *Antiques*, Dec., 1930. MOORE, HARRIS W., *Chip Carving*, 1922. MOORE, MABEL R., *Hitchcock Chairs*, 1933. MORGAN, JOHN H., AND MANTLE FIELDING, *The Life Portraits of Washington and Their Replicas*, 1931. MORGAN, VIVIAN E., "Memorial Wreaths," *Antiques*, Aug., 1935. MORRISON, JOHN L., "The Passing of the Wooden Indian," *Scribner's Magazine*, Oct., 1928. MORTON, STRATFORD L., "Bishop Hill: An Experiment in Communal Living," *Antiques*, Feb., 1943. MURRAY, ANNE W., "Van Buren Versus Harrison: The Campaign of 1840," *American Collector*, Oct., 1948; "Zachary Taylor for President: The Campaign of 1848," *American Collector*, Nov., 1948. MYERS, LOUIS G., "Queen Anne Chairs of Colonial Days," *Antiques*, Dec., 1932. NEWCOMB, REXFORD, *The Old Mission Churches and Historic Houses of California*, 1925. NORMAN-WILCOX, GREGOR, "Is It Pennsylvania-Dutch?" *Antiques*, Mar., 1944 (see also HUMPHREYS). NORTON, C. A. QUINCEY, "Lamp," *Encyclopedia Americana*, vol. 16, 1940. NUTTING, WALLACE, *A Windsor Handbook*, 1917; *Furniture Treasury*, 1928 and 1948. ORMSBEE, THOMAS H., *Early American Furniture Makers*, 1930; "Poughkeepsie Was Also a Jugtown," *American Collector*, Feb., 1936. OMWAKE, JOHN, *The Conestoga Six-Horse Bell Teams*, 1930. PETO, FLORENCE, "The Age of Heirloom Quilts," *Antiques*, July, 1942. PICKEN, MARY B., *The Language of Fashion*, 1939. PIERCE, ENID C., "The Dolls of Springfield, Vermont," *Antiques*, Oct., 1942. PINCKNEY, PAULINE A., *American Figureheads and Their Carvers*, 1940. PINCKNEY, PAULINE A., AND ROSALIND WRIGHT, "Tobacconist Figures," Index of American Design, Federal Art Project (W.P.A. MS.). PITKIN, ALBERT H., *Early American Folk Pottery* (including the History of the Bennington Pottery), 1918. PITZ, HARRY (see WARWICK). PORTER, REV. EDWARD G., *Rambles in Old Boston*, 1887. PORTER, JAMES A., *Modern Negro Art*, 1943. RAMSAY, JOHN, "Early American Pottery: A Résumé," *Antiques*, Oct., 1931; *American Potters and Pottery*, 1939; "Zoar and Its Industries," *Antiques*, Dec., 1944. RAVENSWAAY, CHARLES VAN, "Creole 'Armoires' in Missouri," *Antiques*, Feb., 1943. RAWSON, MARION, *Handwrought Ancestors*, 1936. READ, HERBERT, *Staffordshire Pottery Figures*, 1929. RILEY, PHIL M. (see COUSINS). RIPLEY, VERNETTE SNYDER, "The Age of Dolls," *Antiques*, May, 1936. ROBACKER, EARL F., "The Case for Pennsylvania German Painted Tin," *Antiques*, Oct., 1947. ROBERTSON, ELIZABETH W., *American Quilts*, 1948. ROBINS, F. W., *The Story of the Lamp (and the Candle)*, 1939. ROBINSON, ELINOR (see CAHILL). ROE, F. GORDON, "In the Likeness of Books,"

Antiques, Feb., 1940. ROGERS, CLARENCE N., "Figureheads," *Shipyard Bulletin*, Feb., 1946. ROURKE, CONSTANCE, "Index of American Design," *Magazine of Art*, Apr., 1937; *The Roots of American Culture*, 1942. SAFFORD, VICTOR, "John Haley Bellamy," *Antiques*, Mar., 1935. ST. GEORGE, ELEANOR, *The Dolls of Yesterday*, 1948. SCHMIDT, ROBERT, *Das Glas*, 1912. SEYBOLT, ROBERT F., *The Private Schools of Colonial Boston*, 1935. SEYMOUR, CHARLES, "Houdon's Washington at Mount Vernon Re-examined," *Gazette des Beaux-Arts*, Mar., 1948. SHAW, CHARLES G., "Black Boys and Their Playfellows," *Antiques*, Mar., 1934; "Ancient Trade Signs in Modern New York," *Antiques*, Oct., 1938; "Speaking of Wooden Indians," *Antiques*, Sept., 1939. SHELLEY, DONALD A., "Illuminated Birth Certificates," New York Historical Society *Quarterly*, July, 1945. SINGLETON, ESTHER, *Dolls*, 1927. SMITH, JEROME I., "Painted Fire Engine Panels," *Antiques*, Nov., 1937. SMITH, WINSTON O., *The Sharps Rifle*, 1943. SONN, ALBERT H., *Early American Wrought Iron*, 1928. SPARGO, JOHN, *Potters and Pottery of Bennington*, 1926. STEPHENSON, NATHANIEL W., *Abraham Lincoln and the Union*, 1918. STEWARD, JULIAN H., *Petroglyphs of California and Adjoining States*, 1929. STODDARD, HENRY B., "Windsors: Suggested Criteria," *Antiques*, Jan., 1938. STOKES, I. N. PHELPS, *Iconography of Manhattan Island*, 1928. STOKES, J. STOGDELL, "The American Windsor Chair," *Antiques*, Apr., 1926. STOUDT, JOHN J., *Pennsylvania Folk Art*, 1948. STOVALL, SARAH F., "Two Aspects of Victorianism," *Antiques*, Nov., 1932. SWAN, MABEL M., "The Village Tinsmith," *Antiques*, Mar., 1928; "The Man Who Made Simon Willard's Clock Cases: John Doggett of Roxbury," *Antiques*, Mar., 1929; "The Man Who Made Brass Work for Willard Clocks," *Antiques*, June, 1930; "A Revised Estimate of McIntire," *Antiques*, Dec., 1931; "On Weathervanes," *Antiques*, Feb., 1933; "McIntire Vindicated," *Antiques*, Oct., 1934; *Samuel McIntire, Carver, and the Sandersons*, 1934; "The Johnstons and the Reas—Japanners," *Antiques*, May, 1943; "Ship Carvers of Newburyport," *Antiques*, Aug., 1945; "The Goddard and Townsend Joiners," *Antiques*, Apr. and May, 1946; "Boston Carvers and Joiners," *Antiques*, Mar. and Apr., 1948. TANGERMAN, ELMER J., *Whittling and Woodcarving*, 1936. TERRY, MARIAN D., *Old Inns of Connecticut*, 1937. THOMPSON, MRS. GUION, "Hitchcock of Hitchcocks-ville," *Antiques*, Aug., 1923. THOMPSON, J. H., *Bitters Bottles*, 1947. THWING, LEROY L., "The Four Carving Skillins," *Antiques*, June, 1938; "A Note About Rushlight," *Antiques*, Aug., 1944. TOWER, ELIZABETH (see HALSEY). TOWNSEND, GERTRUDE, "A Set of Eighteenth Century Embroidered Bed Curtains," *Bulletin* of Boston Museum of Fine Arts, Dec., 1942; "Eighteenth Century Brocade Costume," *Antiques*, May, 1945. TRYON, ROLLA M., *Household Manufactures in the United States, 1640–1860*, 1917. TYLER, ALICE F., *Freedom's Ferment*, 1944. WARING, JANET, *Early American Stencils on Walls and Furniture*, 1937. WARNER, ROGER, "Latch and Door Knocker," *Antiques*, Feb., 1923. WARWICK, EDWARD, AND HENRY PITZ, *Early American Costume*, 1929. WASHINGTON, W. LANIER, "Apple Parers," *Antiques*, Nov., 1925. WATKINS, C. MALCOLM, "The Whale-Oil Burner: Its Invention and Development," *Antiques*, Apr., 1935; "The Lamps of Colonial America," *Antiques*, Oct., 1937; "The Early American Domestic Machine," *Antiques*, Feb., 1940; "Notes on the New England Blacksmith," *Antiques*, Mar., 1947. WATKINS, LURA W., *Cambridge Glass*, 1930; "American Glass Lamps," *Antiques*, Apr., 1936. WATKINS, LURA W., AND EVAN W. LONG, "Old-Time Foot Stoves," *Antiques*, Mar., 1939. WEITENKAMPF, FRANK, "Cigar-Store Indians," *Magazine of Art*, Dec., 1948. WELLMAN, RITA, "American Design," *House and Garden*, July, 1938; "American Weathervanes," *House Beautiful*, Jan., 1939. WINCHESTER, ALICE, "American Tin Candle Sconces," *Antiques*, Aug., 1936; "Transportation Textile," *Antiques*, Mar., 1940; "The ABC's of Hitchcock Chairs," *Antiques*, June, 1942; "Antiques and Business," *Antiques*, Sept., 1942; *American Antiques in Words and Pictures*, 1943. WESTROPP, M. S. DUDLEY, *Irish Glass*, 1920. WHEELER, CANDACE, *The Development of Embroidery in America*, 1921. WHITE, HARRY H., "Migrations of Early Glassworkers," *Antiques*, Aug., 1937. WHITMORE, ELEANORE M., "Origins of Pennsylvania Folk Art," *Antiques*, Sept., 1940. WILDER, MITCHELL A., AND EDGAR BREITENBACH, *Santos*, 1943. WILLIAMSON, SCOTT W., *The American Craftsman*, 1940. WILSON, CLAGGETT, "Scrimshaw, the Whaleman's Art," *Antiques*, Nov., 1944. WOOD, T. KENNETH, "Mediaeval Art Among Pennsylvania Germans," *Antiques*, May, 1925. WOODSIDE, CHARLES L., "Marked American Pewter," *Antiques*, May, 1926; "Early American Lamps," *Antiques*, Dec., 1927, and Jan., 1928; "Further Light on the Betty Lamp," *Antiques*, Apr., 1929. WRIGHT, RICHARDSON, *Hawkers and Walkers in Early America*, 1927. WRIGHT, ROSALIND, AND PAULINE PINCKNEY, "Tobacconist Figures," Index of American Design, Federal Art Project (W.P.A. MS.). WYATT, EDWIN M., *Common Woodworking Tools*, 1936.

INDEX

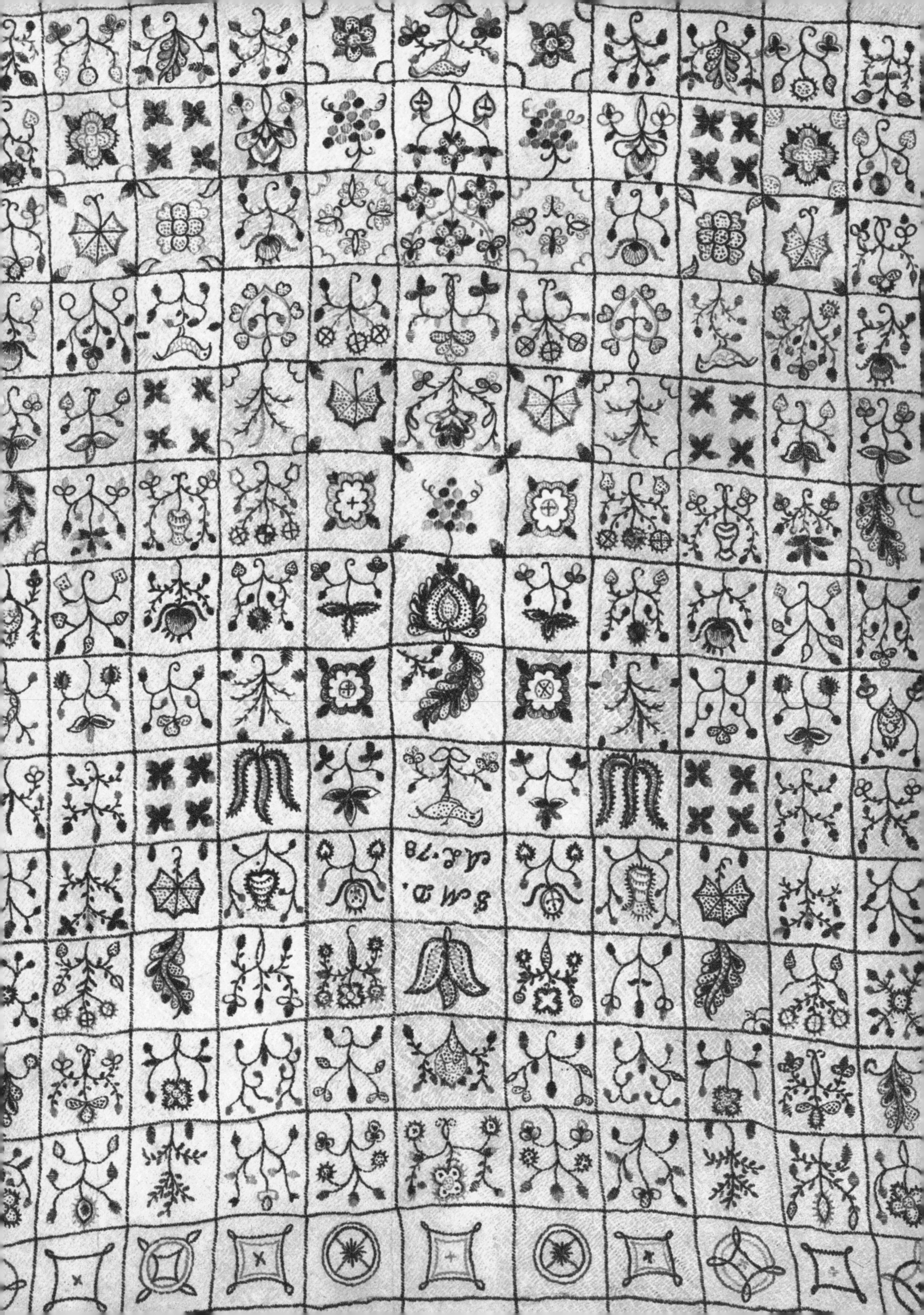